The Crown
and
Local Communities

In England and
France In
The Fifteenth Century

The Crown and Local Communities

In England and France In The Fifteenth Century

Edited by J. R. L. Highfield
and
Robin Jeffs

Alan Sutton
1981

First published in Great Britain in 1981 by
Alan Sutton Publishing Limited
17a Brunswick Road
Gloucester GL1 1HG

British Library Cataloguing in Publication Data

The crown and local communities in England and France
  in the fifteenth century.
  1. Monarchy, English — History — Addresses, essays,
  lectures.
  2. Monarchy, French — History — Addresses, essays,
  lectures
  3. Great Britain — Politics and government — 1399-1485
  4. France — Politics and government — 1328-1589
  I. Highfield, J.R.L. II. Jeffs, Robin
  354.4208'3   JS3137

  ISBN 0-904387-67-4
  ISBN 0-904387-79-8 Pbk

Typesetting and origination by
Alan Sutton Publishing Limited.
Photoset Baskerville 10/11
Printed in Great Britain
by Robert MacLehose & Co. Ltd.
Glasgow

Contents

		Page
PREFACE		7
ABBREVIATIONS		8
INTRODUCTION J.R.L. Highfield, *Merton College, Oxford*		10
1.	Political Theory and the Relationship in England and France between the Crown and the Local Communities .... J.-P. GENET, *University of Paris I*	19
2.	The Centre, the Periphery, and Power Distribution of Fifteenth-Century France .... P.S. LEWIS, *All Souls College, Oxford*	33
3.	The Breton Nobility and their Masters from the Civil War of 1341-64 to the Late Fifteenth Century .... M.C.E. JONES, *University of Nottingham*	51
4.	The Crown, Magnates and Local Government in Fifteenth-Century East Anglia .... ROGER VIRGOE, *University of East Anglia*	72
5.	London and the Crown 1451-61 .... CAROLINE M. BARRON, *Bedford College, University of London*	88
6.	*The bonnes villes* and the King's Council in Fifteenth-Century France .... B. CHEVALIER, *University of François Rabelais, Tours*	110
7.	The Relations between the Towns of Burgundy and the French Crown in the Fifteenth Century .... A. LEGUAI, *University of Dijon*	129
8.	Local Reaction to the French Reconquest of Normandy: The Case of Rouen .... C.T. ALLMAND, *University of Liverpool*	146
APPENDIX		
	Dissension in the Provinces under Henry III, 1574-85 ..... M. GREENGRASS, *University of Sheffield*	162
Glossary	....	183

Chevalier's Tables;   I   114

                          II   114

                          III   120

Barron's Tables   I   102

                          II   103

Maps

Urban Communities to whom Letters Patent were sent   115

The 'Bonnes Villes' to whom Letters 'De par le Roi' were sent, 1461-98'   121

The Duchy of Burgundy in the Fifteenth Century   130

Index   185

Preface

The nine papers published in this volume are revised versions of those read, or communicated, by their authors to an Anglo-French Historical Colloquium held at Tapton Hall of Residence, University of Sheffield, on 23-26 September 1976.

The Colloquium was the third in a triennial series of such colloquia to be held since 1970; previous colloquia took place at Cardiff (1970) and Bristol (1973). A grant from the British Academy enabled the sponsors to invite four French historians: Professor B. Chevalier (President, Université de François Rabelais, Tours); Professor R. Scheurer (Doyen de Faculté des Lettres, Université de Neuchâtel); Professor A. Leguai (Faculté des Sciences Humaines, Université de Dijon); and M. J-P. Genet (U.E.R. d'Histoire, Université de Paris I). All members much enjoyed the hospitality given by the University of Sheffield.

As editors of this volume, Dr Robin Jeffs and I are grateful to Dr C. T. Allmand. He translated the papers of Professors Chevalier and Leguai. He also helped us as editors on several points about the history of France.

August 1980   J.R.L.HIGHFIELD

This book is published with the help of a generous subsidy from the British Academy.
June, 1981   J.R.L.H.

Abbreviations

A.A.S.R.P.	*Associated Architectural Societies Reports and Papers*
A.B.	*Annales de Bourgogne*
A.Bret.	*Annales de Bretagne*
Add.Ch.	Additional Charter
Add.MS.	Additional Manuscript
A.H.G.	*Archives Historiques de la Gironde*
A.M.B.	*Archives Municipales de Bordeaux*
Annales E.S.C.	*Annales, Économies, Sociétés, Civilisations*
Arch.Dép.	Archives Départementales
Arch.Nat.	Archives Nationales
B.E.C.	*Bibliothèque de l'École des Chartes*
B.E.F.A.R.	*Bibliothèque des Écoles Françaises d' Athènes et de Rome*
B.I.H.R.	*Bulletin of the Institute of Historical Research*
B.L.	British Library (formerly British Museum)
B.N.	Bibliothèque Nationale
C.C.R.	*Calendar of Close Rolls*
C.P.R.	*Calendar of Patent Rolls*
C.S.	Camden Series
C.&Y.S.	Canterbury and York Society
E.E.T.S.	Early English Text Society
E.H.R.	*English Historical Review*
Foedera	*Foedera, Conventiones, Litterae, etc.* of Thomas Rymer, various editions
H.J.	*Historical Journal*
M.A.	*Le Moyen Âge*
Morice, Preuves	Dom P.H. Morice, *Mémoires pour servis de preuves à l'histoire ecclésiastique et civile de Bretagne* (3 vols., Paris, 1742-6)
MS.fr.	Manuscrit français
MS.lat.	Manuscrit latin
nouv.acqs.frs.	nouvelles acquisitions françaises
P.P.C.	*Proceedings and Ordinances of the Privy Council of England*, ed. N.H. Nicolas (7vols., Record Commission, 1834-7).

P.R.O.   Public Record Office
Reg.Vat.   [Archivio Segreto Vaticano], Registra Vaticana.
Rev.Hist.   *Revue Historique*
Rot.Parl.   *Rotuli Parliamentorum . . . 1278-1503*
R.S.   Rolls Series
S.A.T.F.   Société des Anciens Textes Français
S.H.F.   Société de l'Histoire de France
S.T.S.   Scottish Text Society
T. R. Hist. S.   *Transactions of the Royal Historical Society*

A Note on Currency

'The money of account in later medieval France was the familiar *l(ivre)*, *s(ou)* and *d(enier)*, either *t(ournois)* or, less commonly *p(arisis)*; the latter was rated from the mid-fourteenth century 25 per cent higher than the former. The actual coins in use, which themselves varied in bullion content, had different values as the government 'cried' them.' See P.S. Lewis, *Later Medieval France. The Polity*, pp. xi-xii (1968). In the time of Philip IV the gold agnel had been equal to 1 *livre* or 20 *sous* (M. Bloch, *Esquisse d' une histoire monétaire de l'Europe*. Cahiers des Annales no. 9 (Paris, 1954), p.44). Under St Louis 12 *deniers tournois* = 1 *gros tournois* = 1 *sou*. In the fifteenth century the English noble was usually rated at 2 *écus*; the *écu* = 20 *sous tournois* and c. 1400 was worth 22 *sous* 6 *deniers* (M. Vale, *Charles VII* (London, 1974), p.241). The *franc d'or* = 20 *sous tournois*. The value of all coins in terms of money of account was subject to marked fluctuations as their gold or silver content was altered by the mints. See further: P. Spufford 'Coinage and Currency' in *The Cambridge Economic History*, iii (Cambridge, 1963) Appendix, pp. 576-602; also his *Monetary Problems and Policies in the Burgundian Netherlands 1433-1496* (Leyden, 1970); A. Blanchet and A. Dieudonné, *Manuel de numismatique française* (4 vols. Paris, 1912-36) ii; M. Wolfe, *The Fiscal System of Renaissance France* (New Haven: London, 1972); G. Dickinson, *The Congress of Arras, 1435* (Oxford, 1955); J. Lafaurie, *Les Monnaies des rois de France* (Paris: Basle, 1951).

Introduction

This collection of essays is concerned with the problem of the relationship between the Crown and local communities, both in England and France. My purpose in introducing them is not only to discuss that relationship, but to extend English and French horizons by adducing examples from the kingdoms of the Iberian peninsula.

The history of central government in both England and France has been much studied. For England, the names of Stubbs and Tout need only be invoked; for France, those of Petit-Dutaillis and Fawtier. Yet scant attention is still paid to the relationships between the Crown and the local communities. This volume represents a partial attempt to supply a deficiency in the history of England and France in the fifteenth century.

Jean-Paul Genet demonstrates that in the history of political thought facts all too frequently run ahead of theory. This collection shows the importance of local communities, and also how the Crown, both in England and in France, was noticing them. Yet late medieval political thought scarcely suggests this. The literature of the *Miroirs aux Princes*, to the study of which Professor Genet has recently made a notable contribution,[1] was personally cast in the framework of a royal court. The tradition of Aristotle which lay so heavily on the minds of late medieval thinkers did not envisage a theory by which the parts might control the centre through the local communities. It was left to the Church during the Great Schism (1378-1417) to evolve conciliar ideas. Yet the Church never made them a practical reality. For that it could thank the papacy.

Dr. Lewis discusses the pluralistic distribution of power in late medieval France. The capacity to make decisions, he tells us, was equally informal, both at the centre and in the provinces. Just as strong, if not a stronger case, can be made for Castile and Aragon between 1400 and 1500. Take, for instance, three examples of the fate of the Castilian *corregidor*. In 1401 the abbot of Sahagún in León forced the *corregidor* to resign in order that he could maintain the abbey's ecclesiastical immunities against the aldermen of the town (the *regidores*).[2] When in 1441 John II was asked to send a *corregidor* to Jerez in Andalusia, he (or his advisers) did not choose an official from the Court. The third count of Niebla, a member of the house of

Guzmán and, therefore, of the most powerful Andalusian noble family, was appointed.[3] The *corregidor* of Jerez from 1471 to 1477 was another local nobleman, Rodrigo Ponce de León, second marquis of Cadiz.[4] Then came the legislation of 1493 by which the institution of the *corregidores* was regulated[5] and it seemed that the Crown was to take an active and a controlling role. But the change was fitful, as a case in 1508 was to show. The Crown then sent a *pesquisidor*, an investigator, to Córdoba to inquire into a disturbance between a faction of the bishop and the men of the *corregidor*; but the marquis of Priego, as *alcalde mayor*, imprisoned the *pesquisidor*. The marquis was eventually fined 20 million maravedis, perpetually banished from Córdoba and its district, and compelled to surrender all his fortresses. His castle of Montilla was razed. Nor was he helped by the intervention of the Constable of Castile. Henceforth, however, the Crown did not rule all at Córdoba; five years later the Aguilar family and its allies again controlled the municipality.[6]

What happened to those who sought patronage at the centre, the Royal Court, rather than in distant Andalusia? Emphasis was put on service as well as on lineage; petitioners appear also to have had to curry favour with bureaucrats as well as noblemen. Furthermore, petitioners had to bring letters of introduction from men in power in the localities. But such letters might not avail. In 1519 a young *hidalgo* from Seville, Alonso Enriquez de Guzmán, went to Barcelona to seek an appointment in the royal household and a habit of the Order of Santiago. He carried letters from the duke of Béjar and the Admiral of Castile. These letters secured him an interview with Charles V. But his case was referred, and nothing happened until he went to call on the king's secretary, Francisco de los Cobos. He then took another letter of introduction, written in the name of the count of Bailén. De los Cobos advised him not only to go home before he had wasted any more money, but to come back to see him when times were more favourable. 'And even then', he said, 'do not think that merely because of your lineage you will gain what you are asking, because other men who are of as noble birth as you and have served better than you, have been here for many days in the same quest and cannot gain it. They must be dealt with before you because they have a record of service.'[7] In fifteenth-century France, as Professor Chevalier shows in his essay, non-noble members of the king's council as well as princes likewise had the king's ear and acted as intercessors for petitioners.[8]

Dr Jones, when discussing the Breton nobility in the fourteenth and fifteenth centuries, directly concerns himself with the periphery of France. Brittany indeed enjoyed a distinct history. Its inhabitants were largely Celtic in origin; it was isolated; and its dukes from time to time claimed to be independent. But Brittany cannot be compared very closely either with Cornwall or Galicia. Though Cornwall was similar geographically and in many ways to Brittany, it was, from 1337 onwards, a royal duchy, controlled directly either by the king or by his eldest son. Similarly Galicia, in the distant north-west of Spain, was a kingdom which had been linked to León, and so to Castile, since the thirteenth century. It is perhaps worth noting that the theory of Professor Meyer to which reference is made by Dr Jones for a renewal of the Breton *noblesse*[9] can be paralleled in Castile, where Salvador de Moxó has shown beyond all doubt that the 'new nobility' of the Trastamaran usurpation of the fourteenth and fifteenth centuries far outweighed and outnumbered the 'old nobility' of their predecessors.[10] The little independent kingdom of Navarre may perhaps be compared with Brittany more pertinently. For there the rulers and the rival factions of the nobility, the Agramonts and Beaumonts, had, like the Bretons, sought to play off kings against one another: in their case the kings of France, Aragon, Castile, and England (as dukes of Aquitaine). But the disappearance of Gascony as an independent unit in 1453 and the linking of the crowns of Aragon and Castile in 1479 greatly reduced the diplomatic possibilities, and the chance of the ultimate division of Navarre came much closer.

For England Dr Virgoe's paper enables the reader to test out what was happening in East Anglia across the whole of the fifteenth century. This is particularly valuable not only because of the existence of that first-rate primary source for East Anglian history, the *Paston Letters*, but also because of the recent study of the same area in the reign of Elizabeth by Mr Hassell Smith to which Dr Virgoe refers. For it is now possible to make meaningful comparisons between East Anglia in the fourteenth and the fifteenth centuries and again at the end of the sixteenth century.[11] In a review of Mr Hassell Smith's book[12] Mrs Pearl observed that it is a fairly straightforward task to describe and to evaluate in varying degrees of completeness 'the machinery of law and order, the provision of social services, the raising of taxation', and 'the personnel of a local governing-class, analysed in terms of prestige, wealth and ideology'; all of which adds up to 'an interpretation of authority in a locality and how it functioned'. But the much more complicated task is to 'demonstrate that what went on at the centre was ultimately affected by local activities and in turn in what ways the centre influenced the periphery'. It ought not to be difficult to agree that Dr Virgoe has made an important contribution to the first part of Mrs Pearl's equation and some very useful suggestions for dealing with the second.

Mrs Barron shows us the political reaction of the English capital to the change of régime when Edward IV seized power from the Lancastrians. We are already in her debt for illuminating the relations between the King and the capital in her article on the 'quarrel of Richard II with London, 1392-7'.[13] This showed quite clearly how the honeymoon period at the beginning of Richard's reign when he had been known mockingly as 'Rex Londonie' could change into the wrangling of the 1390s, and how the capital was forced to come to terms with its monarch. No wonder that the same capital should have behaved with great caution in the uncertainties of the 1450s. She has completely overhauled the existing account of how the city switched over from Lancastrian to Yorkist obedience and in the process has thrown new light on the processes of government finance. Two papers on urban history follow which also demonstrate the nature of the changing relationship between the Crown and the towns. That of Professor Chevalier writing on the *bonnes villes* in the fifteenth century, partly as a result of his quantitative approach, has produced some notable results. The great importance of Flanders, Picardy, and Outre-Seine-et-Yonne has been clearly indicated. By contrast royal letters sent to the towns of the Midi seem to have been few and far between. This fits in well with other evidence such as the maps produced by M. Dupont-Ferrier for the levying of the salt gabelle (1355-1483).[14] Professor Chevalier's treatment reminds us that the French towns of the Middle Ages were markedly freer than the English. In England, by contrast, to quote Mrs Lobel[15] 'the limited powers granted by the Angevin kings and the continued control exercised by them over town affairs, even to the point of making charter rights dependent on good behaviour, has been recognized since Madox's *Firma Burgi* as a most important characteristic of English towns and one that markedly distinguished them from continental ones'. The story of the English royal towns (and indeed of the seignorial ones) in the late Middle Ages is that of the slow growth of limited self-government. The concept of the 'communitas' remained strong, as at York where it seems to have meant as many as could be got into the guildhall; and the community in most towns had a common seal and a common chest. But in fact town governments were increasingly oligarchical. In many places from the middle of the fourteenth century onwards they concentrated on the acquisition of charters of incorporation, or like Bristol in 1373 on county status as well. As a result they largely became independent of the royal officials in the shires. However, though they often became responsible for the payment of their farm, for the administration of food prices, for the collection of tallages and aids, and for the repair and rebuilding of their walls, they remained under the fairly close control of the royal chancery. Petitions ran regularly to Westminster and more regularly writs ran down to the mayor and bailiffs. If a law-suit threatened, as at Oxford in 1429, we read of the eighty burgesses of the city who rode up to London where money was laid out to the justices of the Common Bench.[16] When disputes arose, as at Lynn in 1413, the chancellor, in that case Archbishop Arundel, might well be called in to settle them.[17] The reign of Henry VI proved especially fruitful for the granting of incorporations to towns and to their guilds. In addition to the classic and sophisticated charter granted in 1440 to Hull, other towns — Southampton,

Portsmouth, Norwich, and Nottingham, to go no further, can also provide comparable charters.[18] So can the guilds of Grocers, Fishmongers, Vintners, Brewers, Drapers, Cordwainers, Leathersellers, Haberdashers, and Armourers.[19] How far on the royal side this was the result of a genuine interest on the part of Henry VI's government in encouraging towns and guilds, and how far a reflection of the state of royal finances it is not at present easy to say. Certainly the Crown by including the towns in the new mortmain legislation of 1391, as Colin Platt has noted,[20] showed that it recognized their importance as landowners. For it stated in that act that they had been included because 'Mayors, Bailiffs and Commons of Cities, Boroughs and other Towns which have a perpetual Commonalty and others which have Offices perpetual, be as perpetual as People of Religion'. Moreover from the towns' point of view, as again Colin Platt has observed,[21] the importance to them of their position as landowners was a factor which strongly stimulated the movement for incorporation. The English towns also seem to have frequently sought and secured confirmations of 'inspeximus' and to have shown an interest in confirmations which is comparable with that of the French towns to which Professor Chevalier has drawn attention.

For Burgundy Professor Leguai has made a detailed and useful analysis of the fate of its towns which may be set against the paper of Dr Allmand on the fate of Rouen. It is good to be reminded that there were only two periods in which the Burgundian dukes sought to check appeals to the Paris *Parlement*, namely 1422-35 and 1471-7. It is also salutary to recall that the dukes themselves, apart from Charles the Bold, were so often able to influence French policy at the centre that it might well have seemed that they were the last people to wish it ever to be forgotten that they were peers of France. Likewise the towns themselves frequently had good cause to be glad that they could appeal to the *Parlement* as in the example quoted by Professor Leguai when Dijon was appealing against the duke of Burgundy himself. It is also good to have attention drawn to the ties between the diocese of Langres and the French kingdom. As to the outright resistance of the towns themselves to the incoming French rule, with some exceptions like Dijon, this seems to have been fiercer in Burgundy than at Rouen. Nevertheless Professor Leguai's 'third period' seems to have seen no united opposition, partly because of the rivalry between Dijon, Beaune, and Chalon and partly owing to social divisions within the towns themselves. Thus it was a fairly easy task for Louis XI to pick off his enemies one by one. The conclusion that the towns of Burgundy became as loyal to the kings of France as they had been to the dukes of Burgundy fits in well with Dr Barron's demonstration that towns like London were basically apolitical. They were chiefly motivated by recognizing on which side their true interest lay. As to Louis's construction of expensive castles at Dijon,

Beaune, and Auxonne to overawe their inhabitants as much as to defend the duchy, that smacks more of the castle-building policy of Cardinal Albornoz in the Papal States in the fourteenth century or of the Sforza and the Castel Sforzescho in Milan than of anything in England or the Iberian peninsula. Dr Allmand's paper by contrast shows the clergy and citizens of Rouen in a less timorous mood than Lancastrian London when the régime of Charles VII was imposed upon their city. Dr Allmand has rightly emphasized the continuity between the regional particularism of Normandy, which had been encouraged during the English occupation by the duke of Bedford and his English successors. Hence the reestablishment of the Norman *Cour des Aides* and the *Echiquier*; and both are forerunners of the *Parlement* of Rouen of the sixteenth century. If the duchy of Normandy ceased to exist and Normandy itself became inalienable, nevertheless a substantial part of its rights and privileges remained, and that they did so was due in no small measure to the efforts of the Rouennais. When it is recalled to what extent the administration of Rouen and of Normandy had been run by the Normans themselves under the English régime,[22] it can be seen that Dr Allmand's picture makes very good sense.

Dr Greengrass's essay belongs to the sixteenth century and so does not fall within the scope of the title of this book. Nevertheless his essay was given as a lecture at the conference and is highly relevant to the general theme. It is printed separately in an appendix of its own.

It was indeed above all in France that the localities, if not the local communities, were to impress themselves on the Crown in the sixteenth century; and in their case the story is taken down to 1585. As Dr Greengrass shows the monarchy under the last Valois virtually came to a standstill. Its subjects could generate ideas about reform, but these could not be put into effect because of its weakness. The steady practice of the sale of offices had in any case removed from the Crown its control over its own local officials, let alone over the local communities. In England, if the localities certainly made themselves felt in a succession of Tudor rebellions finishing in the Northern Rebellion of 1569, the Crown succeeded in mastering them. But its financial weakness, its lack of a standing army, and the dependence of the régime on the justices of the peace and other officials of local government, continued to render its position precarious. Thus not only could local bigwigs obtain the redress of grievances in Parliament, but, if the government indulged in legislation which was disliked in the regions, they could go a long way towards ensuring that it was never properly carried out. In any case in England the crisis of the monarchy was postponed till the mid-seventeenth century. In Spain, as in England, local protests, in the shape of the Revolts of the 'Comuneros' and of the 'Germanías', were successfully broken by the forces of the Crown, backed up in the first case by those of the Castilian nobility. But in Spain the problem of the relationship between the Crown and the local communities was complicated by an intense regionalism. The attempt to 'match in' Portugal in 1580 was to fail sixty years later. While the regionalism of Catalonia and the Basque Provinces, if not of Galicia and Andalusia, has lasted to the present day. In England and in France the modern reactions against bureaucratic government, the call for devolved assemblies and decentralization are there to remind us, should we need reminding, that the problems outlined in this volume have in many instances by no means reached the final stage of their development; and still less have they found their solutions.

Notes

1. *Four English Political Tracts of the Later Middle Ages*, ed. J.-P. Genet, *C.S.* (Fourth Ser.) xviii (1977).
2. E. Mitre Fernández, *La Extensión del régimen de corregidores en el reinado de Enrique III de Castilla*. Universidad de Valladolid. Estudios y Documentos, no. 29 (Valladolid, 1969), p. 38.
3. H. Sancho de Sopranis, *Historia Social de Jerez de la Frontera*, Centro de Estudios Históricos Jerezanos, 2nd series, no. 5 (Jerez de la Frontera, 1959), p. 5.
4. Ibid., no. 3 (1959), p. 10.
5. R.S. Chamberlain, 'The Corregidor in Castile in the sixteenth century', *Hisp. Amer. Hist. Rev.*, xxiii, (1943) quoting Ramírez, *Las Pragmaticas del Reyno* (Seville, 1520), fo. 57. For the sending out of the *corregidores* in 1480 cf. Fernando del Pulgar, *Crónica de los Reyes Católicos*, ed. J. de Mata Carriazo (Madrid, 1943), i, c.cxv, p. 423. The legislation of 6 July 1493 confined *corregidores* to the *letrado* class who had studied civil or canon law for at least ten years and were over twenty-six years old. For the subsequent *pragmática* of 9 June 1500 cf. *Capitulos . . . que han de guardar e cumplir los governadores, asistentes corregidores . . . hechos en Sevilla a 9 de Junio de 1500* (Seville, 1500) in Tarsicio de Azcona, *Isabel la Católica* (Madrid, 1964), p. 344.
6. Andres Bernáldez, *Memorias del reinado de los Reyes Católicos*, ed. M. Gómez-Moreno and J. de Mata Carriazo (Madrid, 1962), pp. 541-3; J. Edwards, 'La Révolte du Marquis de Priego à Cordoue en 1508, un symptome des tensions d'une société urbaine', *Mélanges de la Casa de Velásquez*, xii, (1976) 165-72.
7. H. Keniston, *Francisco de los Cobos* (Pittsburgh, 1958), pp. 53-4.
8. See p. 112.
9. See p. 51.
10. Salvador de Moxó, 'Los señoríos. En torno a una problemática para el estudio del régimen señorial', *Hispania* xxiv, (1964) 216; cf. *Los Antiquos señoríos de Toledo* (Toledo, 1973), pp. 102-5.
11. R. Virgoe, 'The Crown and local government. East Anglia under Richard II' in *Essays in Honour of May McKisack*, ed. F.R.H. du Boulay and Caroline Barron (London, 1971), pp. 218-41; A. Hassell Smith, *County and Court. Government and Politics in Norfolk 1558-1603* (1974).
12. In *Times Literary Supplement* for 8 August 1975.
13. *Essays in Honour of May McKisack*, pp. 173-201.
14. G. Dupont-Ferrier, *Etudes sur les institutions financières de la France* (Paris, 1930), I, facing p. 136.
15. M.D. Lobel, 'Some aspects of the Crown's influence in the development of the borough of Oxford up to 1307', *Beiträge zur Wirtschafts- und Stadtgeschichte*, Festschrift für Hektor Ammann (Wiesbaden, 1965), p. 65.
16. *Munimenta Civitatis Oxonie*, ed. H.E. Salter (Oxford Hist. Soc., 1920), lxxi, 284-6.
17. E.F. Jacob, *The Fifteenth Century* (Oxford, 1961), pp. 388-9.
18. C. Platt, *The English Medieval Town* (London, 1976), p.144; cf. Jacob, op.cit., pp. 392-3 and 397.
19. Platt, op.cit., p. 143.

20. Ibid., p. 142.
21. Cf. R.A. Newhall, *The English Conquest of Normandy, 1416-1424* (Yale University Press, 1924), pp. 174-6.
22. T.F. Tout, 'The beginnings of a modern capital: London and Westminster in the fourteenth century', *Collected Papers of Thomas Frederick Tout* (Manchester, 1934), iii. 249-75.

1

Political Theory and Local Communities in Later Medieval France and England

J.P. Genet

When discussing western-European political systems of the later Middle Ages, historians usually recognize the emergence of local communities as a significant development. There being no standard definition of the local community, I shall borrow that used by H. M. Cam for the shire: 'a unit held together by proximity, by local feeling and above all by common living traditions and common responsibilities'.[1] Her definition suits all sorts of local communities, even those which (like the French *commune*) could be defined in a more precise and more technical way. Moreover, the emergence of local communities was not an isolated phenomenon; it was closely linked to the progressive establishment of representative institutions. Although the link between representative institutions and local communities, which is a commonplace of historical writing today, must not always be taken for granted, it was usually obvious in the later Middle Ages. On the one hand, the representative institutions of a kingdom were organized on a local basis, as with the English Parliament[2] where, by the fourteenth century, knights of the shire and borough members were supposed to represent with *plena potestas* the communities which elected them.[3] On the other hand, most local communities were governed by some sort of representative body. Possible exceptions are the community of the vill and the *communauté villageoise*.[4] Outside the political sphere, even the jury may be considered as a representative body.[5]

The later medieval king was, in short, a man of dialogue.[6] He had to take public opinion into account; he needed both to give information to his subjects, in order to justify his actions, and also to be informed of their desires and grievances. In a poem written for the future King John II of France, the author insists on the necessity of dialogue between king and country. 'A prince or good lord should get to know his land . . . He should

visit cities and sites of antiquity, and be ready to listen willingly in both
town and countryside to complaints and grievances, wrongs and acts of
mischief, which his subjects may wish to report . . .'[7] The emergence of
both local communities and representative institutions can be seen as a
reaction against the development of the monarchical state. But it can also
be seen as a response to the stimuli given by kings themselves as and when
these brought to light new problems.[8] Contemporary observers could
hardly fail to notice that the political systems of the west had been much
altered by such developments. It is therefore important to examine the
works of late medieval theorists to try to assess what significance, if any,
they attached to the evolution of local communities. Yet such an assessment
is difficult to make. No theorist was concerned with 'local communities' as
one of his central themes. Whenever he paid them attention, he did so
incidentally; his argument was directed elsewhere. Fortescue's treatment of
the jury is of this kind. A distinct characteristic of late medieval theory is its
failure, both in France and in England,[9] to insert local communities into the
framework of the *politia*. There are many possible explanations for this; I
shall discuss two.

The first explanation derives from the inadequacy of traditional
vocabulary. Medieval political theory borrowed its vocabulary from
classical antiquity, first through Augustine and the Fathers, then through
Roman Law, and finally through Aristotle as amplified and adapted by
Aquinas, Giles of Rome, and the authors of tracts in the style of *Miroir aux
Prince*. For Aristotle, the kingdom (Greek μοναρχία; Latin *regnum*) and the
city (Greek πόλις; Latin *civitas*) were the two political communities worth
mentioning, the two fundamental types of state. He distinguished five forms
of kingship: (i) the Spartan form; (ii) kingship among barbarians; (iii)
dictatorship or elective tyranny; (iv) kingship in the Heroic Age; and (v)
absolute kingship, with the king exercising plenary power in the nature of
patria potestas. Medieval authors may have found these distinctions useful;
but because the *communitas regni* itself was considered in highly abstract
terms,[10] the Aristotelian *regnum* remained for them a concept, a tool for
theoretical demonstrations. Even if the concept was neither clear nor useful,
since kings and kingship were problems of central importance for theorists,
the words *rex* and *regnum* kept their value.[11] For the πόλις Aristotle stated
his ideals in Book VII of the *Politics*. His definitions of the city mark it out
as quite different from existing medieval communities,[12] even urban ones,
with the possible exceptions of the Italian city-state.[13]

Giles of Rome borrows word for word all the definitions of Aristotle
touching the city and its origins.[14] Another strict Aristotelian, Marsilius of
Padua, while defining the state,[15] says that 'city' may be used as a synonym
for state, though in many cases a state is a kingdom composed of many
cities.[16] There is nothing remarkable about this, but Marsilius stresses the

fact that the city is a civil community. Like Aristotle and Giles of Rome, he believes that the origin of civil communities stems first from the household, and then from the village: the household and the village are therefore civil communities, though the model civil community of normal size is the city.[17] Here, as elsewhere, the epithet *civilis* underlines the Roman Law conception of this type of community. Yet even with the addition of the epithet *civilis* this concept of 'community' seems vague;[18] a 'community' is surely characterized by its political and spatial nature; and in Marsilius' vocabulary, the word is applied most readily to what we should call a sovereign state, or, at least, to well defined administrative units.[19] Something of this traditional view of the birth of the state is echoed by Sir John Fortescue in his *Governance of England* when he evokes 'the grete comunalties, as was the felowshippe that came into this land with Brute, wyllynge to be unite and made a body polletike called a reawme . . .' 'body polletike' is here an equivalent of *communitas civilis*.[20] But Fortescue shifts from a purely geographic and economic origin (since the ultimate end of the Aristotelian city is to allow a human group to satisfy its needs in the best conditions) to a constitutional and voluntarist one which, though mythical, may have had some political importance.[21]

Giles of Rome and Marsilius of Padua seem to have been prevented from noticing fully the ambiguities of the word city, perhaps because their technical language was highly sophisticated; the classical culture of most medieval political writers was undoubtedly sufficient to make them aware of the significance of the city in antiquity. But was this so with their audience? By contrast, Nicholas Oresme, when commenting on the *Politica* of Aristotle for Charles V of France and his councillors, felt more concerned with the need to elucidate ambiguities;[22] for Aristotle's statement that a political system of a city may be transformed, he provided a lengthy gloss on the five meanings of 'city'.[23]

(i)   So I say that a city is sometimes taken to be a great multitude of houses or dwellings which are near or close to one another in a single place . . . but this meaning is wrong, just as it would be wrong to say that the chamber of the *Parlement* is the very *Parlement* itself.[24]

(ii) A city is better described as being about men, and for this reason it is stated in the first chapter that a city is a multitude of citizens, living self-sufficiently . . . A city may be regarded as a multitude of citizens, living in one place, taking the city in the first meaning. In this way one says that Paris is a city, Rouen is a city, and so on.

(iii) Each multitude of citizens which governs itself according to certain practices, and which is ruled by princes or a prince, may be called a city, for the practices give the city its character and make it into what it is. In this sense a kingdom or a country is a large city whose whole is made up of a number of parts.

(iv)   The multitude of those who have been or will be of the Catholic Faith of Jesus Christ may be described as forming a city.

(v)   A leading group of people with special responsibilities may be called a city: in this sense whose whom we call Churchmen are like a city. . .'

This set of definitions is particularly interesting, since it provides us with the different meanings which were attributed to the word city in Oresme's times. If we exclude the first meaning (as improper) and the fourth (as confined to theology), we are left with the third meaning, which is purely Aristotelian and recalls the *Defensor Pacis*, and the second and the fifth, both of which can be considered convenient for describing local communities. But a further difficulty arises with the fifth meaning: it may equally apply to corporations and all sorts of corporate bodies.[25] (This is a separate problem with which I deal later.)[26] None the less, Oresme clearly demonstrates that if local communities are at first glance totally absent from the theorists' works, they may in fact be hidden behind an antiquated vocabulary. In other words, if the theorists did not resort to the term 'local communities', it was not impossible for their audience to understand that term.

Evidence of these difficulties of terminology is provided by the *Tractatus De Regimine Principum ad Regem Henricum Sextum*, a tract written for Henry VI of England between 1436 and 1443. As a patchwork of well-chosen quotations and personal comments, it is a good witness to the assumptions underlying the political thought of its time.[27] When quoting almost entire chapters of the *De Regimine Principum*, the author — for he was more than a compiler — suppresses wherever possible *politia* and *civitas* as well as *respublica*; but when this is not possible, he substitutes *regnum* for *politia*, and *communitas* for *civitas*.[28] At times, however, he is confused. He can borrow from Giles of Rome, for instance, when saying that the welfare of the *community* and *kingdom* stems from obedience to the king and observance of the law, but then support his proposition by a quotation which he wrongly attributes to the first book of Aristotle's *Art of Rhetoric*: 'in legibus est salus civitatis'.[29] He probably felt it necessary to try to update political vocabulary in order that he might be understood by his intended audience — the king and his immediate circle. This suggests that by the mid-fifteenth century words such as *city* (*civitas*) were inadequate to describe political reality. But even if medieval political vocabulary is submitted to some distortions, and its terminology is recognized to be antiquated and therefore unreal, it remains true that theorists hardly ever discussed local communities.

The second explanation of the lack of concern shown by medieval

political theorists for local communities lies in their fundamental preoc-
cupations. Medieval political theory is found in a variety of materials. First
there is what may be described as technical literature. Though political
science has emerged today as a distinct branch of knowledge, this was not
the case in the Middle Ages. Many political concepts were then derived
from theology, and from both civil and canon law.[30] If the writings of theo-
logians and lawyers do not directly concern us, the fact must not be over-
looked that the influence which they exercised on political thought was of
the utmost importance. Besides, commentaries on the political writings of
the Fathers and of Aristotle (the *Politics*, the *Economics*, and even the *Ethics*)
undoubtedly belong to the area of political theory: but medieval
philosophers were often engaged in religious and theological controversies
and did not comment directly on practical problems of the day.[31] Their
contribution to political thought was therefore rather general — though the
discovery of Aristotle in the twelfth century was certainly the turning point
in the evolution of political theory.[32] In fact, most of the literature devoted
to political theory from the twelfth century onwards falls into two distinct
groups. On the one hand, there are tracts written for lay rulers, most of
which take the form of the *Miroir au Prince* and purport to describe good and
bad governments and to provide sound advice for princes. On the other
hand, there is an enormous bulk of tracts, more or less polemical, which
having been instigated by the conflicts between popes and emperors were
further stimulated, first by the quarrels between the Papacy and rulers like
Philip IV of France and the Emperor Lewis of Bavaria, and, secondly, by
the quarrels between the General Council of the Church and the Papacy.

The literature of the *Miroirs* is much neglected. A good definition of this
literary genre does not exist, even in the otherwise reliable and useful catalogue of Wilhelm Berges.[33] In a very general sense, the *Miroir au Prince* is an
expression which describes a work in which the ideal portrait of the Prince
is drawn together with an indication of how this ideal may be achieved.
Thus the most popular *Miroir* is a work usually forgotten by modern critics,
the pseudo-Aristotelian *Secreta Secretorum*,[34] manuscripts of which are found
in almost all important libraries. There is also an important group of
Miroirs written for the Angevin kings of England by Peter of Blois, John of
Salisbury, Giraldus Cambrensis, and perhaps Robert Grosseteste.[35] The
true *Miroir* had four distinct features: its author will be a friar and it has as
its purpose the attempt by the friars to enforce the true principles of
Christian religion upon the laity. Its style is didactic; it does not pretend to
be a piece of rhetoric but is a product of moral theology; and finally its
vocabulary becomes more and more Aristotelian the later the date of its
composition. Such a precisely defined corpus of *Miroirs* is predominantly
French and connected with both the Capetian court and the University of
Paris. There are in fact fewer *Miroirs* than is generally thought; but three at

least had a wide circulation, the *De Regimine Principum* of Giles of Rome, the *De Eruditione Principum* attributed to Guillaume Perault, and the anonymous *Liber de informatione Principum*. Other similar works to have been widely read were those of Vincent of Beauvais, and the *De Regno ad Regem Cypri* (coupled with Ptolemy of Lucca's *De Regimine Principum*, a compound work consisting also of the *De Regno* which was for long traditionally attributed to Aquinas).

In all *Miroirs* political decision results from the will of the ruler. Yet he does not have complete liberty since, as will be seen, despite his being its head, he must not act against the good of the community of which he is but a part. Indeed, the psychological and moral laws which govern the ruler are of crucial importance. There is nothing surprising, therefore, in the existence of the tracts which, though purporting to describe the principles of government, are in fact devoted to a study of the four cardinal virtues. An example is *L'Estat et le gouvernement comme les princes et seigneurs se doivent gouverner* (1347).[36] Such studies are appropriate to a system in which everything depends on the just and the good (or unjust and bad) will of the ruler. Far from being purely idealistic, *Miroirs aux Princes* are strikingly attuned to well-known notions of feudalism and bastard feudalism. The word feudal has been applied to the social order which developed after the Germanic conquests in Europe, and so to all the principle features of that order, including relationships between lords and tenants, whether the latter owned land in their own right or held fees. Bastard feudalism went further. It is certain that by the fourteenth century lords, whether in England or France, seldom enjoyed a strict feudal relationship with any of their tenants.[37] A new structure, the monarchical state, had to be taken into account. The aristocracy, whose landed incomes suffered from the prolonged agrarian and demographic crisis which followed the Black Death, tried to obtain as many favours as possible from the king. The king, in his turn, was able to bestow on the aristocracy offices, salaries and gifts from the proceeds of ever-growing taxation. Aristocratic factions thus appeared everywhere; their aim was to exert as much control as possible over this new source of income. And a lord had to be surrounded, to borrow Plummer's words, by 'retainers, who wore his livery and fought his battles, and were . . . in the law courts and elsewhere, *addicti jurati in verba magistri.*' In his turn, the lord maintained the quarrels of his dependants and sought to shield them from punishment.[38]

During the late medieval period English as well as French government was rooted, even at its highest levels, in the personal relationships between patrons and clients. The moral issues which these relationships involved were cardinal for the writers of *Miroirs aux Princes* and their readers alike. But individuals, civil communities, and local communities, even the smallest, all sought patronage. They all had to look upwards, because they needed patrons who would introduce their petitions for redress or privilege either to the king or to those who dominated his council.[39]

From the twelfth century to the fifteenth political debate, as D'Entrèves, Richard Scholz, Walter Ullmann, and Michael Wilks[40] all demonstrate, centred on the problem of sovereignty. This problem implies a study of the relations between human and divine power on the one hand, and the relations between ecclesiastical and secular power on the other. True, the discovery in the twelfth century of Aristotle's concept of the *civitas* as an organism whose purpose was the common good of all gave a new importance to 'citizens', or *populus*. (*Populus* in this context means the whole body of citizens — not the 'many-headed monster', whose penchant for rebelling against the social order the established classes dreaded.) The ruler and his subjects should be bound by mutual ties of duties and obligations. Indeed, theorists became more and more concerned with (in Professor Ullmann's phrase) 'the ascending theme of government'.[41] This provided many opportunities for a new assessment of the share of the people in government, and consequently of the political organization of the *populus*. At the same time, the introduction from Civil and Canon Law of the maxim *Quod omnes tangit . . .*[42] led the way to the development of assemblies, and also to the practice of representation. Notions of representation, as well as of the *communitas regni*, took shape and strength in England from Stephen Langton (1225-6)[43] to the Statute of York (1322),[44] and in France from the quarrel between the archbishops of Bordeaux and Bourges (1227-41)[45] to the assemblies of Philip IV.

Later medieval theorists, it should be noted, were not concerned either with the working or the attributes of local assemblies. Nor were they concerned with the means whereby such assemblies were elected. They may ultimately have derived a theory of limited monarchy from Aquinas, but they failed to transpose it into a constitutional form. Their failure is the more remarkable because in the Church the same theory led to a 'complete denial of the traditional theory of papal monarchy'.[46] In the course of the Conciliar Movement attention was paid to the rights and prerogatives of the General Council, as representative of the whole *ecclesia*. In the world of lay power it was recognized that the king's actions were limited by natural law: but how was this limitation to be enforced? Even Marsilius, known for his 'democratic' outlook and for whom the *populus* is the *legislator humanus* and the *persona ficta* of the state (as Christ is the *persona Ecclesie*), is content with 'an abstract *persona ficta* of the community which the aristocracy has a natural capacity to stand for . . .'.[47] Fortescue's explicit theory of *dominium politicum et regale* has been heralded as a precursor of the 'constitutional monarchy' of the seventeenth and eighteenth centuries;[48] but he is in fact equally shy, if not more so. He relies on a well-composed council for the control of the king's actions much more than on parliament, about which he writes surprisingly little.[49]

So far words such as 'corporate bodies', *communitas, communitas civilis*, and *civitas* have been used without restriction. This implies that local communities can at least be traced in the works of the theorists. Indeed it can be argued, as Professor Wilks observes, that medieval society was 'a seething mass of corporate institutions stretching from the lower reaches of the manorial courts and town guilds to the lofty conceptions of *communitas regni* and *communitas ecclesiae*'.[50] But what place in this seething mass do theorists attribute to local communities? In fact, the structure of medieval society is nearly always explained in terms of 'estates'. Preachers and poets are the most frequent exponents of this explanation;[51] but theorists also attached much importance to corporate bodies which, organized in a more or less regular way, would represent the elementary components of the *politia*. Some of these corporate bodies might have been conceived as local communities. Thus, in his intended address to the three estates which were to be assembled at Blois in 1433, Jean Juvenal des Ursins described the sins of each estate which shared the responsibility for bringing God's wrath on the kingdom of France. After the *gens de justice*, the clergy, the princes, lords and knights, he considered the *bonnes villes* — but by the *bonnes villes* he meant only the merchants.[52]

In England the situation is more ambiguous: 'the commons' might be understood by reference to the community of the shire as well as to social hierarchy. If, as H. M. Cam points out, the knights of the shire must be taken into account, 'as a social order they merge at either end into the nobility and the burgesses'. Furthermore, 'the community represented, though the country gentlemen might predominate, was the whole body of the shire, inhabitants as well as gentlemen'.[53] And there is ample evidence, especially in Fortescue's well-known analysis of rural society in England,[54] that in later medieval times the commons included a large spectrum of social levels. It is, in short, impossible to describe the English shire in social terms.

This inability to insert commons in the social hierarchy accounts for the ambiguity of the word. It was used more often as a designation for a sort of third estate than in its constitutional sense. In France, by contrast, there was a certain degree of inter-relationship between the political structure and the social hierarchy. That is why Fortescue, an acute observer of the English scene, which does not give such encouragement to the estates theory,[55] says in his *De Natura Legis Naturae* that 'in the English kingdom kings do not make laws without the agreement of the three estates of that kingdom';[56] whereas in the *Governance of England* he points to the similarities between the English Parliament and the French *Etats Généraux*, which 'whan thai bith assembled bith like to the courte of the parlement in Ingelonde'.[57]

The inaccuracy of this statement may be obvious today; but though

Fortescue, who served in every Parliament between 1442 and 1460, was certainly conscious of the wide differences between Parliaments and *Etats Généraux*, he could still adapt French political vocabulary to an English reality. In fact, the divisions of society into three estates was normal in contemporary political theory. As a follower of John Wyclif expressed it,

> 'holy chirche is a gode howswife and made clothis of ray to clothe with hir meynye. Clothis of coloure schuld be prestis that ever more schulde be stable and grounde of other parties of holy chirche by techynge of goddis lawe; tho secunde parte, rude and grete, schulde betho comyns, but tho thrid part, as tho chaumpe sotile of sylk or other mater, schulde be noble men that schulde be bytwixe these two . . .'[58]

Even a professional administrator like Edmund Dudley divided his *Tree of Commonwealth* (1509-10) according to the properties of the four estates, king, clergy, 'chivalrie', and 'artificers'.[59] This is more a tribute to tradition than anything else; but since he speaks later of 'realme, citie, company, felloship or particular person',[60] it is clear that his interpretation of political society is based on a corporate view. True, the English government itself was occasionally able to produce a list of estates of which poets and moralists could have approved, as with the poll-tax of 1379 or in its sumptuary legislation.[61] In France estates are nowhere challenged. I have already mentioned the *Epistre* to the Estates-General of Blois by Jean Juvenal des Ursins.[62] In his *Discours touchant les Questions et Differends entre les rois de France et d'Angleterre*, his complete lack of references to local communities is equally noteworthy. Throughout his lengthy exposition of the problem of Gascony, he makes no mention of its people, of local representatives, or even of the sentiments of loyalty felt by the Gascons towards the kings of France; his argument is firmly based on purely historical elements,[63] going back to Dagobert and (629-39) and Louis the Pious (814-40).[64] This is all the more striking since as bishop of Beauvais Jean Juvenal appears to have been sensitive to the encroachments of the royal administration on local privileges.[65] Among corporate bodies and civil communities, the local communities were outshone by estates; and social estates also had in most cases active and influential political expressions (for example, guilds, leagues, and corporations).

It might be concluded that the study of political literature is entirely irrelevant to the problem of local communities. Yet though they were not primarily concerned with local communities and their specific problems, most political theorists were working on problems the solution to which was crucial to the evolution of such communities. Certainly local communities received decisive help from such concepts as representation and common responsibility. But it must also be remembered that no theorist, in France or England, was concerned with providing a background to the effective working of local communities. The only existing institutions to be thoroughly examined were the Italian city states, the General Council of the Church, and, to some extent, the central administrative institutions of both France and the Empire. Only occasionally are relevant observations available which derive from contemporary events, as, for instance, when the author of the *De Speculo Regis Edwardi III* devoted much space to the practice of purveyance.[66]

This study does not, indeed, survey all the available evidence; it is concerned only with political theory in moral and polemical writings, and it ignores 'technical' literature. As the example of the successful career of the maxim *quod omnes tangit* from the text books of the lawyers to the assemblies of France and England demonstrates, 'technical' works are in fact relevant. In the mind of lawyers, local communities existed as the depositaries of local custom;[67] and in his advocacy of the jury, Fortescue underlines the fact that neighbours are the people most likely to know exactly the circumstances in which a crime had been committed. Nevertheless, the complete absence of local communities from later medieval theory is noteworthy, since, after all, local communities were vigorous and played an essential part in the political life of both France and England. This absence sheds a valuable light on political theory itself, and also on the extent to which we may rely on it. Theorists do not try to explain precisely the institutions they see working; they confine themselves to the philosophical and moral principles which govern those institutions. In a feudal society, ideology was still a matter of religion and of religious ethic. Much can be learned from all the compendious theoretical tracts, as the many papers about political theory read to the International Commission for the History of Representative and Parliamentary Institutions prove: and I think that the *Miroir aux Princes* literature is closely connected with the experience of personal relationships in feudal society. But the fundamental characteristics of this literature remained unaltered until the beginning of the sixteenth century. There are occasional forerunners, and it is not mere chance that I have often mentioned Fortescue.[68] Only with Machiavelli's *Prince* and humanist political thought does a new way emerge of understanding politics.

Notes

1. H.M. Cam, 'The community of the shire and the payment of its representatives in Parliament', *Liberties and Communities in Medieval England* (Cambridge, 1944), p. 247. (Miss Cam first published this paper in *Journées de Droit*, Dijon, June 1939.)

2. Ecclesiastical and lay lords were originally summoned because of their feudal relationship with the king. But 'the commons first achieved a corporate identity and a name just because they were not parliament. They had to be called something: and were called *domus communitatis* because they represented the communities — counties, cities and boroughs . . .' (K. Pickthorn, *Early Tudor Government, Henry VII* (Cambridge, 1934), p. 96). Miss Cam considered the English Parliament to be 'an assembly of estates and a concentration of local communities' ('The study of English medieval history today', *Law Finders and Law Makers in Medieval England* (London, 1962), p. 174).

3. J.G. Edwards, 'The *Plena Potestas* of English parliamentary representatives', *Oxford Essays in Medieval History presented to Herbert E. Salter* (Oxford, 1934), pp. 141-54. For a note of the writings on this point see G. Post, *Studies in Medieval Thought* (Princeton, 1964), p. 92.

4. J. Wake, 'Communitas villae', *E.H.R.* xxxvii (1922), 406-13; H.M. Cam, 'The community of the vill', *Medieval Studies presented to Rose Graham*, ed. Veronica Ruffer and A.J. Taylor (Oxford, 1950), pp. 1-14; reprinted *Law Finders and Law Makers*, pp. 71-84; W.O. Ault, 'English village assemblies', *Album Helen Maud Cam: Etudes présentées à la commission internationale pour l'histoire des assemblées d'état* (Louvain, 1960-1), i. 13-35.

5. 'The jury in England was the oldest and, some would argue, the most important root of later representative practice' (R.S. Hoyt, 'Representation in the administrative practice of Anglo-Norman England', *Album H.M. Cam*,ii. 15).

6. B. Guenée, *L'Occident aux XIVe et XVe siècles, Les Etats* (Paris, 1971), p. 159.

7. *Four English Political Tracts of the Later Middle Ages*, ed. J-P. Genet (C.S., fourth series, xvii (1977)), p. 217.

8. See, for instance, C.H. Taylor, 'Some new texts on the Assembly of 1302', *Speculum*, xi (1936), 38-42.

9. An exception is the writings about the government of Italian cities, for which see F. Hertter, *Die Podestaliteratur Italiens im 12. und 13. Jahrhundert* (Tübingen, 1910) and A. Sorbelli, 'I teorici del Reggimento Communale', *Bollettino dell' Istituto Storico Italiano per il Medio Evo e Archivio Muratoriano*, (Rome, 1944), 31-136. Since I am concerned only with French and English theorists, I have not made general use of these Italian texts. John of Viterbo's *Liber de Regimine* (ed. C. Salvemini, *Bibliotheca Juridica Medii Aevi*, III *Scripta Anedotica Glossatorum* (Bologna, 1901), pp. 215-80) was, however, partly known in both France and England through Brunetto Latini's very popular *Le Livres dou Tresor* (ed. P. Chabaille (Paris, 1863)).

10. L.R. Little, 'The size and governance of medieval communities', *Studia Gratiana Post Scripta*, xv (Rome, 1972), 377-97; R.B. Giesey, 'The French Estates and the *Corpus Mysticum Regni*', *Album H.M. Cam*, i. 153-71.

11. J. Quillet, *La Philosophie politique de Marsile de Padoue* (Paris, 1970), pp. 75-77.

12. M. Grignaschi, 'Nicholas Oresme et son commentaire à la Politique d'Aristote', *Album H.M. Cam*, i. 109-11, shows that Oresme did not hesitate to use *city* (see below p. 21), but that he gives *citizen* an entirely different meaning from that of Aristotle.

13. Whether theorists in general, and Marsilius of Padua in particular, drew their inspiration from the examples of Italian city states is still an open question, J. Quillet,

op.cit., and F. Oakley, *The Political Thought of Pierre d'Ailly* (New Haven, 1964) both think that they did so: but M. Wilks ('Corporation and representation in the *Defensor Pacis*', *Studia Gratiana Post Scripta*, xv (Rome, 1972), 291), denies it.

14. See, for example, *De Regimine Principum* (Rome, 1556: reprinted Frankfurt, 1968), ii. 3, fo. 135, and iii. 4, fos. 241-2.

15. This is A. Gerwirth's translation of *regnum* (Marsilius of Padua, *The Defender of the Peace*, 2nd edn (New York, 1967), p. 8). I prefer it to J. Quillet's *Royaume* (Marsile de Padoue, *Le Défendeur de la Paix* (Paris, 1968), p. 57).

16. See Marsilius von Padua, *Defensor Pacis*, ed. R. Scholz, *Fontes Iuris Germanici Antiqui* (Hanover, 1933), pp. 10-11. 'Quod hec diccio *regnum* in una sui significacione importat pluralitatem civitatum seu provinciarum sub uno regimine contentarum: secundum quam accepcionem, non differt regnum a civitate in policie specie, sed magis secundum quantitatem. In alia vero sui accepcione significat hoc nomen *regnum* speciem quandam policie seu regiminis temperati, quam vocat Aristoteles *monarchiam temperatam*, quo modo potest esse regnum in unica civitate sicut in pluribus, quamadmodum fuit circa ortum communitatum civilium, quasi enim ut in pluribus erat rex unius in unica civitate. Tercia significacio huius nominis et famosior componitur ex prima et secunda. Quarta vero ipsius accepcio est commune quiddam ad omnem regiminis temperati speciem, sive in unica (civitate) sive in pluribus civitatibus. . . .'

17. Ibid., pp. 14-16, 74-76. J. Quillet (ed.), Marsile de Padoue, *Le Défendeur de la Paix*, pp. 57-58, provides a useful collection of quotations on the origins of cities.

18. P. Michaud-Quantin, *Universitas, Expressions du Mouvement Communautaire dans le moyen âge latin* (Paris, 1970), pp. 147-53. Marsilius is not exceptional in this respect.

19. *Defensor Pacis*, ed. Scholz, pp. 119-21. Elsewhere Marsilius gives a different interpretation of the word city: 'Sicut enim ad civilem communitatem et legem ordinandam convenerunt homines a principio . . .' (ibid., p. 434). ('Le Rôle de l'aristotelisme dans le *Defensor Pacis* de Marsile de Padoue', *Revue d'Histoire et Philosophie Religieuse*, iii (1955), 306; and 'L'Interpretation de la "Politique" d'Aristote dans le "Dialogue" de Guillaume d'Ockham', *Liber Memorialis George de Lagarde, Studies presented to the International Commission for the history of Representative and Parliamentary Institutions* (Paris-Louvain, 1970), p. 70).

20. J. Fortescue, *The Governance of England*, ed. C. Plummer (Oxford, 1885), p. 112. See also J-P. Genet, 'Les Idées sociales de Sir John Fortescue', *Economies et sociétés au Moyen Age. Mélanges offerts a Edouard Perroy* (Paris, 1973), pp. 450-2).

21. John of Viterbo, *Liber de Regimine*, ed. C. Salvemini, pp. 218-29, expresses another view about the origin of cities. After quoting Cicero, *De Officiis*, ii. 78 ('Id enim est proprium . . . civitatis atque urbis, ut sit libera et non solicita suae rei cuiusque custodia'), he gives as his example the building of Rome by Romulus. For Giles of Rome, Marsilius of Padua, and Sir John Fortescue the community antedated the town, whereas for John of Viterbo the town antedated the community.

22. M. Grignaschi, 'Nicholas Oresme . . .', pp. 107-9.

23. N. Oresme, 'Le Livre de Politiques d'Aristote', ed. A. Menut, *Transactions of the American Philosophical Society*, new series, lx, pt. 6 (1970), 119-20.

24. Grignaschi, 'Nicholas Oresme . . .', p. 107, provides an example of an improper use by Aristotle himself. See also Oresme, op.cit., p. 161.

25. Grignaschi, op.cit., p. 108.

26. See below p. 26.

27. *Four English Political Tracts*, ed. Genet, pp. 40-173.

28. For example, ibid., p. 66, quoting Giles of Rome, Bk. I, pt. ii, ch. 27; and 74, quoting Bk. III, pt. ii, ch. 34.

29. Ibid., p. 74. The author of the *Tractatus* here glosses his quotation from Giles of Rome by adding community (*communitas*) to the original (*De Regimine Principum*, 324).

30. W. Gilmann, *Law and Politics in the Middle Ages* (Harmondsworth, 1975), ch. II.
31. M. Grignaschi, 'L' Interprétation de la "Politique" d'Aristote . . .', pp. 71-72. See also Aquinas, *De Regno ad Regem Cypri*, trans. and ed. as *St. Thomas Aquinas on Kingship to the King of Cyprus*, G.B. Phelan and I. Th. Eschmann (Toronto, 1949); reprinted (Amsterdam, 1967), pp. ix-xxxix.
32. W. Ullmann, *Principles of Government and Politics in the Middle Ages* (London, 1961), pp. 231-7; and also his *Medieval Political Thought*, pp. 179 ff.
33. W. Berges, *Die Fürstenspiegel des hohen und späten Mittelalters* (Stuttgart, 1938).
34. See M.A. Manzalaoui, 'The *Secreta Secretorum* in English thought and literature from the fourteenth to the seventeenth century' (unpublished D. Phil. thesis, 1954, Bodleian Library, Oxford), and his edition of *Secretum Secretorum. Nine English Versions* (E.E.T.S., 1977).
35. For Grosseteste's lost 'Abbreviacio de Principatu regni et Tiranidis', see S.H. Thomson, *The Writings of Robert Grosseteste, Bishop of Lincoln* (Cambridge–New York, 1940), p. 145.
36. Rouen, Bibliothèque Municipale, MS. 1223, fos. 156^v, 165^r -182^r; and B.N.MS. fr. 15352, fos. 151-208. A fifteenth-century English translation, 'The III Consideracions right necesserye to the good governaunce of a prince', is printed in *Four English Political Tracts*, ed. Genet, pp. 174-219.
37. K.B. McFarlane, 'Bastard feudalism', *B.I.H.R.* xx (1945), 161-80; and also his 'Parliament and bastard feudalism', *T.R.Hist.S.* 4th series, xxvi (1944), 53-79 (reprinted *Essays in Medieval History*, ed. R.W. Southern (London, 1968), pp. 240-63).
38. *The Governance of England*, ed. C. Plummer, pp. 15-16.
39. For petitioning by communities through an intermediary, see below B. Chevalier, pp. 112 ff.; P.S. Lewis, p. 37.
40. A.P. D'Entrèves, *The Medieval Contribution to Political Thought* (Oxford, 1939); R. Scholz, *Unbekannte kirchenpolitische Streitschriften aus der Zeit Ludwigs des Bayern (1327-1354)* (Rome, 1911), I; W. Ullmann, op.cit., above n. 30; M. Wilks, *The Problem of Sovereignty in the Later Middle Ages* (Cambridge, 1963).
41. Ullmann, *Principles of Government and Politics in the Middle Ages*, p. 30ff. He means that the power to make laws originally resided in the people, instead of being transmitted from God (as with the theme of 'descending power').
42. Post, *Studies in Medieval Legal Thought*, 163 ff. Y.J.M. Congar, 'Quod omnes tangit, ab omnibus tractari et approbari debet', *Revue Historique de Droit Français et Etranger*, 4e série, lvi (1958), 210-59.
43. E. Hall, 'King Henry III and the reception of the Roman Law maxim Quod omnes tangit', *Studia Gratiana Post Scripta*,xv (Rome, 1972), 125-45.
44. G. Post, 'The two laws and the Statute of York', *Speculum*, xxix (1954), 416-32; D. Clementi, 'That the Statute of York is no longer ambiguous', *Album H.M. Cam*, ii. 93-100.
45. Post, *Studies in Medieval Legal Thought*, pp. 138-40.
46. Wilks, *The Problem of Sovereignty in the Later Middle Ages*, p. 229.
47. Wilks, 'Corporations and Representation in the Defensor Pacis', p. 278.
48. C.A.J. Skeel, 'The influence of the writings of Sir John Fortescue', *T.R.Hist.S.*, 3rd series, x (1916), 74-114.
49. S.B. Chrimes, *English Constitutional Ideas in the Fifteenth Century* (Cambridge, 1936), p. 67. In *The Governance of England* Fortescue uses *council* thirty-eight times and *parliament* only six times.
50. Wilks, op.cit., p. 253.
51. R. Mohl, *The Three Estates in Medieval and Renaissance Literature* (New York, 1933).
52. B.N.MS. fr. 2701, fo. 2^v ff.

53. H.M. Cam, 'The community of the shire . . .', *Liberties and Communities in Medieval England*, pp. 246, 247. See also A.R. Myers, 'The English Parliament and the French Estates General in the Middle Ages', *Album H.M. Cam*, ii. 144.

54. *De Laudibus Legum Anglie*, ed. and trans. S.B. Chrimes (Cambridge, 1942), pp. 118-19.

55. See H.M. Cam's answer to the corporative theories of Emile Lousse in her 'Theory and practice of representation in medieval England', *History*, n.s. xxviii (1931), 11-26, reprinted *Law Finders and Law Makers*, pp. 159-75.

56. *The Works of Sir John Fortescue*, collected by Thomas, Lord Clermont (London 1869), i. 77. 'In regno . . . Anglie reges *sine trium statutum regni illius* consensu leges non condunt, nec subsidia imponent subditis suis.' My translation varies slightly from that given ibid., p. 205. The italics are mine.

57. *The Governance of England*, p. 113.

58. *Four English Political Tracts*, ed. Genet, p. 6.

59. E. Dudley, *The Tree of Commonwealth*, ed. D.M. Brodie (Cambridge, 1949), pp. 22, 42, 44-45. For the king's estate in English constitutional thought, see S.B. Chrimes, *English Constitutional Ideas in the Fifteenth Century*, ch. I.

60. *The Tree of Commonwealth*, p. 40.

61. R.B. Dobson, *The Peasants' Revolt of 1381* (London, 1970), 106-11; W. Hooper, 'The Tudor sumptuary laws', *E.H.R.* xxx (1915), 433-5.

62. See above p. 26.

63. B.N.MS. fr. 2701, fos. 32ᵛ-32ᵛ.

64. Dagobert, King of the Franks 629-39; Louis the Debonair or Pious, Emperor 814-40. For a similar appeal to the remote past, made by the Estates of Normandy in 1578, see M. Greengrass, below, p. 00.

65. F. Maton, *La Souveraineté dans Jean II Juvénal des Ursins* (Paris, 1917), pp. 106-12.

66. *De Speculo Regis Edwardi III*, ed. J. Moisant (Paris, 1891). For its authorship see L. Boyle, 'William of Pagula and the Speculum Regis Edwardi III', *Medieval Studies*, xxxii (1970), 329 ff. For its comments on purveyance see J.R. Maddicott, *The English Peasantry and the Demands of the Crown, Past and Present Supplements*, i (1975), 27-34.

67. An early example of this belief is found in B.L. Hargrave MS. 313, fos. 131ᵛ-2ʳ — 'Ces sount les franchises et les usuages qe *la communalite de Comite de Salop* cleyment over de droyt et d'ancyane usuage du tens dent nule memoire ne eust.' (The italics are mine.) These rights and customs dated back to the time of Robert de Bellême, earl of Shrewsbury or Salop as palatine (come palays), whose lands were forfeited to Henry I for rebellion in 1102. They included exemption from the *murdrum* fine. The relationship between Hargrave MS. 313 and *The Red Book of the Exchequer* is close. With few exceptions, Hargrave MS. 313 contains every entry in *The Red Book of the Exchequer* down to 1253, but none thereafter. 'Ces sount les franchises . . .' is an exception. Written in a semi-cursive hand, it follows a synopsis, which was apparently compiled by Alexander de Swerfield during the reign of Henry III, of knights' fees for various counties in the time of Henry II and Richard I. Since the synopsis is written in a formal hand, 'ces sount les franchises . . .' perhaps represents a later addition. See *The Red Book of the Exchequer*, ed. H. Hall (3 vols, R.S., 1896), I. cxv. 729 ff. I am grateful to Robin Jeffs for his help with this note.

68. Fortescue's modernity is discussed by A.B. Fergurson, 'Fortescue and the Renaissance: a study in transition', *Studies in the Renaissance* (New York), vi (1959), 175-94.

2

The Centre, the Periphery, and the Problem of Power Distribution in Later Medieval France

P.S. Lewis

Should one wish to sense the attitudes of the communities of the periphery to the government of the centre in the France of the earlier fifteenth century one might well begin in Beauvais.[1] After the débâcle of the siege of Orléans and the counter-drive to Rheims the much-maligned and well-battered Pierre Cauchon had prudently departed and his place as bishop had been taken by Jean Juvenal des Ursins — but the Jouvenels, thoroughly identified with the Orléans-Armagnac side, were impeccably 'French', and Jean Juvenal was a very proper person to stiffen the wavering Beauvaisis and the wavering frontier.[2] For the next twelve years, until 1444, when Jean Juvenal was transferred to Laon (on 3 April) and the truce of Tours (on 28 May) Beauvais was, sometimes literally, in a state of siege.

The municipal archives of Beauvais were destroyed during the Second World War; but extracts from them were made by Victor Leblond and Pierre Champion.[3] Jean Juvenal himself had a considerable amount to say about the state of the town during his episcopate. Looking back from Laon in 1445 — where he does not seem to have thought things were much better — he reminded his brother Guillaume that five years before he had put together his *Loquar in tribulacione* (I will speak in the anguish of my spirit) — the text is suitably from Job.[4]

> I do not say of course that I should in the least be compared to Job, [he admitted] but still I have suffered much tribulation, adversity and affliction, because I am the spiritual father of the diocese of Beauvais, and I have fine lands and lordships which used to be ploughed and grazed, but the enemy and those who say they are on our side have killed the local people, taken them and deported them, robbed them and tyrannized them, and they have lost all their stock, and the region is waste and desolate, and churches and houses are burned down and collapsed in ruins, and they have murdered the poor people by imprisonment and other

B

means, and in short I have lost land, stock and my people who are my children, just like Job did.[5]

These groans were not without their echoes in the municipal council meetings, though recorded more soberly and at very much less length. His service in Beauvais certainly marked Jean Juvenal des Ursins.[6] In 1433 he had already sketched out some of the themes with which he was to deal in his *Loquar* seven years later;[7] and in the 1450s as archbishop of Rheims he could remind Charles VII that 'I was twelve or thirteen years in Beauvais, in the front line, and I wrote to you and to the members of your council to have some help sent; and they made me a whole lot of promises, and you wrote to me and so did your councillors, but I never saw or heard about anything ever happening'.[8]

Beauvais, then, was very much on the periphery. According to Jean Juvenal, 'what a frontier is this town of Beauvais . . . Beauvais is one of the best and principal frontiers'.[9] If one turned away from the westward — from the enemy, twenty kilometres away in Gerberoy — and looked southward, towards the centre, what were one's feelings? But what was the centre? For that good Parisian and quondam Parliamentarian Jean Juvenal clearly Paris was the 'ville capital' of the kingdom, and he reproached Charles VII for avoiding it: 'when you come there it seems as if you would rather not be there'. Charles V, on the other hand, 'came there and stayed there and, aided by Wisdom, Prudence, Force and Patience recovered his lordship and put his kingdom back in order, which he would never have done if he had stuck himself away at Amboise'.[10] The attraction of the Loire for Charles VII does not need emphasis. But Gilles le Bouvier also thought that Paris was 'the mistress-city of the kingdom, and the largest, and the king's palace is there in the middle of the town, with the River Seine on either hand'.[11] The idea that Paris was the centre of France was in fact commonplace. But it was an idea that contemporaries could resist, for, with Bernard Guenée, we should talk of institutional centralization and geographic decentralization.[12] The centre of the kingdom was wherever the king, his court or the great departments of state happened to be.

How was the centre regarded from Beauvais? Beauvais, it is clear, felt isolated. There was a time, Jean Juvenal claimed, 'that there was not between the River Oise, the Seine and the Somme a town in the French obedience except this wretched city, which carried the whole burden of the war, and could rely for help neither upon you (i.e. the king) nor anyone else, but only upon themselves'.[13] The taxation that was raised for the war, but which disappeared into private pockets, was one of Jean Juvenal's favourite grievances. Even the taxes paid by the inhabitants of Beauvais, he thought, 'did not go towards the defence of the town but were frittered away by those you had granted them to'.[14] In 1433 he argued that the 'poor lads in the frontiers' did not even get 'a miserable letter-close to encourage them'.[15] The town councillors felt isolated. As was usual in war soldiery cut communications; beleagured towns lived on the occasional newsletter or on hearsay. Jean Juvenal was not the only citizen of Beauvais who was conscious of 'this frontier', of the daily pillaging by the 'French' garrisons of Gerberoy (which was briefly in French hands in 1435-7) and Clermont of the merchants of Beauvais and others victualling the town.[16]

As a result of its geographical isolation as well as of the misdeeds of the soldiery Beauvais was politically alienated. On 9 June 1432 the city council deliberated upon rumours of disaffection. Some people were saying that if Lagny fell to the English Beauvais should abandon Charles VII; they thought that the urban notables had decided to deliver Beauvais to the English. The council decided, for the sake of peace and union, to do nothing. In February 1433 Senlis wrote to Beauvais that the king should be told about 'the wicked and criminal conduct of the king's troops on our side, and how they tyrannize his wretched subjects, whatever status they are, men, women and children, to show him how it is likely to end up, that is with the loss of his lordship and its transfer into alien hands for ever'.[17] The letter might have been written by Jean Juvenal, who gave an oblique reference to the seductive ways of the English in a harangue to the comte d'Eu about 1438,[18] and returned to the argument in his *Loquar in tribulacione* two years later. Things were far better in areas under English control (and here Thomas Basin might have agreed with him);[19] those who had decided to be French (and the Beauvaisis had been English only because 'their last lord and bishop had made this crazy mistake')[20] found that 'their reduction had been the cause of their destruction' and the English rejoiced at it, because it would make them return to the English fold.[21] 'You have already seen', Jean Juvenal warned Charles VII, 'that your English adversary has had a foot in the door and was held to be king; if he comes back, given the oppression which your wretched people suffer, then there is a danger that things might come to a subverting of your lordship, and that you would be a king without a land or a people, or at least you would have very small ones': and this eleven years after the mission of Joan of Arc. There was hardly much moral conviction here: 'if a powerful prince appeared who was determined to see that justice was done, even if he was a Saracen, it is quite possible that like raving witless madmen they would submit to him'.[22]

Thirty years earlier Bordeaux, too, felt isolated, alienated, and fragmented. Cardinal François Hugotion — like Juvenal des Ursins — was concerned about the miseries of the *pays*. In 1406 he bombarded Henry IV of England with letters saying that he had said so much about the *pays* 'that his voice was hoarse with shouting'. He warned that since no help was coming to the 'barbacanas' (the frontiers with the French) the Gascons were much discouraged. It is gravely to be feared that they will decide upon another course of action to their advantage rather than to decide to remain as they are without a remedy'. Furthermore the seigneur de Limeul, 'whom one certainly thought one could trust, has gone French, or so everyone is saying'. Hugotion, like Jean Juvenal, finally adopted a note of elegiac resignation: 'as I have learned by bitter experience, none of my letters does any good, and so it seems that no-one takes any notice of what I say'.[23] Beauvais from Paris is 48 miles; Bordeaux from Southampton is something like 563 miles; and Westminster to Southampton about 75 miles. Although that pious pilgrim William Wey could make the direct crossing from Plymouth to Coruña in four days in 1456, and forty years earlier a letter from the mayor of Bordeaux to the Jurade took ten days to arrive from London,[24] the Bordelais was nevertheless beset by the insecurity of its routes to the centre of power.[25] As the furthest rampart of the old Plantagenet dominions it was remote.

The centre itself could seem remote: in December 1359 the consuls of Albi decided 'that we should send into France or into England, if we cannot get justice done in France, about the vexatious things' which commissioners of the comte de Poitiers, sent at the request of the bishop (of Albi), were bent on doing. The comte de Poitiers, the king's lieutenant in Languedoc, had been at Grenade near Toulouse at the beginning of the month and had already been appealed to there. The mission to England was presumably to the 'sovereign remedy', the captive John II. In the end R. Vidal went to Paris: his mission was successful, but he had to go by water eleven days and at night 'to keep clear of the English, and his horse got catarrh and he sold it in Paris, and so he lost the horse'. He was given five florins compensation.[26] But the constant travelling from the periphery to its capital is too well-known to need comment. The roads of France seem constantly to have been populated with litigants and petitioners wending their more or less uncomfortable way to the court or the central offices, dodging about to avoid the soldiery, their escorts putting up the rate for dangerous passages; some moving pompously as befitted their dignity at a mere twenty-five miles a day; or others like the legendary foot-messenger Malsafava who sprinted the 281 miles from Périgueux to Paris twice in the summer of 1337 at an average of 47 miles a day, and who only laid up for a day before he started back on his second journey.[27] A specialized system of relay horsemen could of course outdo such travellers, but the need for it was exceptional.

The periphery, therefore, did not lack its lines of communication, both moral and physical, with the centre.[28] The history of another frontier town — though its front line, being in the east, was perhaps softer — also bears this out. Lyons could complain about the misdeeds of soldiers. In 1423 its consuls thought that it was 'in the thick of war', but they felt more aggrieved by the effects of taxation. 'Nearly a third of the inhabitants, both rich and poor (the consuls wrote) have left the town and still go off every day, to Savoy where they are not taxed at all, to Dauphiné and Avignon, where they do very well for themselves and almost nothing for the town of Lyons: which *pays* of Savoy and Dauphiné march with the town of Lyons.'[29] The mission of the procureur of Lyons, Rolin de Mâcon, to the peripatetic court of Charles VII in the autumn of 1425 is also instructive.[30]

In November 1424 the *Estates* of Eastern Languedoil at Riom had granted a tax of which the quota of Lyons was 6,400 francs; on 27 November the city had received at Châteaugay a remission of 2,400 francs which was conditional on its making no further requests for one; and from 25 January 1425 the first payment of the tax had been raised in the city. Those who had assignations on the receipt of the receiver of Lyons quickly came forward. On 27 January the officers of the *Parlement* of Poitiers informed the consuls that 400 *livres tournois* as part of their wages were assigned on the tax. In March they informed the consuls that they were assigned on the second payment, and asked them to ensure that their 400 *livres tournois* 'were not converted to other uses'.[31] By June one Colin Jarlot was putting out rather unsuccessful feelers at Bourges: the interest of the Constable de Richemont in the tax was also involved. On 8 June the consuls decided to defer the second payment until 22 July and to send to the king for a further remission (if the journey could be made safely), or otherwise to Yolande of Aragon (the mother-in-law of Charles VII) and Richemont. Possibly about this time the town succeeded in getting a rebate. The news of this was brought by its messenger La Barbe, but otherwise nothing was of avail. The day after the *Parlement* of Poitiers wrote again rather crossly about its 400 *livres tournois*; Richemont had proved inflexible over the raising of his 1000 and on 20 June the bailli of Mâcon and the *sénéchal* of Lyons interned the consuls in the *maison de Roanne*. There they languished until the summer. On 31 July a new and a different tax was ordered to be raised in anticipation of a meeting of the *Estates* of Languedoil at Poitiers in October; Richemont was also assigned on Lyons for this tax. In September the *Parlement* of Poitiers complained to the consuls of Lyons that they had heard that Caqueran, 'the one-eyed' captain of the Milanese contingents in France, and others had been assigned on the Riom tax after it had been granted, and also that they were trying to get themselves paid first.

At this point Rolin de Mâcon set out for the royal court, 'the centre' of the kingdom. On 26 September he wrote from Bourges.[32] He had seen Maître Gérard Blanchet, who was the commissioner for Lyonnais of the so-called 'Poitiers' tax, had exchanged compliments with him, and had also got his promise that he would do his best, either on his own or through his friends, to ensure that Lyons was allowed its largest possible rebate. Mâcon told Blanchet everything that he could think of which might be helpful about the woes of Lyons, and particularly about the assignments on the

Riom tax. Having heard Mâcon, Blanchet wrote letters of recommendation on his behalf to the *généraux des aides*, and particularly to Mâitre Jean Châtagnier. The *généraux*, Blanchet thought, were the people with whom to deal because Richemont did not interfere in financial matters, and, in any case, he was then north of the Loire and therefore inaccessible. Mâcon complained that Richemont's receiver in Lyons was putting the consuls under pressure; Blanchet promised to do something about this; and when Mâcon found that some people were starting for Poitiers — 'the roads are so very dangerous' — he hurriedly set off with them. But at Poitiers at the end of September he found that the members of the *Parlement* were absent because the fairs were then taking place. He also found that the royal council had departed with the king, some said to Thouars, some to Saumur. But· he did manage to catch the *généraux* (Châtagnier was particularly welcoming); they said that Mâcon would have to discuss the question of Richemont's assignments with Richemont himself.

Fortunately, the *généraux* were leaving Bourges; because they would enjoy safety Mâcon travelled with them northwards. By 12 October he was back in Poitiers. He had found at Saumur Buffart, a Lyonnais, who had introduced him to Richemont, though not without difficulty because of the crowd around him. Richemont told him that the question of a rebate on the Poitiers tax was not his business, and also that the king or other people could give Lyons any rebate it liked 'as long as he (Richemont) had the total amount which had been assigned to him' on Lyons or elsewhere. Further representations to Richemont and to the Chancellor had been in vain: Richemont, thought Rolin de Mâcon, had probably better be paid. He would see what he could do with humble petitions to the king and the council, and so on. But also at Saumur Rolin de Mâcon had found Théode de Valpergue, a commander under Caqueran, the one-eyed, that nightmare of the *Parlement* of Poitiers in pursuit of its cut of the Riom tax. Some hard bargaining followed, 'through someone' (wrote Rolin de Mâcon) who is well in with both of us, whom I promised a couple of *écus* for his trouble'. 'If you did not pay up soon', Théode had said, 'you would be in danger of paying the lot without the advantage of any favour the king would have given you.' 'Impossible', Mâcon replied, 'given what you had to pay . . ., and I told him . . . that if I were in his place that I would settle for 400 francs. But though I haggled away on this one . . . he would not have anything to do with it, . . . and so I left him like that. I do not know what he will do about it . . .' 'I talked about it afterwards', Mâcon also said, 'to one of our friends from our region, who is over here, and who knows how to deal with things, who told me that things should not be pushed too far for the moment, because soon there are going to be changes. We do not have many friends over here, which is a great pity for us.'

The arrival of Charles VII in Poitiers on 9 October revived Rolin de

Mâcon's melancholy spirits. He at once had a petition drafted for a rebate on the last tax for Richemont and had submitted to the council by a *maître des requêtes*. He returned, saying that the council would not interfere except according to Richemont's wishes. This was, of course, useless. Mâcon asked the *généraux* to tell the Chancellor what Gérard Blanchet had written to them about, but they refused. 'The whole lot of them turned on me', wrote Mâcon plaintively, 'goodness they did, saying that there was not a town in the kingdom on our side which had always been asking for so much in grants from the king, and getting them, and paying less than the town of Lyons . . . Why did not we go to the *élus*', the Chancellor had asked, 'who were better informed than anyone about it, to modify the tax for us as they saw fit?' 'I told him,' Mâcon said rather weakly, 'that all that could have been done had been done, but that they did not want to do anything about it, and so resort had been had to the sovereign remedy.'

Yet another blow was to descend. 'Messeigneurs of *Parlement*', wrote Mâcon, 'are not at all pleased with you, and monsieur the *premier président* told me in the Chancery, and all the other officers, both of *Parlement* and of the *Requêtes*, Charrier (Richemont's secretary) and all the others, that they would do me as much harm as they could and that they would get the 400 francs'. Worse, the Chancellor had said that the La Barbe remission was worthless, because of the proviso on the first Riom remission that it should not have been made. The *Parlement's* 400 francs, thought Mâcon, should probably be paid; but the Chancellor, on the other hand, seems to have said to somebody who was leaving with the messenger carrying the letter Mâcon was engaged in writing that Richemont never had an assignment for 1,000 francs on the Riom tax; and the fine Piedmontese hand of Théode de Valpergue began to show itself on the way back from Saumur. Mâcon seems to have got 300 francs out of Richemont on his own, and La Barbe's remission was not worth a penny: both the king and the council were determined to take it out on the importunate Lyonnais. 'But', Mâcon wrote with a certain amount of relish, 'after a great deal of "fixing" by messire Théode de Valpergue, you have been excused, with an enormous amount of difficulty, about 900 livres. So you will have to pay messire Caqueran, the one-eyed, 1,250 livres, and *Parlement* 400 livres . . . and nothing else can be done . . . I have not been able to have (the letters yet) . . .; but I should have them tomorrow morning, for messire Théode is being very helpful about them and if he was not, I would not get anywhere . . ."I am fed up" he added equally understandably, 'with being stuck over here.' But all was well: letters *Par le Roi, messire Theode de Valpargue present*, providing for all this, and a *non obstant* for the Châteaugay remission, did eventually arrive safely home in Lyons.[33]

Thus, war produced desperation in Beauvais or Bordeaux; lesser and slower evils like taxation produced negotiation — like that of Rolin de

Mâcon. The expert fixers were, of course, active at all times and in all places: but we might look more closely at some who were busy in later medieval France. Mâcon seems hardly to have been successful, Maître Raymond Queu as agent for Saint-Jean-d'Angély some years earlier seems to have been either more lucky or more wily.[34] *Echevin* and sometime *échevin* by rank, before April 1391 he suceeded in obtaining from the government a *grace* of 400 *livres* for repairs in the town and other matters; he also succeeded in having the gift ratified by the *généraux des finances*. His reward was 40 *livres* on the first payment of the 400 and 20 *livres* on the second payment; but 'should he busy himself and do something profitable for the town' (which meant getting the grant verified by the receiver of Saintonge at La Rochelle) he should have the whole 60 at the first go. In June he was off again to the centre 'on the town's business', getting some of Saint-Jean-d'Angély's privileges confirmed, talking to monsieur de Coucy, who was in charge of the *pays*, about billeting, and doing anything else that was useful. In August he was off yet again, to get a further 200 *livres*; and in January 1392 to get a further 600. In May he was perhaps still in Paris; in August he was asked by letter for a report, and told that if he did not send one his expenses would not be paid; but in September he had yet to reply.

On 7 February 1393[35] in the assembly at Saint-Jean-d'Angély Raymond Queu summed up his services to the town. He had spent a 'long time in France waiting upon the king and his noble council'; he had obtained a letter of 1,200 *livres*, another of 400 *livres*, a third of 200 *livres* for repairs, and other things necessary for the town, and also to help pay the *pâtis*, (the local levies for the maintenance of the soldiery), and finally a letter arranging for the *sénéchal* of Saintonge and the mayor of Saint-Jean to oversee the account of the receiver of the *pâtis*. He had brought back 'all these things at his own cost and expense and out of his own purse, including the drawing up of the letters and their sealing, and without being paid by the town or anyone else, or being advanced anything, to have all these things done and paid for, nor for his own expenses, trouble and salary, and he had paid out a great deal, all out of his own pocket, and would like to be paid and rewarded, or otherwise he would suffer grievous loss'. It was agreed he should be paid 200 *livres*; later in February the methods of payment were worked out and in March 1393 the arrangement was confirmed in assembly. But already it had been agreed that Mâitre Raymond should go back to France for the town, to get its privileges confirmed, to notify the centre of the dolours of the periphery, to get a renewal of the *souchet* (the local tax on wine) and other things necessary for the town's business, and to appear in the *Parlement* of Paris. Sixty *livres* were assigned to him, and 'Raymond Queu shall not be obliged to pay either for the drawing up or for the sealing of what he obtains of the money granted him'. In January 1394 Queu seems again to have been in Paris about the same kind of business.

Thereafter there is silence on the *échevinal* registers of Saint-Jean-d'Angély for over ten years;[36] but early in 1406 Raymond Queu was in Paris getting royal gifts ratified; with a slight sense of *déjà vu* we find him going to La Rochelle to fix things with the receiver there. Again in 1408 he got royal letters ratified and reported that 'someone called Colinet, a clerk of the *grand-maître's*, is willing to take on the business of having the letters verified for the sum of 50 francs to be taken from the assignment'. But he appears to have become testy as a result of being frustrated in his negotiations: probably in the spring of the following year he said to Guillaume Barilh's mother that 'your son is a . . . son of a monk', which would hardly have done for 'someone called Colinet's mother'. But worse was to come. In December 1412 and June 1413 he was again in France, tirelessly getting gifts of *aides* for the town, and tiresomely refusing to hand the letters over until he was paid, so that the *échevinage*, which had determined that he should be 'very well and generously satisfied', lost its temper and threatened to proceed against him. At sunset on 24 August 1413 the mayor of Saint-Jean-d'Angély discovered him beating up Papaillon, son of Jean Papaillon, tailor. A shouting match (at least on Raymond Queu's side) was alleged to have taken place, which ended by Maître Raymond's remarking that he did not think that the mayor was a good mayor. Condemned by the mayor and *échevins*, he appealed against them, and did not abandon his appeal for three years. Just before then, in the spring of 1416, he made his last journey recorded upon the registers 'to Paris to wait upon the king and his council upon the town's business'.

Hélie de Papassol, notary of Périgueux, is a comparatively wellknown fixer; he was at the centre in the spring and summer of 1337.[37] Already the wiles are familiar: slipping the 'esquire' of Guillaume de Villars, *maître des requêtes* of the household, 5 *sous parisis* 'so that he would help us and be favourable to us in our business'; the chief usher of the *Parlement* of Paris the same 'to have his favour in what we have to do in *Parlement*', besides a host of minor presents; dealing with vendors of purloined documents from the other side; and slipping the son of Maître Geoffroy Malicorne, a commissioner in one matter, 5 *sous parisis* 'so that he would help us in our affairs and tell us some of the things that had been done in our absence'. Then there was the pursuit of the king to Val-Notre-Dame, to Pont-Sainte-Maxence, Gisors, Bécoisel, Pontoise, Poissy, Compiègne, and the difficulty of getting to see him. On Tuesday 5 August de Papassol 'did not go to Paris because the king went off towards Compiègne, and it was impossible to follow him on foot because of the crowd of people following'. But it was very possible to obtain, as it were, a season ticket for entry into the king's presence. On 21 July Jean Teulier, usher of the royal chamber, was paid 20 *sous parisis* to give Hélie and his coadjutors the entry; 'he promised us that every time we wanted to go in there he would let us in there and that he

would help us as much as he could in our affairs'. And already there was
the shadow of the great man 'Mossen Ferri de Picquigny, master of the
king's household and a most powerful man', who was given 5 pounds of
lemons and 5 pounds of sugar on Thursday 7 August at Compiègne at a
cost of 35 *sous parisis*. He, in a sense, was the forbear of '*messire* Pierre des
Essars, who was master of the king's household (from 1409); and his
position was such that no chancellor or president of the *Parlement* would dare
cross him'.[38]

The most succinct portrait of the fixer is perhaps to be found in the
powers granted to sire Aymeri Seignouret, proctor of Saint-Jean-d'Angély
on 30 June 1396:

> that he should have authority to pursue, ask, and request from the king our lord
> and from his most noble council, all favours and grants, gifts of cash and others
> whatever and to the profit of the *échevinage*, the town, *châtellenie* and jurisdiction
> thereof, and each as far as concerns it; to pursue before *nosseigneurs* of the chambre
> des comptes, nosseigneurs the *généraux élus sur le fait des aides pour la guerre* [the
> senior officials dealing with the war taxes], and elsewhere where need be, all that
> which has or shall be given and granted by our said lord

and to give quittances for any proceeds he received.[39] But perhaps more
telling still were the moral qualifications proposed for an emissary from
Lyons in September 1426: 'an important and knowledgeable man, with sufficient understanding of how to deal with the matter that he is certain not
to come back without a favourable reply'. A few years earlier Lyons also
advocated that its emissaries be 'men of importance and position, who
would not be frightened to talk personally to my lord the dauphin'.[40]

Professor Chevalier has dealt, as far as the *bonnes villes* are concerned,
with the *amici in curia*, the 'good "go betweens" from the king's retinue',
who in turn might become the king's agents in dealing with the towns. He
has also dealt with the question of the administrative machinery for the
ratification of the proceeds of their actions.[41] There is thus no need to dwell
on these questions, except, perhaps, to reintroduce a familiar face. Maître
Gérard Blanchet, already seen in his dual role in dealing with Mâcon
and the Lyonnais, came from a Champenois family in favour with Charles
V and Charles VI; early a member of the dauphin's party, he was a
councillor and *maître des requêtes* of the household from 1422 and ambassador
to the duke of Savoy; in the same year he married Isabeau, the sister of
Guillaume de Champeaux, bishop of Laon and sister-in-law of the *trésorier-
général* Macé Héron. Further embassies and commissions followed; and
when he died in 1433 he left a son, Guillaume Blanchet, aged 6, who later
became a counsellor in the *Parlement*.[42] But such 'political' intermarriage in
the administrative offices is familiar; and Professor Chevalier has recently
demonstrated the rise of the Tourangeaux at the court of Louis XI, gloomy
though he is about the prospects of writing its history.[43] I shall now move

from the 'marchans affaictiez' at court — the phrase is Alain Chartier's, the 'merchants by appointment' who buy other people and sell themselves[44] — to the question of the relationship of the 'centre' with the 'periphery' in a different sense: the relationship of the court with political forces other than the 'bonnes villes'.

Professor Chevalier has already introduced us to a pair of heroes, Guillaume de Varye and Pierre Doriole, the first and second husbands respectively of Charlotte de Bar.[45] Their brother-in-law Denis also merits attention. Denis de Bar was an importunate cleric.[46] Son of a former colleague of Varye and Doriole, he was slipped by Varye (after mis-shots at Maguelone and Lodève) into the bishopric of Saint-Papoul in 1468; in 1471 he coveted Tulle. Guillaume de Varye was dead, so Denis wrote to his new brother-in-law Pierre Doriole, who like Guillaume de Varye had been a *général des finances* since the 1450s, and who was soon to succeed Guillaume Jouvenel des Ursins as chancellor of France, to fix him up with the second diocese.[47] Pierre Doriole set the wheels in motion, but also wrote to Denis de Bar, asking him whether he was certain that he wanted Tulle. He pointed out that Saint-Papoul and the archdiaconate of Narbonne, which de Bar held in plurality with his bishopric, were worth more. 'There's no doubt whatsoever', Denis replied, 'that [Tulle] . . . is the more use to me; because my two benefices bring in an absolute maximum of nine hundred *écus* and I do not think there is a single benefice in the kingdom worth less [than Saint-Papoul] . . . With a great deal of time and trouble I have not been able to get back what it cost me, nor have I been able to help my relations, which is the thing I desire more than anything in the world.' Pierre Doriole had already mobilized Louis XI, who had promised to write to the Pope to translate Denis from Saint-Papoul, to the cardinals, especially the Cardinal of Rouen, and to his proctor in Curia. Two royal orders were necessary, Denis thought: one for the seizure of the temporalities of Tulle, and one to inhibit the chapter from electing. The commissioners to whom the orders were addressed should not only be well-thought of, but the friends of Pierre Doriole. Denis de Bar suggested one of his own. Would Doriole write to the chapter of Tulle, and to those who 'knew' the chapter, 'recommending my person and praising it much more than it is worth?' But when Louis XI wrote in mid-September 1471 to the archbishop of Bourges, the metropolitan of Tulle, it was to tell him that the chapter was plotting to elect, and to warn him not to confirm the election. The two commissioners sent by Louis, Jean Yver, and Bertrand Briçonnet, reported in October to Doriole from Tulle. The chapter was cavilling, they said, about its right of election and the seizure of the temporalities, but Jean de Blanchefort, the king's harbinger, who was a relative of the deceased incumbent, was presenting the real difficulty. He was behaving peculiarly. If he did not interfere, then there would be no election; they had 'heard secretly' that many members of the chapter were prepared to let the Pope provide. The chapter, however, was in fact split and some of its members elected Gérard de Maumont. Nevertheless, the Pope translated Denis de Bar from Saint-Papoul on 20 November 1471; he took possession in March 1472. Yet he may eventually have found the chapter of Tulle too much for him, because in 1495 he returned, despite his earlier scorn for it, to his former diocese. But Saint-Papoul also appears not to have wanted him: and he consoled himself by composing a treatise on judicial astrology, *De astronomicorum professorum ordine epitoma*.

Such were the means whereby a would-be episcopal climber got his way. Not that a local ecclesiastical community lacked the ability to resist pressure from the centre, however doubtful the outcome might be. A case in point is the reaction of the chapter of Notre-Dame to the nomination of Louis de Beaumont, a royal councillor and chamberlain as well as chancellor of the diocese of Paris as bishop of Paris in 1472-3.[48] On the death of Guillaume Chartier on 1 May 1472 Louis XI had, allegedly without Beaumont's knowledge, asked that Beaumont be provided and he was duly preconized on 1 June. That very day a delegation from the chapter arrived — at Saint-Jean-d'Angély — to ask Louis XI for license to elect.[49] As soon as he saw them, Louis said, characteristically, that he knew what they were up to; that the Pragmatic Sanction was not in force, he had submitted to the Pope; that many of the canons were also royal officers, who ought to mind their behaviour; and that the delegation should see the *premier président* of the *Parlement*. On 17 June the chapter decided to postpone the election, fixed for 25 June, to 24 July. On 10 July Louis wrote to the *premier président* that he was 'most happy' about Louis de Beaumont's provision. He also told the *président* to go with Charles de Gaucourt, governor of Paris, and Denis Hesselin, *prévôt des marchands*, and present his bulls to the canons and inform them of 'my will in the matter, which is that they should receive him without contradiction or delay; and that if they do this I will be most mindful of their affairs and those of their church; and also that if they want to be contrary, I shall give them such a "provision" that they will know I am displeased'. On 20 July Louis's emissaries fulfilled the order, and on 24 July the canons refused the provision on grounds of 'conscience'; but for fear of royal wrath, they also did not proceed to an election, though they drew up a line of defence in case Beaumont fulminated: an appeal to the Pope, or to a future council, 'seu illum vel illos, etc.' On 29 July, though a hardy minority still wished to elect, the election was again postponed; and it continued to be postponed, and the provision of Louis de Beaumont to be resisted, throughout the summer and the autumn and into the winter. Resistance began to crumble in the New Year. On 18 January the chapter again decided, since there were so many different opinions and it was getting late, to postpone matters, this time until 20 January. Then after debate, the 'maior et sanior pars' agreed to let de Beaumont in, but under protest. They would not receive him as true bishop of Paris, recognize his title or abandon their right of election, even though they were not at liberty to elect. On 7 February Louis de Beaumont was received as bishop. Though the chapter eventually gave in, it had stood out against the pressures of the 'centre' for eight months and still, in theory, was doing so: indeed, for whatever reasons, Louis de Beaumont was not consecrated until five years later.

Unlike Louis de Beaumont, a son of the seigneur of La Forêt and a 'courtier' in his own right, the chapter of Notre-Dame perhaps lacked friends at court. 'Friends' of whatever rank were as necessary to a great individual as to a 'community'. Professor Rey has shown how at the turn of the fourteenth century the very great found it necessary to have friends in the departments of state.[50] They continued to be necessary; Charles d'Orléans, comte d'Angoulême, in 1477 obtained the gift of the revenues of the *gabelle* and 1,000 francs for the repair of the fortresses in the county of Angoulême by slipping Louis Tindon, the king's secretary, 100 *livres tournois* for having persuaded the king to make the gift, and Tindon's clerk 4 *livres* for having solicited his master to get the warrant for the gift put through.[51] The 'friends' could also do the wooing: Jacques de Filescamps, receiver of Amiens, told the servants of Jean d'Arly that he would do marvels for d'Arly if d'Arly's new pension was on his receipt.[52] Like importunate clerks in search of expectatives *in forma pauperum* (or for that matter bishops in search of better bishoprics), petitioners besieged the king 'while he was getting up, in his closet, at eight o'clock in the morning', after Mass, after his lunch, after his siesta, during his strolls in the fields around Vincennes, after dinner, even at three o'clock after midnight.[53] Even Louis had to give in. Just before Denis de Bar began to badger him about Tulle Louis wrote to Pierre Doriole, saying that 'I have been under heavy pressure from some of monsieur de Guyenne's people to give the *grenetier* of Rheims leave to resign his office . . . to the benefit of his son. And since I was not able to hedge any longer I ordered the letters to be made out; but I want *you* to hedge about sealing them for as long as you can — say that he will have to pay caution money, or that there is something else wrong, as you think fit, so that the letters are *not* sealed. And warn the chancellor and anyone else you think, so that they are not sealed; and do not show this letter to anyone, and burn it at once.'[54]

If more letters of this kind had survived we would be better informed about what kings really wanted. In 1483 one of Louis's emissaries in Rome, when trying to get Jean d'Armagnac translated from Castres, made it clear that 'the prosecution of this case issues from the personal initiative, instance and proper judgement of the king, without favour to another'.[55] Was 'favour to another' regarded by the importunate petitioner operating through his friends those famous *rouages* of administration the real norm? Admittedly there were administrative traps for petitioners. The Constable Richemont obtained the grant of the much-disputed lordship of Parthenay in 1425, supposedly 'by the king in council'; but, as Jean Juvenal des Ursins, as king's advocate, argued a few years later,

> when the king in his council had been told of it all had been amazed: and the king asked Villebresme [the secretary who had signed the donation] what had happened. And then Villebresme said that at the end of a council Richemont had made out his request by a certain clerk; the king had granted it and ordered Villebresme to make out the letters. The king might have said that Villebresme was telling the truth; but none of his council had heard of it, and one can only say that it was importunity and worthless, and such things are revoked every day: the king is powerless to make such alienations, and it is null . . .[56]

But even the *gens du roi*, with their paralysing doctrines of the inalienability of sovereignty, were not the be-all and end-all of life: the administration might be there, but in the end politics might get their own back. The politicians might, admittedly, find the process a bore. When Guillaume Jouvenel des Ursins as chancellor of France in 1470 hedged about sending a case before the great council to commissioners in Berry even Louis XI was reduced to something near bluster: 'I beg you, my good sir, not to be so *rigorous* in my affairs; because I have not been in *yours*. . . . Now send the case back as it should be, and do not let me have to write to you again.'[57] Perhaps Louis XI was not such an effective tyrant as he has been made out to be.

Initiative and counter-initiative, decisions taken and decisions resisted: an analysis of the whole, or of as great a part of the whole as we can get — and much of this subterranean process is inevitably obscure — seems to me to provide the basis for a theory of power distribution as pluralistic as any produced by, for example, a present-day American sociologist.[58] Power is everywhere and nowhere; but still to be seized. Arthur de Richemont and Charles d'Angoulême, Louis de Beaumont and Denis de Bar, Hélie de Papassol, Raymond Queu, Rolin de Mâcon, all were as much a part of the power process as Gérard Blanchet and Théode de Valpergue, Pierre Doriole and Guillaume Jouvenel des Ursins, Louis XI; or Jean Juvenal, or Cardinal Hugotion. One should perhaps commiserate with Beauvais and Bordeaux in their agony, imploring help which could never come and that 'policing of the soldiery' which could come, and came, only with peace.[59] But their sense of isolation was equally a product of the war: under anything like the normal coming and going of agents, either of the centre or of the members of the community, was the pulsing lifeblood of later medieval French politics, as of any politics. One played the system: one did not try to break it if one had any sense. Individual nobles or groups of nobles, it is true, sometimes rebelled about the way in which the system seemed at some particular moment to be stacked against them; but local communities had more wit than to be herded into collective, or representative, institutions to 'control' the centre. They did perfectly well out of backstairs negotiations: as, in the end, did members of the other politically important classes. It was, after all, to everyone's advantage. In 1421 the aediles of Poitiers explained that,

> because the reverend father in God Maître Guillaume de Lucé, bishop of Maillezais, had worked upon Monsieur the regent to give and grant us for the repair of the town the sum of 2,000 *livres tournois* to be taken upon the emoluments of the Poitiers mint, some of us thought it would be a good idea to give him something on the occasion of his ceremonial appearance in the town as bishop, . . . and also because Maître Jean Tudert, dean of Paris, had pursued and advanced the issue of the letters for the gift of 11.000 *livres tournois* and sent them to us;

they also decided to give him something. Guillaume de Lucé got a pipe of pinot, twelve fat capons and wax torches weighing 25 pounds; Jean Tudert 100 *sous* worth of fish.[60] But then perhaps the dean and the bishop dined together.

Notes

1. V. Leblond, 'Beauvais dans l'angoisse pendant la guerre de Cent Ans', *M. Soc. acad. Oise*, xxvii (1932), 92-361.

2. As Charles VII, who had arranged it all, wrote in recommending Jean Juvenal to the town, his provision 'was and is to us most gratifying and acceptable, since not only the region but the church has been provided with someone completely loyal to us, and both to you and to the region of great advantage, who, both he and his forbears, has served us and ours long and loyally in great and honourable positions and offices' [P.L. Péchenard, *Jean Juvénal des Ursins* (Paris, 1876), p.140, from apparently a later copy then in private hands].

3. Unfortunately with a considerable amount of duplication: Leblond, see above; Champion, Institut de France, MS.5227, fos. 286-317.

4. 'At the time', he recalled, 'I was worried stiff, because in the way in which the war was going and in the way in which it was being run there was neither rhyme nor reason but simply inefficiency and exploitation, and I was in the hottest spot, that is to say at Beauvais, which was simply falling to bits' (B.N. MS.fr.2701, fo.51^{r}a).

5. B.N., MS. fr. 5022, fo. 1^r.

6. Jean Juvenal was clear that it was political service: 'you instructed me', he told Charles VII in 1440, 'that I should come over here and carry out your orders, because always, as long as I am alive, I would want to serve you and obey you' [ibid., fo. 5^v].

7. B.N. MS. fr. 5038, fos. 4^r ff.

8. B.N. MS. fr. 2701, fo. 89^{r}b.

9. B.N. MS. fr. 5022, fos 20^v, 23^v. The sense of 'frontiere' here is clearly that of 'place fortifiée faisant face aux ennemis' [Godefroy, *Lexique*].

10. B.N. MS. fr. 5022, fos. 5^r, 14^{r-v}.

11. *Le Livre de la description des pays*, ed. E.T. Hamy [Rec. de voyages et de docs. pour servir à l'hist. de la géog., xxii] (Paris, 1908), pp. 50-51.

12. 'Espace et Etat dans la France du Bas Moyen Age', *Annales*, xxiii (1968), 758.

13. B.N. MS. fr. 5022, fo. 3^v.

14. Ibid., fo.20^v.

15. B.N. MS. fr. 5038, fo. 5^r.

16. Leblond, op. cit., pp. 259, 260.

17. Ibid., pp. 210-11, 216-17.

18. B.N. MS. fr. 2701, fo 120^{r}b.

19. B.N. MS. fr. 5022, fos. 3^r ff.; T. Basin, *Histoire de Charles VII*, ed. C. Samaran [Classiques de l'histoire de France au Moyen âge, xv] (Paris, 1964), p. 88.

20. B.N. MS. fr. 5022, fo. 3^r.

21. Ibid., fos. 3^v, 14^r.

22. Ibid., fos. 17^r, 25^r.

23. Printed in *Registres de la Jurade*, i [Arch. municipales de Bordeaux, iii] (Bordeaux, 1873), pp. 87-93.

24. *The Itineraries of William Wey* . . . ed. B. Bandinel [Roxburghe Club] (London, 1857), pp. 153 ff. *Registres de la Jurade*, ii [Arch. municipales de Bordeaux, iv]] (Bordeaux, 1883), 329-31.

25. See, for instance, *Registres de la Jurade*, i 121.

26. *Comptes consulaires d'Albi (1359-1360)*, ed. A. Vidal [Bibliothèque méridional, I. v] (Paris-Toulouse, 1900), pp. 20-21, 16.

27. A. Higounet-Nadal, 'Le Journal des dépenses d'un notaire de Périgueux en mission à Paris (janvier-septembre 1337)', *A. Midi*, lxxvi (1964), 382-83.

28. From this point Professor Chevalier (above, pp. 111 ff.) and I are, to some extent, arguing in parallel. But although we reach broadly similar conclusions, we do so from very different points of view.

29. L. Caillet, *Etude sur les relations de la commune de Lyon avec Charles VII et Louis XI (1417-1483)* (Lyon-Paris, 1909), p. 331.

30. The background of Mâcon's mission can be reconstructed (rather hazardously) from Caillet, op.cit., pp. 40 ff., corrected and amplified by the documents published pp. 345 ff.

31. Ibid., p. 348.

32. His letters are printed by G. du Fresne de Beaucourt, *Histoire de Charles VII*, iii (Paris, 1885), 501-9.

33. Caillet, op.cit., pp. 353-4.

34. The material for the remainder of this paragraph is derived from *Registres de l'échevinage de Saint-Jean-d'Angély*, ed. D. d'Aussy, i [Arch. hist. Saintonge-Aunis, xxiv] (Paris-Saintes, 1895), pp. 325, 356, 361, 367, 381, 383.

35. The material for this paragraph is derived from ibid., pp. 385-90, 413. (The chronology of the documents there printed needs some disentanglement).

36. The material for what follows is derived from ibid. ii [Arch. hist. Saintonge-Aunis, xxvi] (Paris-Saintes, 1897), pp. 144, 149, 264, 269; iii [Arch. hist. Saintonge-Aunis, xxxii] (Paris-Saintes, 1902), pp. 18, 19, 60, 70-71 (cf. 171), 162-63.

37. What follows is derived from the document printed by A. Higounet-Nadal, op.cit., pp. 387-402.

38. *Choix de pièces inédites relatives au règne de Charles VI*, ed. L. Douet-d'Arcq [S.H.F.], i (Paris, 1863), 378.

39. *Registres de l'échevinage de Saint-Jean-d'Angély*, ii. 11-12.

40. Caillet, op.cit., p. 370; *Registres consulaires de la ville de Lyon*, i, ed. M.C. Guigue (Lyon, 1882), p. 331.

41. Above, pp. 113, 116.

42. A. Thomas, *Les Etats provinciaux de la France centrale sous Charles VII* (Paris, 1879), i. 287-91.

43. *Tours, Ville royale (1356-1520)* (Louvain-Paris, 1975), pp. 481 ff.

44. *Le Curial*, ed. F. Heuckenkamp (Halle, 1899), p. 23.

45. *Tours . . .*, pp. 293 ff. Cf. R. Gandilhon, *Politique économique de Louis XI* (Rennes, 1940), pp. 249-50.

46. On Denis de Bar see E. Baluze, *Historiae Tutelensis libri tres* (Paris, 1717), pp. 225-9, 234-6; *Dict. d'hist. et de geog. ecclésiastiques*, vi (Paris, 1932), col. 539; *Dict. de biog. française*, iv (Paris, 1948), cols. 113-15.

47. The letters upon which the remainder of this paragraph is based are printed by J. Vaesen, *Lettres de Louis XI* [S:H.F.], iv (Paris, 1890), 360-1, 268-71, 361-3.

48. On Louis de Beaumont see *Dict. d'hist. et de géog. ecclésiastiques*, vii (Paris, 1934), cols. 217-20; *Dict. de biog. française*, iv, col. 1150.

49. The remainder of this paragraph is based upon the material printed by Vaesen, op.cit. x (Paris, 1908), 474-87; Louis's letter is printed ibid., pp. 329-31.

50. M. Rey, *Le Domaine du roi et les finances extraordinaires sous Charles VI, 1388-1413* (Paris, 1965), pp. 295-7.

51. B.N. MS. fr. 26096, no. 1642.

52. 'Lettres . . . relatifs à la guerre du Bien public', ed. J. Quicherat, in *Documents historiques inédits*, ed. J.J. Champollion Figeac [Documents inédits sur l'histoire de France], ii (Paris, 1843), 290.

53. P.S. Lewis, *Later Medieval France: The Polity* (London, 1968), p. 123.

54. Vaesen, op.cit. iv. 241.

55. F. Pasquier, *Boffile de Juge* (Albi, 1914), p. 155.

56. Lewis, op.cit., pp. 216-17.

57. Vaesen, op.cit. iv. 176.

58. I have in mind R.A. Dahl and his associates [R.A. Dahl, *Who Governs? Democracy and Power in an American City* (New Haven-London, 1961); N.W. Polsby, *Community and Political Theory* (New Haven-London, 1963)].

59. Cf. P.S. Lewis, 'Jean Juvenal des Ursins and the common literary attitude towards tyranny in fifteenth-century France', *Medium Aevum*, xxxiv (1965), 115-16.

60. M. Rédet, 'Extraits des comptes de dépenses de la ville de Poitiers, aux XIVᵉ et XVᵉ siècles', *M. Soc. Antiq. Ouest*, vii (1840), 388 ff.

3

The Breton Nobility and Their Masters from the Civil War of 1341-64 to the Late Fifteenth Century[1]

Michael Jones

In his *La Noblesse bretonne au XVIIIe siècle* Professor Jean Meyer referred to a 'renewal of the *noblesse*' after the civil war of the mid-fourteenth century.[2] The 'multitude of poor nobles who formed a veritable plebeian nobility' ('petite noblesse')[3] that was characteristic of the last century of the *Ancien Régime* is seen to have very clear medieval origins. Likewise many specific features of 'droit nobiliaire' in the later period are evidently based on the customary law of the medieval duchy. But it was not part of Meyer's purpose to examine these antecedents in detail. Yet one may ask what are the elements of continuity? In what ways did the nobility capitalize on their opportunities under dukes who pursued domestic and foreign policies in complete independence of royal France? How did royal annexation of the duchy in 1491 change the underlying social structure? What are the implications of the relationship of Brittany and France for the social, economic and political developments of the duchy during this period? Some of these issues are to be examined here in an attempt to discover general features of noble life in the duchy during the last century of its independent existence. I begin with an example which displays both the wealth of the evidence and some of its shortcomings.

About the year 1492 Guillaume de Rosnyvinen presented a *Mémoire* to the council of his sovereign lady, Anne, queen of France and duchess of Brittany.[4] Rosnyvinen was one of several Breton captains of the royal *ordonnance* companies dismissed on the accession of Louis XI. Since 1461 he had not been re-employed in royal service and, as he wrote in the *Mémoire*, 'Every time that the duke (Francis II) was in dispute with King Louis, I placed in jeopardy all my heritage in France, which was worth a good 600 *livres* in annual rent, in order to come to serve the duke, and I lost thereby more than 4,000 *francs* income.' Nor was this the limit of his sacrifice: 'I have refused all the offers the king made me if I would serve him — a lump sum payment of 6,000 *écus*, a pension of 4,000 *francs* and all the offices which I had formerly held under his father.'[5] In France Guillaume had spent four years in the household of Dauphin Louis and fourteen in the company of Charles VII. He could write succinctly but with pride of the losses sustained by his family in ducal service: 'Item, died in ducal service, four of my nephews, namely Jacques, Louis, Jehan, Olivier and my brother of Vaucoullour.' Like the ageing Antoine de Chabannes, he too could tell of exploits in the wars stretching back forty years and more to the capture of Gilles de Bretagne and the taking of Fougères in 1449. More recently in the critical year 1487 Guillaume was captain of St-Aubin-du-Cormier. This frontier fortress he had eventually surrendered to the invading French but not, he alleged, until he had done everything in his power to prevent the capitulation.[6]

What had been the reward for this conspicuous loyalty? Both Rosnyvinen and his wife had lost much when their houses and farms held by tenants on a share-cropping basis (*metairies*) at Plessis-Bonenffant, together with other possessions, were pillaged by German troops in ducal pay and even by the duke's own officials. His household goods had been auctioned publicly at Rennes; more seriously he had fallen under suspicion of collusion with the French and legal proceedings had been started against him. He would, his *Mémoire* stated, willingly have given 50,000 *écus* to repair his damaged honour. For the moment, payments amounting to over 14,000 *livres* would settle an account which included a debt outstanding from 1432.[7] Special pleading apart, the basic outline of Guillaume's story accords remarkably well with what can be discovered from other sources. This career, in particular in its dual and sometimes equivocal service to the king of France and to the duke of Brittany, is archetypal: Rosnyvinen's experiences were shared by many Breton nobles in the fifteenth century. The ways in which such experiences affected the position and outlook of the Breton nobility in this period have received only limited attention.

Recent surveys, together with detailed investigations of noble fortunes in particular societies, have familiarized us with the general contours of noble life in France in the later Middle Ages.[8] Do the ideals, concepts, aspirations, and social mores of the Breton nobility conform to the established pattern? Likewise, with regard to economic problems, where the chronology has received small attention, does Breton noble experience conform more or less to the lot of the nobility in western Europe? We may assume that landed fortunes were adversely affected by the usual range of climatic, genetic, and man-made disasters. Plague, famine, and war devastation created particular predicaments for landlords with falling prices for agricultural produce, shortages of labour, and excessive wages in Brittany as elsewhere.[9] Some Breton landowners showed themselves willing to adopt new practices or extend old ones in order to exploit their lands more effectively in difficult times. Share cropping, generous leases, and other privileges were offered to attract tenants to lands which had run to waste; forest and mineral rights were exploited, and so on. Some landlords were more conscientious, or just simply luckier, than others.[10] Within the Breton nobility at this point, extremes of wealth and poverty, of rank, social prestige and honour, of political influence and armed might, may be as easily observed as it can be elsewhere. The carefully garnered wealth of Olivier IV, sire de Clisson, or that prodigally expended by Gilles, sire de Rays, at one end of the scale, is balanced by the impecuniosity of the *plèbe nobiliaire* who are already so numerous that Brittany ranks alongside Anjou and Maine as one of the provinces with the highest proportion of nobles in the total population, as it has remained even to this century.[11] Fortunately perhaps, we are not here concerned with the origins of this nobility. Reference is necessary, however, to certain prevailing conditions if some salient characteristics of the late medieval period are to be seen in perspective.

First, the constitutional framework within which Breton political life evolved in this period may be briefly summarized.[12] In 1297 the grant of peerage regulated external relations between the duke and the crown of France to which the duke owed liege homage. In 1341 there arose a disputed succession between the Montfort and Penthièvre branches of the ducal house. With English assistance, the Montfort family eventually emerged as the successful party and John IV and his successors were able henceforward to exploit the political difficulties of the French kings. Charles V recognized, albeit reluctantly, the succession of John IV; though the first treaty of Guérande in 1365, contained a provision which was to prove ultimately fatal for the survival of the independent duchy by limiting succession to the male heirs of the Montfort family, with reversion to the Penthièvre family in case of default. In the 1370s Charles V all but succeeded in annexing the duchy before overplaying his hand and unwittingly causing the reconciliation of the duke and his nobility. The second treaty of Guérande in 1381, very similar to the first, thus registered a rebuff for the crown. On the basis of a fragile accord between the duke and his nobility, John IV established a working relationship with the majority of his leading subjects, whose powers were gradually curbed. This relationship formed the platform on which the independence of the fifteenth-century duchy rested. In 1420, 1437, and on other occasions until the later years of the reign of Francis II, the nobility generally rallied round the ducal family in times of crisis.[13]

Without the co-operation of the nobility, the duke and his immediate circle of advisers were too weak to withstand the pressure which the Crown could bring to bear in its efforts to obtain practical recognition of its theoretical sovereignty. With their co-operation, despite animosities inflamed by the actions of the displaced Penthièvre claimants to the ducal throne, or families like the Rohan and the Rieux, ambitious to exploit the uncertain succession to Francis II, the Montfort family were able to elaborate long-cherished and increasingly grandiose ideas about the status of the duchy,[14] which they governed with an almost total freedom from royal intervention. In addition after 1381 John IV and his successors were generally able to avoid deep and irrevocable commitment to an English alliance, and seem to have striven more or less consistently to maintain a neutral position in the Anglo-French war in its latter stages. Even during the ominous reign of Louis XI for Francis II an English alliance was a *pis aller*.[15] It used to be thought that neutrality brought considerable economic advantages to the duchy; such views require some modification.[16] Nevertheless, until the last third of the fifteenth century, Brittany suffered only marginally from the warfare and internal disputes which racked royalist France during this period. Thus the independent constitutional position of the duchy presented its nobility with opportunities which could be profitably exploited. 'The renewal of the Breton *noblesse*' is in part the exercise of choice and the exploitation of these opportunities.

But before the renewal is examined in greater detail, some further elements of continuity in the feudal and social geography of the duchy deserve attention. An obliging contemporary provides a plausible answer to the simple question of how many Breton nobles there were? At the Council of Basle in 1434 Philippe de Coëtquis, archbishop of Tours, a former Breton councillor, stated that Brittany contained three counts, nine great barons, eighteen bannerets, and 4,700 lesser nobles.[17] What is well exemplified here is a characteristic of all European nobilities, the restricted number of really powerful and wealthy members of this order, and the overwhelming majority of other ranks within the nobility. The origins of this division clearly antedate our period, but it would also appear that within the duchy there are some particularly enduring tenurial arrangements, like the high proportion of large agglomerations formed in the eleventh and twelfth centuries, which survive in a recognizable form throughout the Middle Ages and beyond.[18] That, despite unusual family longevity and individual fecundity, comital, baronial, and knightly families became extinct in Brittany as elsewhere according to the rhythms described by McFarlane, Perroy and others is a likely hypothesis simply requiring statistical demonstration.[19] But underlying kaleidoscopic changes in the ownership of land, the primitive castellany seems to have conserved much of its original territorial and juridical integrity.

This is particularly the case in the eastern and southern parts of the duchy. A series of frontier lordships, some of which had extremely ancient origins, dominated this region in the twelfth century, as with minor modifications they did in the fifteenth.[20] Moving westwards to the interior of the duchy, there was the same phenomenon. Only in the far west had the really large feudal complexes so broken down that, apart from considerable expanses of ducal demesne, the Finistère peninsula contained few of the duchy's major lay landholders. And although a number of the outstanding figures in Franco-Breton affairs in the fifteenth century came from this region — Tanguy du Chastel, who smuggled the future Charles VII out of Paris in 1418, his nephew, Tanguy, vicomte de la Bellière, or the Coëtivy brothers — their patrimony was small and it was only towards the end of our period that occasionally a family like that of the lords of Pont l'Abbé acquired possessions which enabled them to rival the holders of lordships in the centre, east, and south of the duchy.[21]

Reasons for the stability of the great baronial lordships must obviously be first sought in the successoral practices governing the descent of estates. As early as 1185 the *Assize* of Count Geoffrey declared: 'that baronies and knights' fees should not be divided in future, but the eldest son should receive the whole inheritance, making suitable provision, according to his means, for his younger brothers.'[22] *Juveigneurs* (cadets) were to receive a life interest only, which they generally held without performing homage. Modifications to this strict successoral régime were made in 1276. The duke gave up his claim to exercise prolonged wardship during a minority *(bail)*, conceded greater testamentary freedom to his great vassals and allowed them to recover any portion for which homage had been performed of younger brothers dying without heirs. In return he was granted the right to a year's revenue from the estates of a deceased tenant-in-chief (*rachat*) regardless of the heir's age. Remission, suspension or donation of the *rachat* as an act of grace and favour was a valuable weapon in the hands of fifteenth-century dukes. By then *juveigneurs* who had heirs were able to pass on to them some of their landed possessions to dispose by will of rents in perpetuity assigned on the provision made for them by their elder brother. Yet the indivisibility of baronial and knightly holdings, though never an immutable law, was generally accepted and held firm until the reformation of the Breton custom in 1580.[23]

Although in the later Middle Ages Brittany had no exact equivalent of the English 'use' and entail or the Castilian 'mayorazgo', a number of great families, whose direct line was failing, were not prevented from making special provision for their main holdings to pass entire to suitable successors by marriage to an heiress. By this means the adoptive or substitute heir acquired not only an inheritance and a wife, but sometimes also a new name and arms, agreeing to drop entirely his former identity, as did the chosen heir of the Chabot-Rays family in 1401 and that of

Montmorency-Laval in 1405.[24] Another important family, the Rohans, faced by the prospect of proliferating cadet lines, made arrangements in 1422 for the creation of an inalienable family patrimony which, while conforming to the spirit of the *Assize* of Count Geoffrey, ran counter to prevailing custom in an effort to preserve the unity of its holdings.[25] In such ways baronies were preserved by a restricted number of great lords.

But at any one moment these formed numerically a minute proportion, not even 1 per cent of all noble holdings. Examples can be found, even amongst the great baronies shortly after the promulgation of the *Assize* of 1185, of a practice which allowed a lord to distribute up to a third of his possessions, unhindered by customary constraint.[26] This mode of dividing inheritances became well established among knightly families and it moulded the noble law of succession in the later Middle Ages. Professor Meyer has demonstrated the importance of this for the eighteenth-century nobility: 'From the fifteenth century the multiplicity of cadet branches irremediably condemned a section of the nobility, first to an increasing poverty and then to absorption in the ranks of commoners.'[27]

What should be recognized here is that the problem was not new in the period when the legal right of *juveigneurs* to a third was guaranteed by the revised custom of 1580. From the thirteenth century, at latest, many families declined in social status as their landed wealth was fragmented by successive partitions which the *Assize* and custom might slow down but could not prevent. Nor does the story lack pathos, since few families were so entirely and consistently unscrupulous 'in sacrificing junior members for the sake of the family's future'.[28] Virtually nothing is known of the growth of this petty *noblesse*, of its relations, other than strictly feudal, with the greater nobility, or of its economic fortunes prior to the acute crises of the mid — and later — fourteenth century. But for present purposes its existence and numerical importance should be noted, facts borne home by the events of the civil war which broke out in 1341.

A clear polarization was taking place. The lowlands and valleys of the feudal map were already filled by a mass of lesser nobles, whose origins remain obscure, while the great families and their landed properties formed the semi-permanent reference points on the uplands. As in England and elsewhere in Europe after the Black Death, outstanding landed wealth came, if anything, to be concentrated in even fewer hands.

In some respects, then, the 'renewal' of the *noblesse* after the civil war may appear to be more remarkable than it really was, but for present purposes the existence of an already impoverished and numerically important petty *noblesse* by the time of the war of 1341-64 should be noted. The presence of poor Breton nobles was a constant feature of the history of the duchy; I shall now discuss their livelihoods. Despite the comparative lack of documentary evidence,[29] two general matters concerning the position of the nobility deserve emphasis. The first concerns the allegiance of the nobility. Although the precise composition of the opposing sides in the civil war has still to be fully investigated the greater nobility on the whole appear to have supported the Penthièvre family, and the lesser, especially in the west and north, at first supported Jean de Montfort.[30] Yet this simple division may, on the analogy of studies of other disputed regions, prove to be much more complex. Already during the civil war the proportion of the lesser *noblesse* entering French royal service in the companies of greater lords is impressive.[31]

This suggests that the distinction between the differing general allegiance of the two groups within the Breton nobility is inadequate. Certainly by the 1370s support for the Montfortists amongst the lesser *noblesse*, even in Finistère had reached its nadir.[32] But disenchantment may well have set in much earlier in consequence, perhaps, of economic difficulties accentuated by guerilla warfare. In fifteenth-century Guyenne nobles living on the frontier of war devised a régime of local truces and altered the practice of succession in order to protect their lands from the worst effects of warfare.[33] Local truces were arranged in Brittany, but it is not clear whether Breton families adopted the stratagem of dividing their lands amongst relatives with different allegiances, although the occasional hint of such practices may be detected. The balancing act which John IV performed between England and France was paralleled by similar multiple acts of tightrope walking by his nobility and defection could take place on a massive scale.

The traditional, feudal hold which the duke of Brittany might once have had over his nobility had manifestly failed in the civil war to secure its total allegiance. Amongst other things it was considered necessary in the late fourteenth century to devise 'a supplementary oath and a legal contract' which would, it was hoped, reinforce the feudal nexus.[34] The numerous *alliances* (non-feudal political contracts) formed in pursuit of this end have been skilfully described by Peter Lewis: he asks whether such contracts in Brittany ensure the fulfilment of their purpose. The moral constraints of the *alliance* — the fear of dishonour and reproach for perjured knightly faith — or more obvious sanctions like the loss of one's property, pension, or office, must undoubtedly have influenced the actions of those who entered into such agreements. But short of a case study of each *alliance*, the obvious answer is that in some cases it did cement allegiance between the contracting parties while in others breakdown of trust or outright disobedience led to its nullification sooner or later. Yet Mr Lewis and M. Capra entertain doubts. In Guyenne, where the creation of *alliances* has an equally long history, they claim that nobles were a great deal less inconstant in their loyalties than other historians admit.[35] It may well be that with a few exceptions the same is true in Brittany. Some *alliances*, Lewis suggests, were 'imposed upon a contractor because of some dereliction of duty or as a pledge of good behaviour'. Certainly the *alliance* in Brittany was principally used when the relations between the duke and his nobility were strained.

After he returned from exile in 1379, John IV extracted a series of obligations or bonds from a considerable number of nobles, including some of the most influential. The sire de Malestroit was obliged for a fine of 4,000 *livres*; and perhaps in connection with Malestroit's case, the sire du Molac was obliged for 2,000 *livres* in 1383 'because of a certain dispute which had arisen between the lord of Malestroit and himself'.[36] In 1382 the lord of Rostrenen had subscribed an obligation for 1,000 *livres*; Jean, sire du Chastellier d'Yréac, and Rivalen de Rochefort were pledges for Monsieur Rivalen de Ploër in the sum of 2,000 francs. In 1382 again, the sires de Montauban and Montfort stood surety for Jean, sire de Beaumanoir, who was obliged to the duke for 6,000 francs 'because of certain acts of disobedience committed against my lord, the duke'.[37] Many other such pledges are recorded in the first inventory of the ducal archives drawn up in 1395, and since its compiler was careful to note cancelled letters, it must be presumed that many of these obligations were still in force. Some guaranteed the appearance of offenders in court, probably to answer civil charges. Others relate to prisoners of war and those guilty of criminal offences who were, in effect, on parole. The brevity of the entries in the inventory is often tantalizing. But that the majority of such obligations were not just simple actions for debt is made clear by other entries in the inventory. Many of these obligations must have hung suspended over the lesser contracting party in a way reminiscent not only of King John's practices in England, but also foreshadowing the punitive recognizances taken by Henry VII a century later.[38] Like the *alliance* or the pension, such bonds represented a weapon in the duke's armoury which could be used to compel allegiance and determine political behaviour.

The second general matter which needs to be stressed with regard to the position of the nobility during the civil war and succeeding military actions is the way in which these circumstances helped at the time to differentiate the *noblesse* from other sectors of Breton society. Traditionally it was the pre-eminent role of the nobility in medieval societies to fight. Nor had the nobles of the duchy shirked their duties before the civil war.[39] But traditions of military service outside the duchy took on an entirely new dimension from the mid-fourteenth century. In thirteenth-century Paris immigrant Bretons were satirized as carriers of bundles and cleaners of latrines.[40] From 1341 to the early sixteenth century it was the *noblesse* who temporarily emigrated, not only to theatres of war elsewhere in France but also to Italy and Spain.[41] Many reasons for emphasis amongst the Breton nobility on its military role during this period may be postulated. From the fifth century A.D. the duchy has acted as a human reservoir. Overpopulation, economic recession and civil war may be held responsible for releasing a particular flood in the mid-fourteenth century. The duchy appears to have largely escaped early visitations of the plague.[42] Royal service provided an income which was welcome in difficult days. There is little remarkable in a poor region capitalizing on one of its few assets — a relative abundance of manpower in a period of general population decline — as the analagous examples of Scotland and Switzerland in the later Middle Ages also demonstrate.

Though the result of the predominating concern of the Breton nobility in the later Middle Ages with warfare may have led to a hardening of its social attitudes. Long after it had lost its military reputation, it remained conservative, obstinate, and jealous of its feudal and judicial privileges.[43]

Although many noble families in the duchy had ancient origins, for the mass of the *noblesse* continuous family histories begin with the names of those who were mustered, especially under the two successive Breton constables, Bertrand du Guesclin and Olivier de Clisson. This is an accident of surviving documentation. Thus Prigent de Coëtivy, knight, is recorded in the late thirteenth century, but there is then a long gap until we meet Guillaume de Coëtivy, esquire, in Clisson's company in 1379, together with Alain, sire de Coëtivy, father of the Admiral and his brothers.[44] The earliest forbears of Guillaume de Rosnyvinen who can be easily traced all appear under the constable in the years following 1370.[45] The Chastels were an old family, but about this time many of its members served in royal armies. Examples could be cited from many more families besides those of de Coëtivy, de Rosnyvinen, or du Chastel. During the late fourteenth century it becomes possible to trace descents from among the amorphous mass of nobility. In the late seventeenth century 28 per cent (a high survival rate) of the *noblesse* appear to have been directly descended in the male line from families which were already noble in the fifteenth century.[46]

The survival of an increasing number of records from the Breton *Chambre des Comptes* also gives an impression that there was a 'renewal' of the nobility. The development of general taxation in the duchy *c.* 1345-70 was achieved at the price of allowing the nobility to retain their personal immunity from *fouages*, *impôts*, and *aides*.[47] There is only one full surviving letter of John IV by which he ennobled land. Additional records show that individually or corporately others sometimes enjoyed respite from *fouages*.[48] After 1417, however, letters of ennoblement and enfranchisement were issued in increasing numbers.[49] From the later fourteenth century, there survive a series of general or local 'réformations des feux'.[50] Tax records thus provide some crude minimal averages for recruitment to the nobility, their distribution and density.[51] More accurate lists for fiscal purposes at this time also presented added advantages to the dukes who were now in a much better position to control entry into the nobility and as a facet of their patronage they keenly exploited rights to ennoble.

Accession to the lowest ranks of the Breton nobility seems to have been relatively easy. 'Arms', wrote the author of Le Jouvencel 'ennoble a man whoever he may be.'[52] And fifteenth-century Bretons, unlike their seventeenth-century successors, accepted in practice that 'when one has been counted twice at the musters then one is henceforward reputed noble'.[53] Many families passed into the ranks of the *noblesse* by service in arms. The acquisition of noble fiefs had been another traditional means of achieving nobility. Families who practised partition of estates according to the principles adopted by the nobility were themselves, *ipso facto*, considered noble. In both these instances, the acquisition and enjoyment of nobility is fairly simply described. In the next instance, strict definition is impossible.

In Burgundy and the *bailliage* of Senlis, 'It is not the office which ennobles'.[54] The same would appear to be true in Brittany, but hints of change can be found. Letters of enfranchisement for lands reveal that this privilege, often an early step towards the acquisition of nobility, was particularly a reward for office holders. Ducal officials also benefited from personal grants of franchise from taxation.[55] In 1428, for example, Henri Faiaust, assistant to Jean Mauléon, *trésorier de l'épargne*, a practising 'lawyer, clerk and notary of our court of Ploermel, who is accustomed to living and conducting himself as a noble without in any way concerning himself with any craft or commercial practice except with writing and notarial arts' was freed from contributing to *fouages*.[56] In 1433 Guillaume Jahou, 'homme de science, avocat d'assise' went one better and had his lands ennobled because he was 'a noble person issuing and descending from noble persons', even though he held various lands in the diocese of Rennes which were subject to partible inheritance 'according to the manner of those of low estate and condition'.[57] In the following year Jean Jouguet was ennobled, and the reasons for this are explained in some detail.[58] In none of these three cases did the holding of an office ennoble on its own account. Faiaust lived in a noble style; Jahou was a noble by blood and race; and Jouguet was a noble by arms. Though lowly, their offices were compatible with nobility.

There has been an increasing appreciation in recent years of this conjunction of office and nobility in later medieval France,[59] but for what range of offices was this true in Brittany? Was venality systematized by Francis I in 1522-3 already a general characteristic of office-holding under the dukes? How far were the nobility in competition with others for office? Although the questions have yet to be fully studied, it is clear that many nobles, whatever their rank, accepted office and acquired training in such practical subjects as law in order to compete for ducal, seigneurial, and municipal employment.[60] A number of ducal secretaries, forefathers of the *noblesse de robe*, may have come from ancient noble families; many received patents of nobility and thus paralleled the social rise of secretaries in royal service who automatically acquired nobility following an ordonnance of Charles VIII.[61] The fortunes of the descendants of Jean Gibon, illustrate the point. Gibon's holdings were freed from *fouages* in 1436 as a reward for his services as secretary. In 1496 his grandson, Maître Jean Gibon, 'écuyer, sire du Grisso, procureur de la Chambre des Comptes de Bretagne', came to terms with his fellow parishioners over the demolition of 'a length of the choir of the church of Notre-Dame du Mené next to the presbytery' in order to build as a chapel a family burial place, and in whose great window the arms of Gibon and his wife were to be displayed. In 1523 Maître Jean's grandson married Adèle de Carné, a representative of another family which had risen even more dramatically in ducal service. Both families were to survive to the eighteenth century when the Carnés married into the 'high royal court nobility', while the Gibons du Grisso et du Pargo continued to provide members of the Breton parlement.[62] The medieval antecedents of *noblesse de robe* are still little understood. Nor is representation of the *ancienne noblesse* in branches of the legal profession which were considered compatible with nobility.[63] But it seems clear that as a result of acquiring seigneuries and offices, and also of intermarriage among its members, the bureaucratic class was rising quickly to prominence.[64]

The most usual way to acquire nobility in Brittany was by letters patent, and those who were granted patents of nobility form a very miscellaneous group. That in Brittany ducal surgeons and apothecaries and the relatives of clerks of the ducal chapel became members of the *noblesse* scarcely appears surprising when carpenters and those endowed with little but abnormal physical strength were likewise ennobled.[65] Those willing to marry the illegitimate daughters of the high nobility were sometimes lucky enough to acquire nobility themselves.[66] It is common knowledge that participation in retail trade as opposed to international commerce, raising of livestock, keeping of taverns and sundry other allegedly demeaning occupations was not as elsewhere in France in the first half of the fifteenth century an automatic derogation of noble status in Brittany.[67] There developed the notion of *dormition* of *noblesse*. Individuals, even whole families, practised commerce and after they had made modest fortunes, they reassumed noble status.[68] Acknowledged practice in the fifteenth century, *dormition* became an article of the Breton custom in the sixteenth and remained a unique and, to royal officials, a disturbing feature of Breton noble law in the seventeenth.[69] In the world of commerce, high finance and office holding the interests of the old and new families of the *noblesse*, and of the socially indeterminate, merged in the late fifteenth century though the pattern which can then be distinguished was probably much older.[70]

As a result average annual recruitment to the nobility under John V, as measured by the issue of patents, far exceeded such averages in Valois Burgundy, where Philip the Good created only one new noble family a year during the course of his reign. The Breton average of about six families a year for the period 1417-42 is very similar to the rate of royal promotions for the whole of France during the reigns of Charles VII and Louis XI.[71] Military emergencies in particular presented opportunities for aspiring candidates to present themselves as willing to undertake service as other nobles were accustomed to do. Many who were thus without formal ties with the *noblesse* were admitted; others who had proved themselves in the wars likewise gained admission. Under Francis I the average number of promotions remains almost the same, at about six a year, though the correlation with warfare is not quite so obvious. It can therefore be understood why such a constantly high level of ennoblement by contemporary standards should have been criticized. The main concern of Peter II seems to have been to appease *roturiers* (commoners), who were left to pay the tax burden which fell proportionately more heavily upon them with each ennoblement, and to protect his own income. In the great set of constitutions issued in the *Estates* of 1451 it was decreed that:

> henceforward commoners of simple and low condition, retailers, those practising law and others who are not of noble descent cannot by any means acquire nor obtain in hereditary possession in our country and duchy of Brittany, heritages or noble fees, held nobly, and by fealty, of us or lords of our country, nor appropriate in any manner whatsoever such heritages and noble fees except by our permission and licence.[72]

A brake was applied — the average number of ennoblements for Peter's reign falls to under four a year. One only is recorded for the brief reign of Arthur III.

From a review of similar evidence for the reigns of Francis II and Anne, it would seem that there was a distinct fall in the number of ennoblements in the last half of the century. Under Francis II promotions at an average of a little over one a year, and under Anne, of less than one a year, suggest that the *noblesse* was becoming increasingly closed, a feature which was common to other contemporary nobilities.[73] After a period of relatively easy access during which a 'renewal' took place as new families acquired noble status or old ones had theirs confirmed, the qualifications for admission to the nobility appear to have been tightened. The ducal legislation of 1451, repeated in 1455, was echoed sixty years later when nobles in the *Estates* of 1517 petitioned to prevent *roturiers* obtaining noble *fiefs*.[74] Whether it was a response to such requests or not, Francis I gave critics of excessive ennoblement by patent little to quarrel about in Brittany and the virtual cessation of official promotions in Brittany after its annexation to France may well have served to strengthen the provincial exclusiveness of the Breton nobility.[75] Though much more research on the full social consequences of the absorption of the duchy into the kingdom remains to be done, before the cycles opening and closing the *noblesse* are plotted in detail.

Another index of increasing noble consciousness and exclusivism is differentiation of rank. Such differences had existed long before the civil war, but from the reign of John V, the process of promotion within the nobility by ducal patent can also be observed. In 1433, for example, Jean de Beaumanoir, sire du Bois de la Motte et du Treméreuc, was created a banneret, for the reason that he was:

> descended in all lines from great and noble families . . . and also he possesses the power and faculty, both in subjects as in rents and revenues, to hold the estate of banneret . . . with the right to keep, have and maintain in perpetuity, arms and banners on the battlefield, in the army at funerals and obsequies and in all other places where it is appropriate and necessary for him to do so, as do the ancient barons and bannerets of our duchy.[76]

In 1440 Guillaume de Sévigné, knight, received a similar privilege to have his own banner, together with 'a gibbet with three posts'; in the same year the seigneury of Fresnay was erected into a barony.[77] Between 1451 and 1455 Peter II created six bannerets, and Francis II and Anne continued to confer this dignity on leading subjects.[78] Promotion to banneret was originally closely linked with particular forms of army organization. Because of the development of royal ordonnance companies in the 1440s the military grade of 'banneret', with special rates of pay, was suppressed in France.[79] Its use in Brittany thereafter would appear to have been primarily social.

That such questions of status and dignity were much in the mind of a duke like Peter II is also made plain by his promotion of the lords of Derval, Malestroit, and Quintin to the ranks of the nine great barons in the *Estates* of 1451. Francis II again followed suit. The myth of the nine ancient baronies of Brittany emerged in the early fifteenth century. It was perhaps fostered by the Rohan family, but was more probably developed as a conscious imitation of the twelve peers of France or the cult of the nine worthies as part of a deliberate effort to create a court mystique.[80] Like the creation of orders of knighthood, such an institution increased the range of patronage available to a ruler, reflected glory on him and his leading subjects, created tangible and intangible bonds among the higher nobility, and strengthened their cohesion. The importance of such considerations cannot be measured, but they obviously mattered to a society, which was increasingly dominated by men of rank and prestige.

Since at least the late fourteenth century patents of creation as well as other grants of privileges to the nobility, were normally presented to the *Estates* for their acknowledgement.[81] In the *Estates* there were frequent disputes, such as that about the baronies created in 1451, about precedence which often held up the other business. Such disputes, apparently over fine

points of honour, are too easily dismissed as absurd. They do in fact reveal
how conscious the nobility was becoming about its status. In many respects
they may be considered as part of the proper business of the *Estates*, which
were, it appears, often indifferent to the serious business of politics,
especially since the grant of a particular privilege implied, enhanced, or
conferred judicial and other rights which might have detrimental effects on
another seigneur. A mark of honour for one family might be interpreted as
a slight by another. Even the numerous disputes over the positioning of
knightly tombs, pews, and armorial bearings in parish churches and
chapels may thus be important for the light they throw on tensions that
arose among the higher nobility, and also on the role of the duke when he
reconciled nobles whose quarrels appear, on first sight, to have been oc-
casioned by fits of pique.[82] Deeply cherished assumptions about order and
precedence sometimes came under fire and political action might as easily
be determined by injured pride as by strictly economic factors. The
surviving council minutes for 1459 – 63 show how closely the duke's
advisers kept an eye on the private affairs of the nobility; they vetted, for
example, all royal mandates concerning litigation in the *Parlement* of Paris,
oversaw marriage contracts, protected the interests of minors, rebated the
rachat, and consented to a whole series of personal privileges. The broken
series of chancery registers reflect similar discussions of which we have no
record. But they tell the same tale.[83] If a separate Breton identity was to be
maintained in the fifteenth century, the dukes not only had to depend on
continuing social harmony among the nobility, but also had to satisfy its
aspirations at all levels.

But the duke by no means monopolized the services of his nobility,
however much on occasion he tried to circumscribe their actions.[84] For
some who ventured beyond the Breton frontiers in the fifteenth century the
rewards, or the opportunities in the short term at least to run up bigger
debts, may have been considerable; with a flow of offices, dignities,
pensions, lands, and other marks of royal favour. In succession to Du
Guesclin and Clisson in the fourteenth century, Brittany provided a
number of leading officers for the royal administration in the fifteenth,
Arthur, comte de Richemont became Constable of France in 1425, thirty-
two years before he became duke in 1457. In his entourage Chastels,
Rosnyvinens, Coëtivys, and many others served the King.[85]

Jean, sire de Rieux, Marshal of France, ceded his office in 1417 to his
son, Pierre. Gilles, sire de Rays, was appointed a marshal of France in
1429, losing his place only when his monstrous crimes became manifest in
1440. He was succeeded shortly afterwards by André de Laval, sire de
Lohéac.[86] At the same time Prigent de Coëtivy was appointed admiral, a
post which was later held by Jean, sire de Montauban.[87] Towards the end
of the century there was Pierre, sire de Gié, a cousin of the vicomte de

Rohan, and a man who according to Louis XI was 'greatly avaricious and loved money'. Louis nevertheless made him a marshal a position eventually lost as a result of court intrigues in 1506.[88] A number of other families gained a lesser prominence like the Pontbriants, who were implicated in the fall of Gié.[89]

But a survey of the names listed in *Gallia Regia* suggests a number of observations. First, and in confirmation of the primarily military role adopted by the Breton *noblesse* from the mid-fourteenth century, Bretons serving the king are chiefly to be found in army commands. Secondly, the number of Breton nobles holding civil office in France seems to have been a very restricted one, if their total numbers and potential suitability is considered. Few Bretons were appointed royal *baillis* or seneschals. Little evidence survives for the interchange of personnel between the ducal and royal administrations. Nor is there much surviving evidence for extensive movement among the financial officers of the duke and king.[90] Unlike other great provincial later medieval rulers the dukes of Brittany were either unlucky in placing their servants about the royal court, or in royal employment or they were less concerned to do so.[91] This is yet another aspect of the independence of the duchy in the fifteenth century.

Especially during the reign of Louis XI, some ducal pensioners might be found at the royal court, and some royal pensioners at the ducal court. Charles V made considerable use of pensions to subvert the position of John IV; but in normal circumstances kings of France found such outlay a poor investment and when they were being economical pensions were stopped.[92] Only during the last years of the reign of Francis II did the king use more costly and also more regularly paid pensions to outbid the duke and the inducements he could offer to his nobility. Neither the number of royal pensioners, nor the material rewards which the majority of Breton nobles acquired from their service to France, should be overestimated.[93]

To judge by the rebuilding of manor houses, or châteaux, which imitated the latest styles of the Loire valley, some royal pensioners derived from their service to the kings of France more than a taste for beautiful things.[94] But ducal support was pervading and important. Both Peter II and Francis II were concerned with castles. They urged their owners to repair them, seized the revenues of those who refused to comply, and destroyed weak places. Whereas in the rest of France seigneurs were becoming much more aware of domestic comforts and kings kept an alert watch on the military works of their leading lords 'Brittany undertook, on the contrary, the most extensive and complete reconstruction of its defensive system', with a massive rebuilding of ducal and seigneurial castles from *c*.1450.[95]

Concessions of taxes like the *billot* on wine and other products multiplied and were carefully licensed, accounts being rendered to the duke's own financial officers by seigneurial receivers. But the duchy may not have

c

footed the total costs of this rebuilding programme, for as Rosnyvinen's *Mémoire* relates, individual captains might have to find finances themselves and in doing so they might draw on revenues derived in France.[96] As it transpired this modernization was inadequate; royal artillery played a decisive role in reducing fortresses in 1487-91, though the defence of Nantes (19 June-16 August 1487) shows what could be done with up-to-date urban defences and a resolute garrison.[97] Factors such as these must undoubtedly be remembered, even though it is not yet possible either to measure the strain which building operations put on noble finances or to determine the effects of the transfer to the duchy of specie in the form of wages and pensions. There may well have been a crisis in noble fortunes, which in individual cases was clearly exacerbated by the political turmoil of the 1480s and early 1490s. But the extent and nature of this crisis cannot be determined until such matters as the normal contributions of estate revenues to the income of the nobility are investigated.

Thus there are many problems to be resolved before the role of the nobility in the history of the duchy can be critically assessed. Politically their posture throughout the fifteenth century was Janus-like; the ambivalence which Rosnyvinen showed at the outset of his career is but one example. Loyalties were divided; the divisions of the 1480s proved fatal to the survival of the independent duchy. But who gained and who lost on the political merry-go-round remains obscure, and what of the benefits gained over the preceding century by Bretons in royal and ducal service?

Even disregarding the longer perspectives, problems of the survival of old families, recruitment of new, differences of rank within the nobility, definition of noble privileges and their exercise all require much closer attention. Concluding his remarkable book, Professor Meyer writes:

> from the end of the Middle Ages to the beginning of the twentieth century Brittany indubitably offers the unique example of a region dominated by the same order, formed for the most part of the same families. Certainly there was a partial renewal of this social framework but the newcomers were absorbed into the governing body whether they came from the noble stock of other regions . . . or from the ranks of richer townspeople. This permanence of the noble framework of Breton provincial life has contributed not inconsiderably to the reinforcement of the irreducible originality of the province and has thus perpetuated the problems bound up with its very existence.[98]

When future investigations into some of the problems which I have discussed are completed, a similar conclusion, though with suitable modifications, may be reached for the later Middle Ages and the early modern period. Such investigations will not only lead to a better understanding of the nature of French society, crown and community; they will add yet another dimension to a long and complex story.

Notes

1. Since this essay is a general statement about work in progress, references have been
    kept to a minimum. I am grateful for particular help from Malcolm Vale, Alan
    Cameron, Peter Lewis, and the late John Cooper, and to the Wolfson Foundation for a
    scholarship which enabled me to consult some of the manuscripts cited.
2. J. Meyer, *La Noblesse bretonne au XVIIIe siècle* (2 vols., Paris, 1966), i, 57.
3. 'Abondance de la noblesse pauvre qui forme une véritable plèbe nobiliaire', ibid. i. 21.
4. Morice, *Preuves*, iii. 558-63.
5. 'Premier echanson, son conseiller, Grant-Reformateur des eaux et forests de France'
    (Morice, *Preuves*, ii. 1299, 1409, 1642).
6. P. Contamine, *Guerre, état et société à la fin du moyen âge. Etudes sur les armées des rois de
    France, 1337-1494* (Paris, 1972), pp. 447-8. B.N. MS. 15541 f. 28, report on state of
    St-Aubin; A. Dupuy, *Histoire de la réunion de la Bretagne à la France* (2 vols., Paris, 1880),
    ii. 118, 448-50.
7. Cf. *Lettres et mandements de Jean V, duc de Bretagne*, ed. R. Blanchard (5 vols., Nantes
    1889-95, cited as *Lettres de Jean V*), no. 2041 *contra* B.A. Pocquet du Haut-Jussé, *François
    II, duc de Bretagne, et l'Angleterre (1458-1488)* (Paris, 1928), p.169 n.33.
8. Bibliography in *La Noblesse au Moyen Age XIe — XVe siècles*, ed. P. Contamine (Paris,
    1976), pp. 19-35.
9. Morice, *Preuves*, ii. 1152-61, constitutions of 1425 combatting these developments.
10. Cf. Bois, in *La Noblesse*, ed. Contamine, pp.219-33.
11. B-A. Pocquet du Haut-Jussé, 'De la vassalité à la noblesse dans le duché de Bretagne',
    Bulletin philologique et historique (jusqu' à 1610) du comité des travaux historiques et scientifiques,
    1963, pp.785-800, Meyer, op.cit., i.21ff., 440-2. P. Contamine, 'The French nobility
    and the war', *The Hundred Years War*, ed. K. Fowler (London, 1971), p.138.
12. Michael Jones, *Ducal Brittany 1364-1399* (Oxford, 1970), *passim* for this paragraph.
13. A. de la Borderie, *Histoire de Bretagne*, continuée par B. Pocquet (6 vols., Paris-Rennes,
    1896-1914), iv.197-214, 247, 524-5.
14. Michael Jones, '"Mon pais et ma nation"; Breton identity in the fourteenth century',
    War, Literature, and Politics in the Late Middle Ages, ed. C.T. Allmand (Liverpool, 1976),
    pp. 144-68.
15. Cf. M. Keen and M. Daniel, 'English diplomacy and the sack of Fougères in 1449',
    History, lix (1974), 383-7. Pocquet, *François II, passim*.
16. H. Touchard, *Le Commerce maritime breton* (Paris, 1967), pp. 157-74.
17. *Concilium Basiliense*, ed. J. Haller *et al.*, iii. *Protokolle des Concils von 1434 und 1435* (Basel,
    1900), p.50.
18. La Borderie, *Histoire*, iii. 56-92 and map.
19. Cf. K.B. McFarlane, *The Nobility of Later Medieval England* (Oxford, 1972), pp.xxiii,
    142-76.
20. J. Boussard, *Le Gouvernement d'Henri II Plantagenêt* (Paris, 1956), pp. 103-12.
21. A. de la Borderie, *Etude historique sur les neuf barons de Bretagne* (Rennes, 1895) for the
    fluctuating numbers and composition of baronial lordships.
22. *La très ancienne coutume de Bretagne*, ed. M. Planiol (Rennes, 1896), pp. 321-3.
23. M. Planiol, 'L'Assise au comte Geoffroi. Etude sur les successions féodales en
    Bretagne', *Nouvelle revue historique de droit français et étranger*, xi (1887), 117-162, 652-708,
    is fondamental.

24. 'Cartulaire des sires de Rays', ed. R. Blanchard, *Archives historiques du Poitou*, xxviii (1898), pp. cvii-cviii; and xxx (1900), no. CCCXVI. A. du Chesne, *Histoire généalogique de la maison de Montmorency et de Laval* (Paris, 1624), pp. 573-5.
25. Lyon, Bibliothèque municipale, Coll. Henry Morin-Pons, 24 December 1422, published by L. Caillet, *A. Bret.* xxvi (1910-11), 100-4.
26. Planiol, art. cit., p. 688, and also J. Yver, 'Les Conditions originaux du groupe de coutumes de l'ouest de France', *Revue historique de droit français et étranger*, 4ème sér., xxx (1952), esp. pp. 41-43.
27. Meyer, op. cit. i. 166; for the problems of an heir with indulgent parents see Morice, *Preuves*, ii. 1357-8.
28. Planiol, art. cit., p. 699.
29. Cf. Bois, in *La Noblesse*, ed. Contamine, p. 225 for general reasons for the growth of documentation in the later fourteenth century, though some earlier accounts do survive (for example, from the barony of Vitré, Arch. Dép. Ille-et-Vilaine, 1 F 1527, 1535-6, 1542, 1549-50).
30. Jones, *Ducal Brittany*, pp. 11-12.
31. Morice, *Preuves*, i. 1469-74, 1478-84, 1489, etc., and cf. Contamine, *Guerre, état et société*, p. 153.
32. On 10 September 1372 ten Breton knights and esquires, several of whom possessed lands in Finistère, were given *fiefs-rentes* by Charles V, (B.N. MS. Nouv. acq. fr. 20026, no. 172).
33. M. G. A. Vale, *English Gascony 1399-1453* (Oxford, 1970), pp. 154-215.
34. P.S. Lewis, 'Of Breton *alliances* and other matters', *War, Literature, and Politics* ed. Allmand, p. 137.
35. Idem, 'Decayed and non-feudalism in later medieval France', *B.I.H.R.* xxxvii (1964), 157-84. P. Capra, 'Les Bases sociales du pouvoir anglo-gascon au milieu du XIVe siècle', *M.A.* lxxxi (1975), 293-9.
36. 'à cause de certain débat esmeu entre le sire de Malestroit et luy', Arch. Dép. Loire-Atlantique, E. 238, inventory by Hervé le Grant, 1395, for the following details.
37. 'à cause de certaines desobeissances faites à mons', ibid. f. 46ʳ.
38. J.R. Lander, 'Bonds, coercion and fear: Henry VII and the peerage', *Florilegium Historiale: Essays presented to Wallace K. Fergusson*, ed. J.G. Rowe and W.H. Stockdale (Toronto, 1971), pp. 327-67; reprinted in J.R. Lander, *Crown and Nobility, 1450-1509* (London, 1976), pp. 267-300.
39. In a French host of 1271 the duke of Brittany was obliged to supply 60 knights, including 16 bannerets; Burgundy, 50 or 55 knights (7 bannerets); Flanders, 40 knights (13 bannerets), etc. (B.N. MS. fr. 32510, fo. 27r).
40. A. Chédeville, 'L'immigration bretonne dans le royaume de France on XIe au début du XIVe siècle', *A. Bret.* lxxxi (1974), 321-2.
41. L. Mirot, 'Sylvestre Budes et les Bretons en Italie', *B.E.C.* lviii (1897), 579-614; lix (1898), 262-303; though only a few fought in the Italian wars of the late fifteenth century (cf. F. Lot, *Recherches sur les effectifs des armées français des guerres d'Italie aux guerres de religion, 1494-1562* (Paris, 1962). For Bretons and Spain cf. *Lettres de Jean V*, no. 2282 and J. Duran y Lerchundi, *La Toma de Granada*, ii (Madrid, 1893), 153-5, a reference kindly supplied by Dr. J.R.L. Highfield.
42. Touchard, *Le Commerce maritime*, p.55.
43. Cf. Meyer, op.cit. i. 24-25.
44. *Recueil d'actes inédites des ducs et princes de Bretagne* (XIe, XIIe, XIIIe s.), ed. A. de la Borderie (Rennes, 1889), nos. cxxxvi, clxviii; Morice, *Preuves*, i. 1087, 1110-11; ii. 203, 205, 207, 246; *Lettres de Jean V*, nos. 172, 229.
45. *Morice, Preuves*, i. 1648; ii. 203, 205, 207, 275, etc. A seventeenth century family history traces the descent from a certain Geoffroy and his relatives mentioned *c.* 1338 (Arch. Dép. Ille-et-Vilaine, 2 Er. 299).

46. Meyer, op.cit. i.57.
47. Michael Jones, 'Les Finances de Jean IV, duc de Bretagne', *Mémoires de la société d'histoire et d'archéologie de Bretagne*, lii (1972-4), 29-30. For others exempt cf. *Lettres de Jean V*, no. 2191. *Fouage* a direct tax on households, calculated in Brittany on the theoretical basis of three households to a hearth (feu); *impôts* and *aides* — indirect taxes levied as customs or sales taxes on foodstuffs and other basic products.
48. Arch. Dép. Loire-Atlantique, B.125, no. 8, 1 March 1391; *Lettres de Jean V*, nos. 424, 739, 888.
49. Ibid., no. 1248 (Arch Dép. Loire-Atlantique, B. 126, no. 68, 24 August 1417); letters ennobling Charles Even and his lands, appear to be the first surviving example.
50. Cf. Touchard, *Le Commerce maritime*, pp. 54-55. Réformations des feux — a revision of the official list of households on the basis of which fouage was levied.
51. Catherine Guilmet, 'Etude de la population bretonne d'après le Registre de la Réformation des feux de 1426', (Diplôme d'études supérieures principal, Nantes 1966), already indicates the high density of nobles in the diocese of St-Brieuc, a point graphically demonstrated by Meyer (op.cit. ii, map).
52. A. Bossuat, *Perrinet Gressart et François de Surienne, agents d'Angleterre* (Paris, 1936), p.2.
53. Meyer, op.cit. i. 107-9; Bossuat, loc.cit.
54. J. Bartier, *Légistes et gens de finances au XVe siècle: les Conseillers des ducs de Bourgogne, Philippe le Bon et Charles le Téméraire* (Bruxelles, 1955), p.198, cf. B. Guenée, *Tribunaux et gens de justice dans le Bailliage de Senlis à la fin du moyen âge (vers 1380-vers 1550)* (Paris, 1963), p. 413.
55. *Lettres de Jean V*, nos. 1863, 1872, 2048, 2259, 2360, 2375, 2415, etc.
56. Ibid., no. 1799.
57. Ibid., no. 2124.
58. Ibid., no. 2156.
59. Cf. Guenée, op.cit., pp. 413-15. E. Dravasa, 'Vivre noblement: Recherches sur la dérogeance de Noblesse du XIVe au XVIe siècles', *Revue juridique et économique du Sud-Ouest, série juridique*, (1965) 135-93 and (1966), 23-129, esp. tables, pp. 78-83.
60. Jones, in *War, Literature, and Politics*, ed. Allmand, p.160 and idem, 'L' Enseignement en Bretagne à la fin du moyen âge: quelques terrains de recherche', *Méms. de la soc. d'hist. et d'arch. de Bretagne*, liii (1975-6); 33-49.
61. Bartier, op.cit., p.191. G. Tessier, *Diplomatique royale française* (Paris, 1962), p. 157.
62. Arch. Dép. Morbihan, E. 1542-4. Aspects of this story are highlighted in J. Gallet, 'Les Seigneurs dans le Vannetais: L'exemple des Gibon du Grisso (XVe-XVIIIe siècles)', *Enquêtes et Documents*, iii (Centre de Recherches sur l'histoire de la France Atlantique, Nantes, 1975), 79-104.
63. Cf. J.H.M. Salmon, *Society in Crisis: France in the Sixteenth Century* (London, 1975), pp. 101-12.
64. Cf. Bartier, op. cit., p. 197.
65. *Lettres de Jean V*, nos. 1749, 2245, 2276, 2290, 2551, etc.
66. Ibid., no. 2357. For other varied qualifications, nos. 2250, 2470, 2489.
67. Touchard, *Le Commerce maritime*, pp. 356-63.
68. Dravasa's remarks on the ending of *dérogeance* in Brittany by the acquisition of letters of rehabilitation require re-examination (art. cit. iv (1966), 121 n.364, 126-7 nn.384, 387) because the legal texts cited do not entirely support his views and there is a dearth of historical examples from this period. On occasion the duke confirmed the right of those of noble status to continue trading; alternatively those no longer enjoying noble status nevertheless were enfranchized from taxes normally falling on commoners (cf. Arch. Dép. Loire-Atlantique, B. 4, fo. 107ʳ, 5 August 1466, and B. 5, fo. 151ᵛ, 24 November 1467, for examples).
69. Meyer, op.cit. i. 135 ff.

70. Cf. Touchard, op.cit., pp. 358-61. J. Kerhervé, 'Une Famille d'officiers de finances bretons au XVe siècle: Les Thomas de Nantes', *A. Bret.* lxxxiii (1976), 7-33.
71. Bartier, op.cit., p.195. G. du Fresne de Beaucourt, *Histoire de Charles VII* (6 vols., Paris, 1881-91), ii. 606-7; iii. 457; iv. 422-3; v. 330-1; vi. 373-4. The main source for Breton ennoblements is Arch. Dép. Loire-Atlantique, B. 125-31.
72. *La Très ancienne coutume*, ed. Planiol, pp. 405-20 (quotation, p.417), a better text than that of Morice, *Preuves*, ii. 1582-91.
73. Cf. McFarlane, *Nobility*, pp. 268-78.
74. *Documents inédits relatifs aux Etats de Bretagne de 1491 à 1589* ed. vicomte Ch. de la Lande de Calan (2 vols., Nantes, 1908), i. 26-31.
75. Only two clearly Breton families are cited in J-R. Bloch, *L' Anoblissement en France au temps de François Ier* (Paris, 1934), Catalogue nos. 37, 44, and 265. But cf. Salmon, op.cit., pp.99-100.
76. *Lettres de Jean V*, no. 2096.
77. Ibid., no. 2455. *Musée des Archives Nationales. Documents originaux de l'histoire de France exposés dans l'hôtel Soubise* (Paris, 1872), no. 453 for Fresnay (not in *Lettres de Jean V*).
78. Morice, *Preuves*, ii. 1563-4, 1592-3, 1594-5, 1641-2, 1668-70; iii. 31-32, 902-3.
79. Contamine, *Guerre, état et société*, pp. 250-2.
80. Morice, *Preuves*, ii. 1560-3; iii. 368-70, 480-2, 551-2, 749-50. The full terms of the grant of the barony of Lanvaux to André de Laval, lord of Lohéac, with a clear statement on the theory of the nine baronies, are set out in letters of 24 March 1464 (Arch. Dép. Loire-Atlantique, B 3 fos. 152v-15r), cf. also La Borderie, *Etude, passim*.
81. Cf. Morice, *Preuves*, ii. 459-65, 513-25 and 649-55.
82. H. du Halgouet, 'Droits honorifiques et prééminences dans les églises en Bretagne', *Méms. de la soc. d'hist. et d'arch. de Bretagne*, iv (1923), 31-87, a valuable introduction especially to legal aspects, but the Chancery registers have not been used. In 1466 alone there were no fewer than 12 such disputes (Arch. Dép. Loire-Atlantique, B 4 *passim*.)
83. Ibid., E.131 (council minutes), B.2ff.
84. Jones, *Ducal Brittany*, p. 66; Lewis, in *War, Literature and Politics*, ed. Allmand, p. 133. In 1461 steps were taken to ensure the exclusive service of some ducal officers in ducal employment (Arch. Dép. Loire-Atlantique, E.131, fos. 122v-3v).
85. Cf. M. G. A. Vale, *Charles VII* (London, 1974), p. 119. E. Cosneau, *Le Connétable de Richemont* (Paris, 1886), *passim*. Prigent de Coëtivy left debts totalling £42,230 11s 3d (L. de la Trémoille, *Prigent de Coëtivy, amiral et bibliophile* (Paris, 1906), pp. 84-86).
86. Contamine, *Guerre, état et société*, pp. 236, 239.
87. G. Dupont-Ferrier, *Gallia Regia, ou état des officiers royaux des bailliages et des sénéchaussées de 1328 à 1517* (7 vols., Paris, 1942-65, cited as *G.R.*), nos. 9271, 2013, 20134.
88. Morice, *Preuves*, iii. 301-3. But the essential source for his career is *Procédures politiques du règne de Louis XII*, ed. R. de Maulde (Paris, 1885), pp. xi-cxxxi, 1-786. For Louis's views, p. 244.
89. Ibid., pp. lxxxvi ff. *G.R.*, nos. 6140, 7372, 22358.
90. A remark based on information kindly supplied by M. Jean Kerhervé, who is studying the financial personnel of the duchy.
91. Cf. P.S. Lewis, *Later Medieval France: The Polity* (London, 1968), pp. 153-8.
92. The *fiefs-rentes* granted in 1373 (above n. 32) were cancelled in 1387 (B.N. MS. Clairambault 487, fos.189r-90v).
93. Arch. Dep. Loire-Atlantique, E. 212; Arch. Nat., KK 79. Only a handful of Bretons appear on the remarkable list of some 769 royal pensioners, c.1480 (B.N. MS. fr.2900, fos.7r-16r), of which Peter Lewis kindly gave me a transcript.
94. A. Mussat, 'Le Château de Vitré et l'architecture des châteaux bretons du XIVe au XVIe siècle', *Bulletin monumental*, cxxxiii (1975) 132-64.

95. R. Grand, 'L'Architecture militaire en Bretagne jusqu'à Vauban', *Bulletin monumental*, cix (1951), esp. pp.368-79.
96. Morice, *Preuves*, iii. 558-63.
97. La Borderie, *Histoire*, iv. 533-8; P. Contamine, 'L'Artillerie royale français à la veille des guerres d'Italie', *A. Bret.* lxxi (1964), 221-61. For the defences of Rennes, J-P Leguay, *La Ville de Rennes au XVe siècle à travers les comptes des miseurs* (Paris, 1968).
98. 'de la fin du Moyen Age aux débuts du XXe siècle, la Bretagne offre sans doute l'exemple unique d'une région dominée par la même ordre, formé sur une large part des mêmes familles. Il y a eu certes rennouvellement partiel de ces cadres, mais les nouveaux venus se sont fondus dans le milieu dirigeant qu'ils fussent issus de la noblesse d'autres régions . . . ou de la bourgeoisie. Cette permanence du cadre nobiliaire de la vie provinciale bretonne n'a pas peu contribué à renforcer l'originalité irréductible de la province, et à perpetuer aussi les problèmes liés à son existence.' Meyer, op.cit. ii.1255.

4

The Crown, Magnates, and Local Government in Fifteenth-Century East Anglia

Roger Virgoe

Some years ago I published an article on the relations between the Crown and local government during the reign of Richard II.[1] A study of the parliament rolls of the period and analysis of office-holding and commissions in one region — East Anglia — appeared to show that though local government was certainly an important political issue it was the knights and squires of the counties who took the initiative for change: the Crown was conducting a holding operation rather than seeking to extend its authority. During the last three years of his reign, however, Richard II did pursue a more aggressive policy in local government matters: opposition to this policy helped to produce support for Henry Bolingbroke and is reflected in the articles drawn up against the king in 1399.[2] Finally it was argued that the Lancastrian usurpation marked the success of the Commons' policy of local self-government by the knights and squires of the counties and very limited involvement of the Crown. With the weakening of Crown control, however, the great magnates, both through their influence on appointments made by the Crown to local offices and through their accumulation of clients and retainers from among the classes which filled these offices, were able in many shires to dominate for long periods the Crown's local officials. Consequently all other men of the county had to seek 'good lordship' in order to maintain or increase their status and 'lyvelode'.

This paper pursues some of these themes into the fifteenth century, examining briefly some of the changes in local government and attitudes towards it, and assessing the importance of other structures of authority within the counties. This is a preliminary exploration which makes no claim to have examined all the relevant sources, and two more specific reservations must be made. First, the article deals only with county government, and ignores the towns, as well as ecclesiastical administration. Secondly, it draws its evidence largely from East Anglia, being part of a more general study of the region in the late Middle Ages. Socially and politically East Anglia was not typical of the whole of England in the fifteenth century and the more specific points made in the latter part of the paper may not be equally applicable to other counties.

The fifteenth century was not a period of radical departures or, indeed, of really new institutions in local government, though the acquisition of great new estates by the Crown gave a new status to the local officials of the duchy of Lancaster from the beginning of the century and to other stewards, receivers, and feodaries from 1461. There were, of course, in all counties numerous officials appointed by the king or one of the great officers — keepers of manors and constables of castles, customs officials, vice-admirals, and the like — and any comprehensive study of the relations of central and local government ought to include some consideration of these, as well as of the officers of the great franchises. It is not, however, proposed to deal with these offices and their holders here, except in passing, nor to consider minor or subordinate office-holders, such as coroners, bailiffs, and constables. Apart from the justices of assize, who twice a year brought to the counties some of the panoply and power of the authority of the king, it was throughout the fifteenth century the offices of sheriff and escheator and the numerous commissions of the period, above all the commission of the peace, which most clearly connected royal authority, magnate power, and the local community. It was the gentry who filled these positions, the Crown which nominated to them and the magnates who influenced their actions, and it is upon these institutions that the paper will concentrate.

By 1400 the Commons had achieved most of the modifications to the office of sheriff which had been embodied in numerous petitions during the fourteenth century. The sheriff had to be a resident member of the governing class of the county over which he presided, and not the local steward of a magnate; he had to be formally nominated by the council and great officers; he, his under-sheriff and clerks, could serve only for a year at a time.[3] These modifications were not seriously challenged in the fifteenth century and there is consequently much less emphasis on the sheriff's office in the parliamentary petitions of the period. Nevertheless there were a substantial number of such petitions which can be roughly divided into four groups.

The first group, frequent enough in the fourteenth century also, complained of the financial burden of the office, the sheriff's farm being impossible to collect in full in many shires but the Exchequer refusing to modify its demands. Petitions from individual sheriffs to the Council are frequent and during the first two Lancastrian reigns the Commons often supported the claims by groups of sheriffs to be allowed to account by oath for the revenues actually collected.[4] But although the Commons, with some justification, claimed that this principle had been accepted by the Crown in the 1399 parliament,[5] the Exchequer would never acknowledge the concession and the parliamentary petitions were always largely or wholly rejected, though individual sheriffs were encouraged to petition the Council for *ad hoc* relief. Such petitions in parliament cease under Henry VI, perhaps as a result of the Council ordinance of 1423 which granted that all sheriffs who by ancient custom had pardons of their arrears should, without further petition, have a privy seal warrant ordering the Exchequer to allow them what was customary.[6] The problem was not solved, however; on a number of occasions sheriffs refused to make office until further allowances were made to them.[7] It is clear that in some counties, the fees obtained by the sheriff for private business and the various douceurs available could not make up for the burden of the farm. Under Edward IV the Commons again petitioned for the right of the sheriffs to account by oath but it was not until well into the sixteenth century that declaration by oath was generally allowed.[8]

A second group of petitions from the Commons was aimed at abuses and extortions committed by the sheriffs. The best-known of these resulted in the statutes strengthening the controls over the sheriff's role in the election of knights and burgesses to parliament.[9] The evidence suggests that these statutes were largely ineffective, and this also seems to have been true of the acts of 1425 and 1439 which attempted to prevent the impanelling of biased juries and other interference in the due process of law.[10]

By the fifteenth century the execution of legal process and the holding of elections were probably the most important of the sheriff's duties for the society of the county over which he presided. His role in collecting the king's income, his judicial and peacekeeping duties and even his role as leader of the shire posse remained significant, but, as is well-known, declined during the period.[11] The acts of 1461 and 1497 virtually ended the sheriff's judicial role and much diminished his independence in the control of legal processes.[12]

Finally a small group of petitions concerned the qualification to hold the office of sheriff and the term of the appointment. A petition of 1402 asked that the sheriff should be a resident of the shire to which he was appointed and that he should reside there during his term of office.[13] This was enacted but the law was certainly breached during the fifteenth century, especially when the sheriff was a courtier. On the other hand the statutes which limited the sheriff's term to one year were normally obeyed and there was much less petitioning on this theme than during the previous century. An act of 1413 extended the rule to bailiffs and Council ordinances of 1426 confirmed that under-sheriffs and bailiffs should not be reappointed and provided for the incoming sheriff to swear to this effect.[14] There is evidence that for sheriff's officials the law was enforced, though, no doubt, not consistently, even in cities that held county status.[15] In 1445 the Commons petitioned that the law had been extensively broken and the statutes were reaffirmed and penalties increased, but so far as the sheriffs are concerned there is little evidence of breaches of the law: during the previous ten years a sheriff had been immediately reappointed in only four bailiwicks — three of these instances involved Cambridgeshire and Huntingdonshire where there was always difficulty in finding candidates.[16] There were only two short periods in the fifteenth century when there was a general extension of the sheriffs' term. In 1421 the relevant statutes were suspended for four years, the Commons petitioning that war and pestilence had severely reduced the number of qualified men available. This act was repealed in the following year.[17] From 1461 to 1463, at a time of crisis, many sheriffs served two successive terms without statutory sanction, though the breach of the law was ratified by an act of the parliament of 1467.[18] Similar acts were passed to indemnify the sheriffs of 1448-9 who had held the office for more than twelve months because no replacements had been found and those of 1458-9 whose replacements had been delayed by political crisis.[19]

The comparatively small number of petitions concerning the sheriff's office that were presented to fifteenth-century parliaments can be largely explained by the fact that the demands of the Commons had to a great extent been met.[20] Not that fourteenth- and fifteenth-century legislation seems to have changed radically the sort of man appointed to the office. It is true that during the later years of the reign of Richard II and during the Lancastrian régime there was a considerable decrease in the number of knights holding this office but this was mainly due to the shortage of knights in the realm as a whole during that period. Under the Yorkists, however, there does seem to have been a deliberate policy of appointing men of higher rank as sheriffs, even though the total number of knights available does not seem to have increased substantially. Nearly half of the sheriffs of Norfolk and Suffolk under the Yorkist kings were knights and Henry VII took the policy further: two-thirds of the sheriffs of the same bailiwick in his reign were knights. But even under the Lancastrians the great majority of the sheriffs came from the leading gentry families of the counties in which they served, though in Norfolk and Suffolk at least the Council ordinance of 1426 discouraging the appointment of lawyers to the office seems generally to have been observed, and this may have excluded a number of the powerful gentlemen of the region such as the Heydons and the earlier Pastons.[21]

When sheriffs were appointed from outside the circle of the leading gentry political motives may frequently be suspected. Dr Jeffs has shown that at times there existed a deliberate policy of appointing Household men to the office, certainly for political reasons.[22] The sheriff, though losing his omnicompetence in administration, still presided over and represented the shire and his office remained the main channel of communication between the Crown and the county, not only in fiscal and legal process, but also in matters of peace-keeping and politics. It was natural, therefore, that political factors sometimes entered into the choice of the official. Particularly at times of political crisis the appointment of a sheriff with sufficient wealth and status to overawe the shire was essential. It was felt necessary in October 1450 to have 'a man of great birth and livelode' as sheriff of Norfolk and Suffolk at that critical time after the fall of Suffolk and the return of York from Ireland.[23] In 1461, 1471, and 1485 there seems to have been a deliberate policy by the Crown of appointing men of substance, often closely connected with the king, in order to impose royal authority on the counties after a change of dynasty.[24] There are times, too, when a dominant faction at Court clearly used its influence to appoint sheriffs favourable to it. The clearest example of this is during the decade before 1450 when, as the impeachment articles against the duke of Suffolk alleged, he used his influence to nominate friends and clients or those prepared to pay him for the office: thus, they argued, the duke had 'over gret and un-fittyng rule in this your Reame' and those outside his affinity were 'oversette in their country' and 'every matier trewe or fals that he wolde favour went forthe'.[25]

The accusations are, of course, prejudiced, but a scrutiny of the sheriffs for various counties during the 1440s indicates the influence of Suffolk and his Court allies in their appointment: most of those appointed to Norfolk and Suffolk during the period are either his clients or members of the Household, which was under his supervision as its appointed steward.[26] In 1454, on the other hand, many of the sheriffs were certainly connected with the anti-Court factions associated with the duke of York, as John Wingfield, sheriff of Norfolk and Suffolk, certainly was. The clearest example of magnate nomination to the sheriff's office in East Anglia comes, however, from the early years of the reign of Henry VII when clients and servants of the earl of Oxford consistently held the office — but here, of course, there was no conflict between the interests of the king and the local magnate, who was acting virtually as his lieutenant in the region.[27]

Such deliberate policies and consistent magnate control are not, however, frequent in fifteenth-century East Anglia. For most of the century appointments of sheriffs, as of other officials, were the result of a variety of pressures upon the Council, the great officers who drew up the list of three nominees, and the king, who pricked one of them. There is some evidence in the *Paston Letters* of magnate interest in the choice of sheriff, even in non-crisis years,[28] and doubtless the views of those of lesser rank, the assize judges, Chancery and Exchequer officials, and members of the Household, could have force also. The 'old school tie' was already a factor in such appointments. In 1456 John Paston was advised that as Thomas Brown, like Paston a member of the Inner Temple, had been appointed under-treasurer of England, he would probably be willing to grant Paston the nomination of the escheator of Norfolk and Suffolk for the coming year.[29] Such direct evidence of these practices is rare but it can hardly be doubted that they were as common in the fifteenth century as they were to be at any period for the next four hundred years.

The nomination of an escheator could, of course, serve only self-interest, and it is certain that much of the lobbying for the sheriff's appointment had the same motive. The political role of the sheriff was often important to the magnates and leading gentry but far more important was his control of legal process, especially the impanelling of juries. It was for this, for instance, that John Heydon was allegedly prepared to pay £1,000 in 1450: for fear he might succeed, it was alleged, no-one in Norfolk would put in complaints against him or his friends until they were sure of a reliable sheriff and under-sheriff.[30] There are numerous examples in the *Paston Letters* of manipulation of writs and juries that the act of 1439 was concerned to prevent.[31] 'Labouring' the sheriff and his officers was an essential part of litigation.

For the shire, then, the sheriff in normal times was above all an official to be bribed, threatened, and placated in order to hold up or expedite a writ or to secure a favourable jury. For the Crown the sheriff remained a vital link, politically as well as administratively, with the counties but by the fifteenth century annual appointment and local pressure had diminished his ability to strengthen royal rights and impose law and order. Although the prestige of the office, reinforced by the high status of some of its occupants, could at critical times be an effective force in the shire, it was commissions appointed by the Crown, and above all the commission of the peace, that were performing the most important duties of county government during the fifteenth century.

The commission of the peace, too, was not the object of controversy that it has been under Richard II.[32] For the first fifty years of the Lancastrian régime the commission in most shires was more or less established in line with the demands of the Commons during the fourteenth century as a small group of 'the more sufficient' of the shire, appointed by the advice of Chancellor and Council in the form of periodic new commissions and not by individual 'associations'. Consequently there were only two important petitions enacted in parliament which touched upon the membership of the peace commissions. The first, in 1414, confirmed that the J.P.s were to be appointed on the advice of the Chancellor and Council and were to be drawn from 'the most sufficient' residents of the shire, only the lords, judges, and the chief steward of the duchy of Lancaster being permitted to be non-resident.[33] In Norfolk and Suffolk at least these provisions appear to have been observed but in 1439 a petition from the Commons alleged that the commissions had been increased in size by the addition of 'insufficient men' and the consequent act laid down that every J.P. should normally have £20 a year in land.[34]

There is, in fact, no apparent evidence for change in the character and size of the commissions in the years before 1439 and the act had little obvious effect on the composition of the Norfolk and Suffolk commissions. Between 1399 and 1450 the commissions fluctuated in size between twelve and seventeen members, with only a slight tendency to increase.[35] The commissions enrolled in November 1436 are fairly typical.[36] The bishop of Norwich and the Chief Steward of the duchy sat on both, with the two assize judges; the Norfolk commission also included three lords, three knights and four esquires or gentlemen, of whom at least three were lawyers; the Suffolk commission had three lords, three knights, and three gentlemen, all of whom were lawyers. A number had been on the commission since the early twenties and only two in each commission were newcomers, one being the duke of Norfolk who had just received livery of his lands. The active members of each commission were far fewer, of course: in each county one knight and three lawyers were paid for their attendance at quarter sessions.[37] Although the evidence suggests that by the 1450s there was rather greater attendance, there remained a small core, most of them lawyers, who did the majority of the judicial work of the commission.

The comparative stability in the size and composition of the peace commission gave way to a period of more radical changes and increased size during the later years of the reign of Henry VI. There are, however, some difficulties in assessing changes in the composition of the commission. The Council ordinance of 1426 ordered a new commission to be issued annually,[38] but for most of the fifteenth century there is no regularity in the enrollment of commissions and there are some very long gaps: for example there is no Suffolk commission enrolled between 1424 and 1431, for Norfolk none between 1424 and 1428, and there are frequent two or three year intervals. On the other hand some years have three or more commissions enrolled in a single year which suggests that the correct practice was followed of issuing a new commission every time a new J.P. was appointed.[39] There is, in fact, some evidence that, as in the sixteenth century, not all commissions were enrolled and this makes it hazardous to comment in detail upon changes in their membership.[40] Nevertheless the enrolled commissions make the general developments fairly clear. In Norfolk and Suffolk, and apparently in other counties too, the greater fluctuations and increased size noticeable during the 1450s were taken much further during the Yorkist period, when the Norfolk commission increased in average membership from something under sixteen to over twenty-four, and the Suffolk commission to over twenty. By the 1480s numbers were to increase to around thirty and after 1500 membership rarely fell below that figure.

The political troubles after 1450 obviously account for the more radical changes in the membership of the commission — in 1455, 1460, and 1470, for instance. Its considerable increase in size, however, must have other causes. Partly, perhaps, it was due to the increased burden of work put upon the justices. Even during the Lancastrian period a number of statutes substantially extended the jurisdiction of the commission — over Lollardy, liveries, and prices and wages, for instance — and, as Putnam showed, the charge to the J.P.s suggests that they also exerted jurisdiction in some areas without statutory basis.[41] In the later part of the century, particularly under Henry VII, the jurisdiction of the commission was extended even further.[42] An increased membership may have been needed in order to cope with the increase in business, but probably more important was the greater attraction of membership to the gentlemen of the shire when so much power was in the hands of the J.P.s. Even in 1422 the Minority Council had recognized the importance of the peace commission when claiming control over nomination to it, and in 1449 John Damme could remind Paston of 'what John Heydon may do, being a justice of the peace'.[43] Apart from the judicial powers proper the right to bind over to keep the peace was of great value, even to the magnates and others who rarely appeared at Quarter Sessions. The increase in the size of the commission came, however, mainly from the addition of more resident knights and squires. The 1504 commission of the peace for Norfolk, for instance, contained only two more lords than that of 1436 but the number of knights had risen from three to twelve and the number of esquires and gentlemen from four to thirteen. By 1504 it is possible that a high enough proportion of the gentlemen of the county sat on the peace commission to produce a sense of humiliation in any wealthy or well-connected gentleman if he were omitted from it. This certainly cannot have been so during the first half of the century when the gentry members of the commission formed a much smaller group. More than half of the knights, for instance, who appear on the 1434 list of those who took the oath in Norfolk not to harbour law-breakers never became J.P.s, whereas of the identifiable Norfolk knights of the first decade of Henry VIII's reign only one — Sir Thomas Wodehouse — apparently never became a J.P.[44]

Nevertheless, the fluctuations in membership that characterize the commission from the middle of the century and the increasing size suggest that already by that time there was some demand from below to sit on the commission and pressure from magnates to nominate their clients to it. Appointment to the commission was formally the responsibility of the

Chancellor and Council: certainly external pressures existed but it is even more difficult than in the case of the sheriff to ascertain why individuals were appointed as J.P.s. There are few references in the Paston and Fastolf correspondence to the personnel and activities of the commission of the peace — the contrast with the Elizabethan Bacon and Gawdy correspondence is very pronounced[45] — but there are one or two useful allusions. During his legal difficulties in the 1450s, for instance, William Worcester wrote a letter to John Paston in which he indicated that Sir John Fastolf had been responsible for the appointment of John Jermyn and Thomas Heigham to the Suffolk commission, the latter on the nomination of 'Mr. Geney'.[46] Later in the decade Thomas Playter was negotiating with the Chancellor to have John Paston and his friends restored to the Norfolk commision.[47] And in May 1465 Margaret Paston wrote to John Paston 'I would right fayn that John Jenney wer putte out of the commission of the peace and my brother William Lomnour wer set in his place. And if there be labour for Dr. Aleyn prevent it as he will take too much upon himself.'[48] And John Paston, in the midst of his troubles, was apparently successful in having Jenney replaced by Lumnour and preventing Aleyn being appointed to the commission. Although there is little direct evidence for it there can be no doubt that magnate nominations were also often successful, though as each J.P. was less powerful politically than the sheriff or knight of the shire there was probably less direct influence exerted. But it is certainly no coincidence, for instance, that during the late 1430s and 1440s a high proportion of the new J.P.s appointed to the Norfolk and Suffolk commissions were clients and retainers of the duke of Suffolk and that a number of these lost their place on the commission in 1450.[49]

In spite of its increasing duties the commission of the peace was not the governing body of the shire that it was to become during the sixteenth century. Apart from the important duties carried out by the sheriff and other officials many other functions were performed by *ad hoc* commissions with a much wider membership, though even so not encompassing all the knights and squires of the counties. These *ad hoc* commissions — of inquiry, oyer and terminer, array, sewers, etc. — were very numerous in the Lancastrian period. Again there can be no certainty that all were enrolled but, for instance, sixty-eight such commissions for Norfolk affairs were enrolled on the Chancery rolls between 1437 and 1461.[50] Up to 1450 they were mostly concerned with the normal processes of government — trade and shipping, Crown loans, inquiries into royal rights, etc. — together with commissions of inquiry into disputes between individuals, usually initiated by those concerned; after 1450 there is a decline in such commissions and a great expansion of those implying the necessary involvement of the full force of the Crown by commissions of oyer and terminer, arrest and array to deal with the growing troubles and disorders in the region. Well over a hundred men sat on such commissions between 1437 and 1461 and there is no evidence of any opposition, such as occurred under Richard II and earlier, to the overriding of the powers of the J.P.s by the appointment of large and powerful commissions of oyer and terminer from 1450.[51]

A quick count of the *ad hoc* commissions enrolled on the Chancery rolls of Henry VII, whose reign also occupied twenty-four years, shows a striking contrast.[52] Apart from gaol delivery commissions only fifteen appear to have been issued for Norfolk. Assuming that this is not due to a change in the administrative practices of Chancery, the explanation no doubt is to be found in a variety of developments in Yorkist and Early Tudor government. Partly, perhaps, it was due to the Crown policy of strengthening the authority of the commission of the peace and thus consolidating many of the duties of local government under one body. Partly also, perhaps, to the increasing ability of the Council to settle at Star Chamber or by local delegation disputes that would at an earlier period have necessitated commissions of oyer and terminer or inquiry.[53] In general the increasing control of the Crown in the regions through the employment of a more extensive and efficient group of professional administrators made it less necessary to appoint special groups of often inefficient local gentlemen to inquire into royal rights, check smuggling, settle local disputes, etc. In East Anglia the administrators mainly employed on such tasks were themselves usually men of local origins and residence: men like Sir James Hobart, Sir Thomas Lovell, Sir Robert Drury, Sir Robert Southwell, and Thomas Lucas, who were involved in the central administration of the Crown but also sat on local commissions and filled local offices, both under the Crown and under the great magnates of the region. They had their counterparts during the earlier period, of course, but never before had the link between the working membership of the royal administration and local government been so strong.

It would, however, be wrong to think that the later fifteenth century saw any real 'bureaucratization' of local government. By 1399 the gentry had secured the principle that the administration of their shires should be in the hands of men appointed by the king, but, with few exceptions, drawn from their own ranks. Petitions of the Commons during the fifteenth century show that they continued to be sensitive to breaches of this principle whether these were the responsibility of the Crown or of the great magnates, and the reign of Henry VII saw no radical change. There was clearly more than individual self-interest involved in the Commons' consistent pursuit of this policy but the sentiment behind it is elusive. The petitions for the appointment of resident gentleman as sheriffs and their election as knights of the shire certainly indicate the existence of a sense of 'the community of the shire' and its existence in this context is confirmed by the well-known letter of John Jenney to John Paston in 1455 in which he writes of the 'evil precedent for the shire that a straunge man shulde be chosyn . . . yf the jentilmen of the shire will suffre sech inconvenyens, in good feithe, the shire shall not be called of seche wurshipp as it hathe be'.[54] This is a rare direct reference to the sentiment and it is not surprising that it is found in the context of an election of the knights of the shire. Dr Maddicott has recently emphasized the continued vitality in the fourteenth century of the county court as a political and social event,[55] and, though the evidence is scanty, some of this vitality certainly continued into the fifteenth century, particularly at elections. The election of the knights of the shire was the one occasion when the freeholders of the county performed an act of political will and although most work on parliamentary elections in the fifteenth century has rightly emphasized the influence of the Crown and magnates, there is also evidence, mostly indirect, of participation and independent action not only by gentlemen but also by lesser freeholders.[56]

Lists of witnesses on fifteenth-century election indentures are usually short and do not provide a very accurate impression of attendance at the county courts but Dr Rogers has shown that it is possible to use this source to acquire some insight into the leading 'political' families of the county over a period,[57] and where, as in Suffolk under Henry VI, there are several indentures which, perhaps because of a contested election, contain a much larger number of names, a more accurate knowledge of the attendance at county courts for elections can be obtained.[58] The Suffolk lists of 1435 and November 1449, for instance, each contains a hundred or more names. Among them are many knights, squires, and gentlemen: even among these less than half ever filled major offices or sat on commissions for the county. But two-thirds of the names on each indenture are those of lesser men, yeomen, and other freeholders, who were below the status necessary to fill such positions (though some served as tax-collectors, bailiffs, etc.) but were clearly part of the shire community.[59]

The word men normally used for their county in a non-administrative sense was 'country', and there are a number of examples of this usage in the *Paston Letters*, some of which clearly imply a group wider than the leading gentry who filled the major offices and commissions.[60] Undoubtedly it was not used in a very precise way but when men spoke of their 'country' or 'shire' they normally implied those inhabitants of it who played some part in its communal activities, and these surely included the freeholders who attended shire elections. It is, indeed, rather more doubtful whether the great lords of the region were regarded by their inferiors as belonging to the community. Certainly even the leading gentry families could at times see a sharp contrast between themselves and the lords. McFarlane pointed out that the fifteenth century saw a growing differentiation between the lords and the rest of the aristocracy, and this is illustrated by John Paston's sturdy defiance of the duke of Suffolk in 1465: 'it is not profitable ner the comen well of gentlemen that any gentleman should be compelled by entry of a lord to show his evidence or title to his land nor I will not begine that example ne thralldom of gentlemen ner of other'.[61] The gentry did feel that they belonged to two interlocking groups, one socially and the other geographically defined. This interlocking of status and territorial loyalties can be illustrated by the window which was set by Sir Thomas Erpingham in the Norwich Austin friary to commemorate the names and arms of all those knightly families of Norfolk and Suffolk which had died out in the male line since 1327. Significantly, when William Worcester copied and extended the list he also included esquires.[62] The same local sentiment is shown by the collections made by Worcester towards a history of the gentry families of Norfolk.[63] The evidence is scanty and its geographical source narrow but does suggest that at least in East Anglia there did exist a sense of a historical community based upon the shire which was to have considerable significance for regional and national politics at a later period.

Nevertheless it would be wrong to exaggerate the importance of this community feeling in the fifteenth century. There is no reason to doubt the commonly held view that for most of this period the 'horizontal' relationships of the gentry and yeomanry were less important to most of them than the 'vertical' relationships of bastard feudalism. 'Good lordship', not just for individuals but for the shire as a whole, was the essential political structure in which men acted. It was, for instance, to the duke of Norfolk that in 1450 the gentlemen of Norfolk went to discuss the state of the shire, and it was he, with the duke of York, another East Anglian magnate, who nominated the knights of the shire in 1450, and, by himself, in 1455. It was to the duke of Norfolk again that the Norfolk gentry petitioned in 1452 against the activities of Charles Nowell. At about the same time the duke could proclaim that 'next the King . . . we woll . . . have the princypall rewle and governance throwh all this schir, of whishe we ber our name'. 'If my lord of Norfolk would come he schuld make all weele', wrote Richard Calle in 1465, for 'all the cuntre . . . woll hooly go with him.'[64] And these are some of the 'communal' references in the Paston correspondence: the individual examples of the search for good lordship in the region are, of course, legion

This is not to say that the magnates' own policies and power were not affected by the attitudes and grouping of the gentry that have been discussed above. These interrelations of magnates and gentry constitute a separate power structure within the region to some extent subsuming both the official institutions which theoretically mediated the authority of the Crown and also those that provided the structures for the communal feelings of the gentry. The lords' power was often strengthened by the possession or control of Crown offices, both central and local, but they primarily drew their authority from their own landed wealth, the tradition of deference and subservience towards their dynasties and their consequent ability to muster large numbers of servants, tenants, and clients to enforce their will. Of course the nature of magnate power varied from region to region and could be greatly affected by the personality of the individual lord and, more tangibly, by his position at Court and in the king's Council. For short periods Court influence could outweigh the local advantages held by magnates of greater landed estate and traditional supremacy, though permanent influence depended on the establishment of a great 'lyvelode' and a tradition of obedience within the area. The duke of Suffolk in the 1430s and 1440s used his Court position to dominate East Anglia and temporarily eclipse the influence of the Mowbray duke of Norfolk. In the early years of the reign of Henry VII the earl of Oxford likewise replaced the Howard duke. But in neither case was the power permanent. The inherent landed strength and traditional authority of the dukes of Norfolk survived both periods of eclipse.[65]

It has not, however, been the intention of this paper to analyse the politics of East Anglia or of the nation as a whole during the fifteenth century, but to describe some of the main aspects of the formal and informal institutions of local government in that period. These were certainly at the centre of local politics, though less, perhaps, as the focus of ambitions than as the agencies by which ambitions could be fulfilled. It must be left to another occasion to describe more fully regional politics within this context.

Notes

1. R. Virgoe, 'The Crown and local government: East Anglia under Richard II', *The Reign of Richard II*, ed. F.R.H. Du Boulay and Caroline Barron (1971), pp. 218-41; and cf. R.L. Storey, 'Liveries and commissions of the peace 1388-90', ibid., pp. 131-52.
2. *Rot. Parl.* iii. 419.
3. Virgoe, loc. cit., pp. 220-2, and references given there. For a rather idealized picture of the process of appointment see J. Fortescue, *De Laudibus Legum Anglie*, ed. S.B. Chrimes (1942), pp. 55-56.
4. *Rot. Parl.* iii. 434, 495, 592, 614, 635; iv. 11, 12, 78, 103, 191.
5. Ibid. iii. 434; 1 Hen. IV, c. 11.
6. *P.P.C.* iii. 39.
7. For a detailed discussion of this problem see R.L. Jeffs, 'The later medieval sheriff and the royal household', Oxford, D. Phil. thesis (1960), esp. c.2.
8. *Rot. Parl.* v. 494, 568, 632; vi. 64; and see Jeffs, op.cit., c.4.
9. 7 Hen. IV, c. 5; 11 Hen. IV, c.1; 8 Hen. VI, c.7, etc.
10. *Rot. Parl.* iv. 306; v.29; for examples of the sheriff's crucial role, often abused, in the electoral process, see R. Virgoe, 'The Cambridgeshire election of 1439', *B.I.H.R.* xlvi (1973), 95-101 and articles there referred to.
11. See Jeffs, op. cit., c.1 for illustration of the continued military and peace-keeping role of the sheriff.
12. 1 Ed. IV, c. 2; 11 Hen. VII, c.3.
13. *Rot. Parl.* iii. 495.
14. *Rot. Parl.* iv. 10; *P.P.C.* iii. 220-1.
15. P.R.O., C.255/11/3. nos. 4, 5, 6, 10, 20, 21.
16. *Rot. Parl.* v. 108; 23 Hen. VI, c. 7. Information on individual sheriffs' terms of office is taken here and elsewhere from the *List of Sheriffs for England and Wales from the earliest times to 1831*, P.R.O. Lists and Indexes, no. ix (1896).
17. *Rot. Parl.* iv. 148, 191.
18. Ibid. v. 631.
19. *Rot. Parl.* v. 202, 367.
20. There appears to be only one fifteenth-century petition of any importance concerning the eschaetorship: in 1472 it was complained that many insufficient men held the office and let it to farm (*Rot Parl.* vi. 156-7).
21. *P.P.C.* iii. 219.
22. Jeffs. op.cit, pp. 171-3.
23. *The Paston Letters,* ed. J. Gairdner (1906), ii, no. 146 and cf. 155, 162; cf. iii. 415, 487 for similar interest in 1461.
24. Jeffs, op.cit., pp. 226-9, 233-5.
25. *Rot.Parl.* v. 181; Bodley MS. Eng.Hist. b. 119.
26. William Calthorpe (1441-2), Thomas Brewes (1442-3), and William Tyrell (1445-6) were certainly connected with Suffolk; Thomas Danyell, Philip Wentworth, Giles Seintlow, and John Say, who held office consecutively between 1446 and 1450, were all courtiers.
27. See R. Virgoe, 'The recovery of the Howards in East Anglia, 1485-1529', in *Wealth and Power in Tudor England*, ed. E.W. Ives, J.J. Scarisbrick and R.J. Knecht (1978), pp. 10-11.
28. *Paston Letters,* ii. 220; iii. 348, 415; iv. 690.

29. Ibid. iii. 348.
30. Ibid. ii. 146, 155.
31. E.g. ibid. ii. 175, 179, 188, 193; iii. 487; iv. 586.
32. See n. 1.
33. *Rot.Parl.* iv. 51; 2 Hen. V, stat. 2, c.1.
34. *Rot. Parl.* v. 28; 18 Hen. VI, c. 11.
35. Details of membership here and elsewhere, except when noted, are taken from the tables printed in the *Calendars of Patent Rolls*; but see below for the problems of their reliability.
36. *C.P.R., 1436-41*, pp. 586-7, 590; P.R.O., C.66/440, m. 49d.
37. P.R.O., E. 101/575/32 and 33. A similar pattern of three or four main working members, most of them lawyers of the quorum, existed under Richard II and Henry IV — P.R.O., E. 101/575/29 (1), (2), (3); G.E. Morey, 'The administration of the counties of Norfolk and Suffolk in the reign of Henry IV', London M.A. thesis (1941), pp. 91-99.
38. *P.P.C.* iii. 220.
39. Once the practice of 'associations' was ended there should have been a new commission at every new appointment, and this certainly appears to have happened by the Elizabethan period — T.G. Barnes and A. Hassell Smith, 'Justices of the peace from 1558 to 1688 — a revised list of sources', *B.I.H.R.* xxxii (1959), 221-42; A. Hassell Smith, *County and Court* (Oxford, 1974), pp. 73-75.
40. Ibid., *Proceedings before the Justices of the Peace in the Fourteenth and Fifteenth Centuries*, ed. B.H. Putman (1938), p. 3, introductory note (ii).
41. *Proceedings*, ed. Putnam, pp. xx-xxv; e.g. 13 Hen. IV, c.7; and 2 Hen. V, c. 4.
42. E.g. 3 Hen VII, cc. 1, 3; 11 Hen. VII, cc. 2, 3, 7, 24. See, e.g., S.B. Chrimes, *Henry VII* (1972), pp. 166-71; W. Holdsworth, *History of English Law* (7th edn, 1956), i. 288-9.
43. *Rot. Parl.* iv. 176; *Paston Letters*, ii. 95.
44. *C.P.R., 1429-36*, pp. 404-7; W.J. Blake, 'Fuller's list of Norfolk gentry', *Norfolk Archaeology*, xxxii (1961), 261-91.
45. See the numerous references in Smith, *County and Court*, *passim*.
46. *Paston Letters*, iii. 316.
47. Ibid. ii. 253.
48. Ibid. iv. 582.
49. Obvious examples are Thomas Tuddenham and John Heydon (Norfolk) and John Ulveston and John Andrew (Suffolk) who were omitted from the October 1450 commissions. To these may be added Reynold Rous, Thomas Brews, John Heveningham, and John Harleston (Suffolk) who remained on the commission after 1450.
50. The information is taken from the *Calendars of Patent Rolls* and *Calendars of Fine Rolls*. Gaol Delivery Commissions are omitted from the figures.
51. Virgoe, 'Crown and local government', loc. cit., pp. 222-3.
52. See n. 50.
53. Cf. *Select Cases before the King's Council in the Star Chamber*, ed. I. S. Leadam, Selden Society, xvi (1903), p. li.; J. Guy, *The Cardinals' Court* (Sussex, 1977).
54. *Paston Letters*, iii. 295.
55. J.R. Maddicott, 'The county community in fourteenth-century England', *T.R.H.S.*, 5th series, 28 (1978), 27-43; cf. Helen Cam, 'The community of the shire and the payment of its representatives in Parliament', *Liberties and Communities in Medieval England* (Cambridge, 1933), pp. 236-50.
56. For instance at the Norfolk election of 1460, the Cambridgeshire election of 1439 and the Huntingdon election of 1450 — see n. 10 above.
57. A. Rogers, 'The Lincolnshire county court in the fifteenth century', *Lincolnshire History and Archaeology*, i (1966), 64-78.

58. The Suffolk indentures of 1433, 1435, 1437, February and November 1449, 1453 and 1455 each have more than sixty names on the witness list (P.R.O., C. 219/14/4/51, 14/5/51, 15/1/72, 15/6/60, 15/7/57, 16/2/25, 16/3/37); cf. the analysis of the Huntingdonshire electorate in 1450 in J.G. Edwards, 'The Huntingdonshire parliamentary election of 1450', *Essays in Medieval History presented to Bertie Wilkinson*, ed. T.A. Sandquist and M.R. Powicke (Toronto, 1969), pp. 383-95.

59. In 1433 the knights of the shire from each county were ordered to name to the Chancellor those persons who ought to take the oath not to harbour or maintain lawbreakers — *Rot. Parl.* iv. 456. The counties seem to have interpreted this instruction in various ways, but the Norfolk list contains nearly 400 names and of these less than one-fifth are ecclesiastics, knights and squires see n. 44 above.

60. E.g. *Paston Letters*, ii, nos. 69, 75, 145; iii. 449; iv. 593.

61. K.B. McFarlane, *The Nobility of Later Medieval England* (Oxford, 1973), pp. 122-5; *Paston Letters*, iv. 595.

62. F. Blomefield, *An Essay towards a Topographical History of the County of Norfolk*, 2nd edn (1806-10), iv. 86-88; Bodley MS. 860, fos. 381-2; K.B. McFarlane, 'William Worcester: a preliminary survey', *Studies presented to Sir Hilary Jenkinson* (1957), pp. 196-221.

63. McFarlane, 'William Worcester', pp. 216-18.

64. *Paston Letters*, ii, nos. 132-4, 148-9, 210-11; iii. 288; iv. 593.

65. For Suffolk's position in the 1440s see *Paston Letters*, vol. ii *passim*, and cf. R.L. Storey, *The End of the House of Lancaster* (1966), pp. 55-57, 217-25. For Oxford see reference under n. 27.

5

London and the Crown 1451-61

Caroline M. Barron

The strength of Edward of York as he approached London in February 1461 lay not only in his armed retinue, but also 'in the commonalty of London who were delirious with joy and obviously prepared for a change of dynasty'. Such is the accepted view.[1] It was propagated by his most consequential supporters and, equally inevitably, by London chroniclers writing after Edward's accession.[2] But what was the 'commonalty of London'? Historians have often written of London welcoming Henry Bolingbroke, or supporting Henry V, or failing to support Henry VI during the 1450s, as if the city during this period was a homogeneous body. This was not so.

In the mid-fifteenth century 30,000 to 40,000 people lived in the city and its immediate suburbs.[3] Of the 12,000 to 14,000 adult males only those who were 'free' (i.e. citizens) mattered politically. The freemen numbered between 3,000 and 4,000.[4] The distinction between free and un-free in the city was important. A man acquired the freedom if he had served a lengthy apprenticeship, or by patrimony if his father were free, or if, indeed, he could purchase it. A freeman was a person of substance with a stake in the community, who shared the burdens of administration and defence and, in return, enjoyed certain trading privileges and exemptions from taxation. A wealthy, successful freeman could hardly avoid the expensive office of alderman. The freemen of the city, called the commonalty, met every October at Guildhall to elect the mayor for the succeeding year from among the twenty-five aldermen. Although all freemen stood an equal chance of shouldering this burden, members of merchant, rather than artisan, companies were usually elected. Of the 159 aldermen between 1400 and 1485 all but eleven came from the established merchant companies of Drapers, Mercers, Grocers, Fishmongers, Skinners, Goldsmiths, Ironmongers, and Vintners.[5] The artisan freemen resented this merchant monopoly of office and occasionally expressed their feelings violently.

Between 1437 and 1444 there was a consistent, but unsuccessful, attempt to elect Ralph Holland, a tailor, as mayor.[6]

On occasion, bitterness may have existed between wealthy merchant freemen and their poorer artisan brethren. Yet the gulf between them was never so wide as that which separated the minority of freemen from the majority of the unfree. Among the unfree there were, of course, stable elements: Italian and Hanseatic merchants, secular clerks and members of religious orders, the thousand or so law-abiding 'Doche'.[7] But the bulk of the 10,000 unenfranchized comprised skilled and unskilled day labourers, apprentices, and vagrants, as well as the retainers and servants of magnates whose town houses lay in or near the city. In times of crisis the desires and activities of the unenfranchized were as much a preoccupation of the Court of Aldermen as the external threat from the approach of armies. When law and order seemed likely to break down, the unenfranchized became quick-witted and nimble-fingered. At best, they enjoyed the chance of plunder; at least, a spectacle and a few days holiday. Such a prospect dismayed propertied freemen.

Two incidents illustrate this division of interest. After Warwick's defeat at the second battle of St Albans in February 1461 the road to London lay open to Queen Margaret. To prevent the city from being plundered, the mayor and aldermen sent victuals to her army at their own expense.[8] William Gregory records what followed:

> Ande the mayre ordaynyd bothe brede and vytayle to be sende unto the quene, and a certayne sum of money with alle. But whenn men of London and comyns wyste that the cartysse shulde goo to the Quene, they toke the cartys and departyde the brede and vytayle a-monge the comyns . . . But as for the mony, I wot not howe hit was departyd; I trowe the pursse stale the mony.[9]

The author of the *Short English Chronicle* also noted the divergence of interest between the 'worthy and the Aldremen' and the 'comones'. The former wanted to come to terms with the queen to avoid the sacking of the city, while the latter were anxious to hold it for the Yorkist lords.[10] A similar division arose in May 1471, when Thomas Fauconberg besieged London with an army of Kentishmen in the name of Henry VI. The author of the *Arrival of King Edward IV* observed that there were many who were inclined to admit Fauconberg: 'some for they were powre; some, men's servants, men's prentises, which would have bene right glade of a comon robery, to th'entent they might largely have put theyr hands in riche mens coffres'.[11] London was not, therefore, homogeneous. But its divisions were horizontal, separating the wealthy from the poor, merchants from artisans, citizens from the unenfranchized. In 1461 the aldermen were Lancastrian and the mob was Yorkist; in 1471 the aldermen were Yorkist and the mob largely Lancastrian. Although the unenfranchised mob was a powerful force in city affairs and the enfranchized rulers could ignore its wishes only at their peril, yet the normal voice of the city was that of its wealthy governing minority, characterized by conservatism and caution.

This governing élite usually conducted the normal relations between the city and the Crown. The best-documented aspect of these relations is that of finance. But although the government of Henry VI was dependent on loans from London, London itself was equally dependent upon the Crown for the exercise of those privileges and exemptions upon which its economic prosperity was founded. For all its wealth and national importance in the fifteenth century, London still operated only within a framework of privileges granted by royal charters. Its officers were answerable to the king for the maintenance of law and order, for the execution of royal writs, and also for the protection of foreign merchants. The Londoners still remembered the events of 1392 when Richard II had seized the city's liberties, and their recovery had cost some £30,000. They could not, therefore, lightly refuse royal requests for financial help, nor effectively demand redress of grievances before supply.[12]

Throughout the fifteenth century the city rulers were constantly on their guard to protect the liberties and privileges of London, not only from the challenges of other towns, but also from claims by the Crown. They were concerned with financial advantages, which might be won or lost as the Crown decided. Although most disputes were perennial, a new area of friction arose during the 1430s. In order to augment his dwindling resources, Henry VI began to grant monopolies of certain indispensable offices in the city to royal servants by letters patent. In 1432 Thomas Multon was granted the office of wine-gauger. In the fourteenth century the gauger had charged buyer and seller a halfpenny each for gauging a tun of wine, but by the mid 1440s the mayor and aldermen complained to the King's Council that he was charging $4d$ a tun.[13] In November 1440 six esquires of the king's household were sold the office of cloth-packer in London in survivorship for £48. The Londoners keenly resented this monopoly, particularly because Henry IV had granted them the right to pack their own cloths.[14] In December 1440 Henry VI granted the monopoly of the office of wine-drawer to Wiliam Styce and Thomas Quyne; they were empowered to exercise the office through deputies and to draw the accustomed fees.[15] In 1394 the fees had been established at $10d$ a tun for carrying wine from the port to a destination within the walls, and at $16d$ for a tun carried beyond the walls.[16] Here the citizens complained not so much about the rates charged, but about the monopoly itself, since it effectively destroyed their right to draw their own wine.[17] Finally, in October 1442 the king granted the office of garbeller in the ports of London, Southampton, and Sandwich jointly to Richard Hakedy, a grocer, and William Aunsell, a royal sergeant.[18] This grant particularly affected the Grocers, who complained in 1446 that garbelling in the city was carried out by men of 'little behaviour or value'.[19]

The king's motives in granting such patents are understandable. He could realize in hard cash a hitherto unexploited asset and by doing so obtain income as well as a means of rewarding royal servants. But monopolies cut across long-established vested interests and tended to raise the price of the inescapable services which patentees offered. Several companies might feel particularly aggrieved — the Drapers about the cloth-packer, the Vintners about the gauger and wine-drawers, and the Grocers about the garbeller. Yet everyone in the city was affected: the burdens of increased costs had to be shared. The aldermen, therefore, on behalf of the citizens at large, constantly complained about patents. In 1442 they tried, but without success, to make the grant of a royal loan conditional upon the revocation of the cloth-packers' and wine-drawers' patents.[20] They claimed that such patents conflicted with the city's chartered rights and infringed the jurisdiction of the mayor. As a deterrent, they ordained that any freeman who accepted such an office by royal grant should lose his freedom and pay a £20 fine.[21] In 1444 the citizens achieved a partial but unsatisfactory concession: occupiers of disputed offices already granted by royal patent were to enjoy them for life, but their reversion was to belong to the mayor and citizens. The Londoners continued to press for a grant of such offices in perpetuity — and not least when they negotiated with Edward of York in the months before and after his accession.

The conflict over patents is only one area where a watchful and indigent Crown questioned the customary privileges of London. These conflicts occurred within the better-known context of the financial relationships between the Crown and the city. The Londoners' unsuccessful attempt in 1442 to make the grant of a loan conditional upon the withdrawal of the royal patents demonstrates the interplay of finance and privilege. The Londoners were very important royal creditors, although at times their importance might be eclipsed by, for example, Cardinal Beaufort.[22] London loans to the crown might be raised from individuals, from merchants of the Calais Staple, many of whom were Londoners; or from the city in its corporate capacity. Such loans were interconnected, for a large advance by the Staplers or by a group of prominent citizens might well make it difficult for the city to raise a corporate loan if it were asked for one soon afterwards.

The City Journals reveal something about the negotiations which preceded a corporate London loan. The king usually sent a letter to the mayor and citizens explaining his need. A meeting of the Common Council would be especially summoned, at which the king's letter would be read and discussed.[23] From time to time the king employed more direct methods. Thus in March 1415 the archbishop of Canterbury and other royal councillors went to Guildhall to argue the merits of the policy to invade

France: and in July 1444 the earl of Suffolk explained the need for a loan to finance the embassy which would bring Margaret of Anjou to England as Henry's bride and thus achieve a final peace with France.[24] Also, the city from time to time received direct requests from France, as in June 1435 and July 1451 when the mayor and aldermen of Calais sent letters asking for assistance; or in January 1453 when the earl of Shrewsbury wrote from Aquitaine.[25] Between 1416 and 1448 the citizens very rarely refused to lend; but on no occasion did they lend as much as the king requested. This was a custom which both parties probably well understood.[26] When the Londoners did refuse a request they always pleaded poverty. Their primary concern, once they had agreed to advance money, was to achieve good security for repayment. They were important lenders who had to be kept in good heart; thus they fared better than many other creditors at the Lancastrian Exchequer.

The copious information which the Exchequer records provide is opaque. They never reveal, for example, whether a loan for which tallies of assignment were issued was ever repaid. On occasion, irredeemable tallies were returned to the Exchequer and new ones issued under the guise of a 'fictitious loan'.[27] Unless another source survives which supplements the Exchequer's record of tallies issued, it is impossible to know whether, or how, a creditor received his money. For corporate London loans, however, the City Journals provide a partial check. On two occasions the City Chamberlain made a statement to the Common Council about the king's indebtedness to the city. In February 1439 John Chichele reported that the king's outstanding debt amounted to £2,666 13s 4d.[28] At least £333 6s 8d of this dated back to a loan made to the Crown in March 1431, and in the intervening eight years the Londoners had corporately lent £14,333 6s 8d. Hence the amount outstanding in 1439 was a small, and not an unreasonable, proportion of their outlay since 1431. In March 1450 John Middleton reported that the king then owed the Londoners £3,230 12s 4½d.[29] Since 1431 the city had advanced twenty-two loans to the Crown and only five of these were still outstanding. The evidence of the Journals suggests, therefore, that the Londoners received preferential treatment at the Exchequer, and also that their tallies of assignment were largely honoured by the sources on which they were drawn.[30]

The relationship between the Crown and the city in the fifteenth century was delicately balanced. On the one hand, the financial need of the Crown; on the other, the anxiety of the city about its privileges.[31] The political shifts of the period 1450-61 made it hard for either party to maintain the customary equilibrium. The relations between the Crown and the city during these years have to be carefully examined, for it cannot be assumed that decisions taken by the Londoners were politically inspired. By 1449 Henry VI was considerably in debt. According to Professor Fryde, 'the business community was becoming indifferent to the fate of the régime and had lost all trust in it: the repeated refusals of Londoners to lend money to Henry VI during the last disastrous campaigns in France in 1448-52 show this very clearly. The financial bankruptcy of the Lancastrian monarchy was as complete on the eve of the Wars of the Roses as was its political collapse.'[32] Professor Storey has also argued, but not with reference to the merchant community, that it was the bankruptcy of Lancaster which drove York to rebellion.[33]

Although after 1448 the Crown is likely to have been very short of ready cash, the evidence that the Londoners were indifferent to the fate of Henry VI's régime is less convincing. Although the City Journals record seven occasions between 1448 and 1460 when the Londoners refused the king's requests for loans, yet during the same period they did, in fact, make fourteen loans or gifts.[34] This represents a slightly higher rate of support than had been customary between 1416 and 1448 when they had provided, on average, a gift or a loan each year. The unprecedented number of refusals to lend did not reflect indifference, but arose from the unprecedented number of royal requests for assistance. When the citizens refused such requests they pleaded 'insufficiency' — and often in good faith. For, apart from the corporate loans of those years, the Londoners had advanced considerable sums either as individuals or as merchants of the Calais Staple. Between 1448 and 1460 the Receipt Rolls of the Exchequer record loans from the Staplers amounting to over £37,000, as well as loans totalling £21,500 made by eighty-three individual Londoners. Moreover, the Staplers are known to have provided at least a further £24,000.[35] Nor do the Receipt Rolls record all the corporate loans or gifts made by London from 1448 to 1461. In fact only two such advances are recorded: a loan of £666 13s 4d in October 1449, and a gift of £1,333 6s 8d in January 1453.[36] Yet the City Journals reveal the existence of a further twelve loans or gifts. The loans amounted to over £2,000 (the exact amounts of three are not known), and gifts to over £1,000.[37] Thus the incompleteness of the Receipt and Issue Rolls is revealed when they are checked against the City Journals. Any assessment of the degree of support for Henry VI's government based upon them is bound to be faulty. Indeed it was not the Londoners who failed Henry VI, but the Exchequer itself.

The Exchequer had originally dealt mainly with cash; its procedures could hardly cope when revenue was anticipated as extensively as it was by the government of Henry VI. Early in the fifteenth century a loan from London was usually recorded as received in the Receipt Roll and the issue of tallies for repayment similarly noted a few days later. But the process of acknowledging receipt of a loan became indivisible from the process of issuing tallies of assignment. If all the sources of royal revenue were so desperately overburdened with unpaid tallies that the Exchequer could issue no more, then the loan would not be recorded on the Receipt Rolls. In July 1444 Common Council agreed to make a loan to the Crown, but instructed its agents not to hand over the money without obtaining a written receipt from the officials of the Exchequer as well as an assignment upon the next parliamentary tenth and fifteenth. In fact, the agents could obtain only a note of receipt from John Poutrell, a collector of the wool subsidy in London.[38] There is no record of the loan in either the Receipt or Issue Rolls. A loan for the defence of Calais in 1451 amounting to £1,333 6s 8d was acknowledged in a similar way: the four treasurers of the parliamentary subsidy, together with William Beaufitz, one of the collectors of tunnage and poundage in London, entered into a semi-private obligation to guarantee repayment to Thomas Catworth, the mayor, and two aldermen.[39] There is no mention of this loan in the Exchequer records. In both these cases the Londoners appear to have negotiated directly with the collectors of royal revenue and the Exchequer itself was innocent of the transaction.

When the derelict state of the Exchequer between 1448 and 1460 is considered, the extent of London support for the government may be reassessed. Individual Londoners and the city corporately gave or lent at least £30,000, and the merchants of Calais at least £60,000. The London merchant community was primarily concerned with the safety of Calais, and it was certainly fretful about the repayment of loans. Yet the pattern and extent of their lending does not suggest that they were indifferent to the fate of the régime. Throughout the 1450s they continued to have a financial stake in the government and this was an important consideration in their response to overtures from those who planned to dislodge the Lancastrian dynasty and, in so doing, render its debts irredeemable.

The policy of the mayor, aldermen, and Common Council was to maintain the city's neutrality and the *status quo*. In January 1452 Richard, duke of York, marched towards London, was refused entry by the citizens, and withdrew to Dartford.[40] When Henry VI's illness between August 1453 and December 1454 made him unable to conduct the government himself, the city rulers were careful to maintain good relations not only with York, but also with Queen Margaret. When York was staying at Baynard Castle in November 1453, the mayor and aldermen were in two minds whether to visit him or not. In the end they decided to wait for instructions from the royal council and not to commit themselves or to show favour to either party 'except as commanded by the king and his council'.[41] In the same spirit the Court of Aldermen decided later to greet the Queen on her arrival in the city in their scarlet liveries, and also to do the same for the duke of York on the following Friday.[42]

On the eve of the battle of St Albans in May 1455 the mayor and aldermen sent messages to the lords supporting York to refuse them entry into the city on the king's orders.[43] During the period of York's ascendancy and second protectorship, lasting until February 1456, there is no evidence that the Londoners corporately lent money to the government.[44] The city had its own troubles in 1456. Fierce fighting broke out between the London mercers and the Italian merchants; and the failure of the city authorities to curb this violence resulted in the imprisonment of an alderman, William Cantelowe, and other mercers.[45] This showed that the city was not immune from the general lawlessness and unrest which permeated the country at large.[46] Early in 1458 King Henry tried to reconcile York and the Nevill earls with the heirs of the magnates slain at St Albans three years earlier. The presence of so many armed retinues in or near London posed a formidable task for the civic authorities; the Journals indicate their efforts to keep the peace. 535 men were enrolled to patrol the wards; a river curfew was imposed from 6 p.m. to 6 a.m.; the gates were to be closed during the same hours; and a rota of night watches was drawn up for the aldermen.[47] Whereas the duke of York and the earls of Warwick and Salisbury lodged within the city, the duke of Somerset, the earl of Northumberland, and Lords Egremont and Clifford remained outside — in Fleet Street and Westminster.[48] York, Warwick, and Salisbury all possessed town houses within the city walls: York at Baynard Castle, Warwick in Old Dean Street, west of St Paul's, and Salisbury at the Erber in Dowgate ward.[49] The other lords did not. On this occasion the Londoners successfully maintained the peace; and the king commended their efforts.[50]

Whether through fear or ambition the supporters of the duke of York began to arm in 1459. On 23 September they fought an indecisive battle at Blore Heath in Cheshire. This battle provoked the king to write from Nottingham to the mayor and citizens of London. When his letters had been read sergeants were sent to the Venetians and the Florentines, and also to the wardens of the Gunners, Armourers, Bowyers, Fletchers, Mercers, Haberdashers, Joiners, Tailors, and Upholders instructing them to come to the Court of Aldermen the next day to hear the king's command. Meanwhile no arms were to be sold openly or privately to any adherent of the duke of York or the earls of Warwick or Salisbury.[51] The city was to be defended in the king's name.[52] But after the rout of Ludford on 12 October the earls of Warwick and Salisbury, together with York's eldest son, the earl of March (the future Edward IV) fled to Calais; and York himself fled to Ireland. On 11 October the aldermen had assured the king of the good disposition of the city, as well as of their daily labours to preserve the peace.[53] On 16 October Common Council agreed to give the king £666 13s 4d 'to relieve his great expenses after the recent perturbations'.[54] There is little evidence, therefore, of Yorkist sentiment in the city at this time.

At the Coventry Parliament of November 1459, York, Warwick, and Salisbury were attainted. On 8 November Common Council made a further loan for the relief of Calais.[55] Two months later, however, the city resisted the king's commissioners of array on the grounds that such commissions infringed the liberties of the city. Yet the mayor and aldermen gave £33 6s 8d towards the wages of soldiers mustering at Sandwich under the earl of Wiltshire for embarkation to Calais.[56] In return, the citizens received 'gracious' letters from the king, which promised them his support in their long-standing quarrel with the London clergy over tithes, and also assured them that he would not infringe their liberties if they remained loyal.[57]

In February 1460 the citizens were once more put upon the alert; the city companies contributed towards the cost of new artillery; and on 1 March Henry VI was honourably received at Cripplegate.[58] The earls of March, Warwick, and Salisbury planned their return from the comparative safety of Calais. But when a letter announcing that Warwick's fleet was anchoring off Hastings on 8 June was brought to the Court of Aldermen, the court decided not to forward it to the king because it was of no great matter.[59] Nevertheless the mayor and aldermen made careful provision for the defence of the bridge, the burning of the drawbridge, the mustering of archers, and the guarding of the Tower. At the same time, many citizens were enlisted to maintain continuous watch.[60] London was not therefore taken by surprise when the earls of March, Warwick, and Salisbury landed at Sandwich on 26 June. As they advanced, a meeting of Common Council was held 'for guarding the city in these times of trouble'. The Council agreed to assist the mayor and aldermen in holding London for the king. Yet it stipulated that Lords Hungerford and Scales, the commanders of the Tower garrison, should not help to defend the city.[61] Thus the Londoners hedged their bets. Whatever the outcome of the rebellion, they could plead that they had held the city for the victor.

On 28 June Common Council took detailed measures to defend the bridge; but they were measures which would also allow the passage of non-combatants. A deputation was sent to the insurgent earls 'to try to move them to take another route or not come through the city: but if they, or any of them, were to come to the city, they would find it defended by the whole authority of the mayor, aldermen and common council'. This deputation was sent with the approval of those royal councillors who were lodged in the Tower. The keeping of the city gates that night was entrusted to reliable aldermen.[62] The next day was Sunday, the feast of St. Peter and St Paul, and, by tradition, a day of civic ceremony. But the mayor and aldermen abandoned their usual procession to St Paul's. They also decided that any messenger coming from the insurgent lords should not be received.[63] On Tuesday 1 July the deputation sent three days before returned, and the determination of the Londoners to resist crumbled.[64] They were not prepared to see the city sacked for the cause of Henry VI, and so the earls of March, Warwick, and Salisbury entered peacefully. London became Yorkist on 2 July 1460, but not before. It was a decision born of realism and self-interest, not of principle and altruism. Once, however, the city governors had agreed to open the gates to the earls, it was imperative that the latter should gain control of the government, if not of the Crown itself. It is not surprising, therefore, to find the city throwing its whole weight behind the Yorkist campaigns during the next months; for if Henry VI were to return in triumph to his rebellious capital, the privileges and purses of the city would inevitably suffer.

London support for the Yorkist cause after July 1460 was of two kinds: the practical support of money and fighting men, and the moral support of organized cheering crowds. Between 4 July 1460 and 7 April 1461 the citizens corporately lent the Yorkists £11,000.[65] There is nothing remotely comparable to this scale of lending over so short a period in the pattern of corporate London support to the Crown during the Lancastrian period. But even this large sum does not represent the full extent of London support for the Yorkist cause. At least three city companies lent over £500 to the future Edward IV, and individual Londoners also provided quite substantial amounts.[66] *Ad hoc* sums of money were also produced for the earls of Warwick and Salisbury, which were never recorded in the royal Exchequer: it seems unlikely that they were repaid.[67] This very extensive financial help, amounting to at least £13,000, was crucial to Edward IV's triumph and helps to explain how his cause was able to survive its defeats at Wakefield and the second battle of St Albans.

But London help was not confined solely to finance, important though that was. When the citizens allowed the retinues of March, Warwick, and Salisbury to enter the city on 4 July 1460, Henry VI's remaining partisans withdrew to the Tower under the leadership of the earl of Kendal, Lords Scales, Hungerford, and Lovel, and Sir Edmund Hampden. From this vantage point a considerable bombardment of the city took place and, in retaliation, the Tower was blockaded.[68] Common Council made this decision reluctantly, 'for the security and defence of the city' since no other way seemed to be safe for the city.[69] In spite of a defiant exchange of letters between the defenders of the Tower and the Londoners, the royal defeat at Northampton on 10 July and the successful capture of Henry VI made the surrender of the Tower inevitable.[70] On 16 July the mayor, aldermen, and commons of London agreed under their common seal to accept the terms of the Lancastrian surrender.[71] Soon afterwards the hapless supporters of Henry VI, now prisoners in the Tower, suffered 'pleyn execucion and due administracion of justice . . . in all hast possible according to his saide lawes and theire demerites in that behalve.'[72] The earl of Warwick headed a commission of oyer and terminer which sat at the Guildhall on 23 July. Sir Thomas Brown, a former under-treasurer of England (1447-9) and currently sheriff of Kent, was attainted for treason, together with three other leading defenders of the Tower. Two more defenders were attainted

D

on 28 July. All six were drawn, hanged, and quartered the next day. On 2 August John Archer, a member of the Inner Temple who was also councillor of the duke of Exeter, the Constable of the Tower, underwent a like fate.[73]

Although the mayor and aldermen decided to dress in their liveries to welcome the duke of York in November 1460, the Londoners were no more anxious than his Nevill allies to make him king.[74] Moreover Lancastrian support was swelling, especially in the north and south-west. Jasper Tudor, earl of Pembroke, was raising forces in Wales in Henry VI's name; early in December letters from him, the queen, and the young Prince Edward, were read in Common Council.[75] A letter from the earl of Northumberland, like-wise a supporter of the king, was also read to Common Council some days later.[76] But in spite of this pressure a contingent of Londoners, led by John Harowe, a mercer, marched north to be defeated with York at Wakefield on 30 December 1460.[77] When the news reached London, Common Council at once agreed to a further loan of 2,000 marks 'on account of the great insur-rections and turbations in the kingdom'.[78] The news of the earl of March's victory at Mortimer's Cross on 3 February must have heartened the Londoners. Yet the northern levies of Queen Margaret were pillaging their way south.[79] In spite of the bows, arms, and bow strings supplied by the Londoners,[80] Warwick's army was defeated at St Albans on 17 February and the road to London lay open to the queen. In this crisis the mayor and aldermen played for time by sending carts of food and money to try to keep her troops away from London.[81] She and her advisers, now strengthened by their possession of Henry VI, made a fatal mistake by not seizing London when it was comparatively undefended. They perhaps knew that the aldermen and Common Council were planning to hold London for the Yorkist cause; they may also have thought the defences of the city a sufficient deterrent.[82] Warwick, however, was able to effect a rendezvous with March and together they moved towards London. On 26 February Common Council received a letter from Henry VI declaring March a traitor and enjoining resistance to him, and also one from March and Warwick requesting entry into the city.[83] Their request was granted. On 1 March 1461 the Londoners joined the retinues of March and Warwick in St John's Fields at Clerkenwell outside the city to provide Edward with the popular acclaim necessary for his seizure of the Crown.[84] Three days later he took possession of the realm and was installed as king. Of the events of 4 March 1461 the Journals' clerk writes in his most laconic manner:

> Memorandum on Wednesday 4 March 1461 Edward duke of York, called earl of March, with various lords & magnates . . . with a great commonalty of the kingdom, entered the royal palace at Westminster and took possession of the kingdom in the royal seat, namely on the south side of the great hall there, and he took it upon himself and obtained it with honour, Richard Lee Mayor, with the

Recorder and Aldermen and many other citizens of the city present there, at the command of the said lord the king.[85]

Edward did not, of course, secure the throne merely by sitting on a royal seat, but by his bloody victory at Towton on 29 March. Common Council received the news with joy and relief. The king's letter from York instructed the citizens to thank God for his victory; it also informed them of the theft of much of his treasure and many of his horses. The Londoners took the hint and, in the euphoria of victory, agreed to lend the king a further 2,000 marks 'for the good conclusion of these events'.[86]

But with the new king securely established the Londoners began to take a firmer line. At the end of April they refused to provide money for Calais; and for his coronation on 28 June they made only a comparatively small gift of 1,000 marks, because their recent expenses in his cause had been so great.[87] Yet the aldermen and common councilmen considerably exercized themselves over the choice of new liveries to wear when greeting Edward on entry into the city, and at the coronation itself. 'Le lyghter grene' cloth was selected by Common Council since it was learnt that the men of Coventry would also be in green.[88] Within weeks of the coronation, Richard Lee, the mayor, was able to report to Common Council that the amounts lent by each citizen had been recorded in a book at the Exchequer.[89] This formal acknowledgement of the London debts on the Receipt roll was an important achievement: it provided a measure of security for repayment such as the Londoners had not enjoyed since 1449.

Only eight days after the coronation, Common Council decided to take up the matter of the cloth-packers patent with the king.[90] At first, Edward appears to have been prepared only to allow the Londoners to have the disposal of the disputed 'offices' for the next six years, but the citizens pressed to have them in perpetuity.[91] They were to be disappointed, for the royal letters patent of 15 August granted them the offices of cloth-packer, gauger, garbeller, and wine-drawer only during the king's pleasure. The mayor and aldermen were not satisfied. Although they managed to secure new letters patent dated 26 August which granted them the offices during good behaviour, they still failed to secure a grant in perpetuity.[92]

The recording of the London loans at the Exchequer and the grant of the long disputed 'offices', albeit only during good behaviour, were tangible concessions.[93] But Edward was not always amenable to the wishes of the Londoners; his negotiations with Hanse merchants, for example, were far from satisfactory for the citizens, and the large corporate loan, for all that it was recorded, remained outstanding.[94]

The end of this story comes in 1478. By then Edward's debt to the city amounted to £12,923 9s 8d: the original £11,000 borrowed in 1460-1, and a further meagre £1,923 9s 8d accumulated in the intervening eighteen years.

Edward's method of dealing with this desperate debt was summary and effective: he sold the Londoners certain privileges, rights, and properties to the sum of his indebtedness[95] First, for £1,923 9s 8d, the right to acquire lands in mortmain to the value of 200 marks a year;[96] secondly, for £7,000, the offices of cloth-packer, garbeller, gauger, and wine-drawer in perpetuity, together with the right to elect their own coroner;[97] and finally, for £9,000, the manor of Blancheappleton together with Stewards Inn, free of rent and in perpetuity.[98]

So the considerable investment of the citizens in the Yorkist cause in 1460 and 1461 eventually proved to have been worthwhile. It is perhaps worth reflecting that, but for the creative meddling of Henry VI and his council in the 1440s over civic offices, Edward IV would have had nothing with which he could bargain for the liquidation of his London debt.

The commonalty of freemen who comprised the political community of London was not therefore indifferent to the fate of the Lancastrian régime, but, rather, continued to support it with loans and gifts until June 1460, only a few days before Warwick and Saisbury's army entered the city. The £30,000 which the Londoners lent to Henry VI either individually or corporately (excluding loans from the Staplers) between 1448 and 1460 compares favourably with the £35,000 which they lent, according to the calculations of Dr Ross, to Edward IV between 1462 and 1475.[99] The pattern of lending in both periods is not noticeably different; and the apparent discrepancy between the respective sums borrowed by Henry VI and Edward IV is almost certainly the result of lacunae in the Lancastrian Exchequer records. The city of London remained loyal to Henry VI until the arrival of Warwick and Salisbury early in July 1460 made a shift of allegiance necessary. Once the citizens had made such a shift, they were bound to ensure the success of the Yorkists; and this explains the massive financial support provided by the Londoners in the succeeding months. Without their support the Yorkists would not have been able to survive their defeats as well as the death of their leader. Without a Yorkist victory, the Londoners had no hope of maintaining their privileges intact, let alone of augmenting them. But with Edward IV on the throne they were able to demand and, ultimately, to secure rights and offices long sought and long denied. The primary concern of the commonalty of London was consistent: it was, as their clerk noted, 'the security and defence of the city'.[100]

Table 1

1. *Sources* This table is based upon information largely derived from Exchequer Records — Receipt and Issue rolls, deeds, and Warrants for Issue. Further information was also found in the Letter Books and the Journals of the city, as well as in the printed calendars of the Patent and the Close rolls. The table itself is imperfect because of the deficiencies of the Exchequer records of the 1450s (see n. 44); the loss of the London Journal for 1429-36; and the very damaged condition of the Journal for 1456-62. The latter, incorrectly bound at a later date, has now been photographed in its entirety, and the photographs are bound according to the original fifteenth century sequence. Throughout this essay when citing Journal 6, I have cited the uncorrected foliation.

2. *Cross-checks* For corporate loans by the city to the Crown the Exchequer records can be checked against entries in the city journals. For the loans of individual Londoners the records of the Exchequer provide the only surviving information.

3. *Staplers' Loans* The table takes account only of those loans made by merchants of the Calais Staple which the Exchequer recorded. Dr G.L. Harriss has shown ('The Struggle for Calais: An Aspect of the Rivalry between Lancaster and York', *E.H.R.* lxxv (1960), 30-53) not only that some of the Staplers' loans — for example that of £24,000 in 1456 to pay the wages of the mutinous Calais garrison — were not recorded, but that the Staplers in 1462 received a formal acknowledgement from the Crown of its total debt to them of nearly £41,000.

4. *Conclusion* Despite its several limitations, the table shows that the most marked support for the Lancastrians came in the early years of the dynasty; that the aggressive campaigns of Henry V in France attracted less support than defensive measures after 1430 to save Calais, Normandy, and Gascony: and that the corporate London loans totalling £11,000 made during the nine months July 1460-April 1461 were unprecedented in amount over so short a period (see above p. 97).

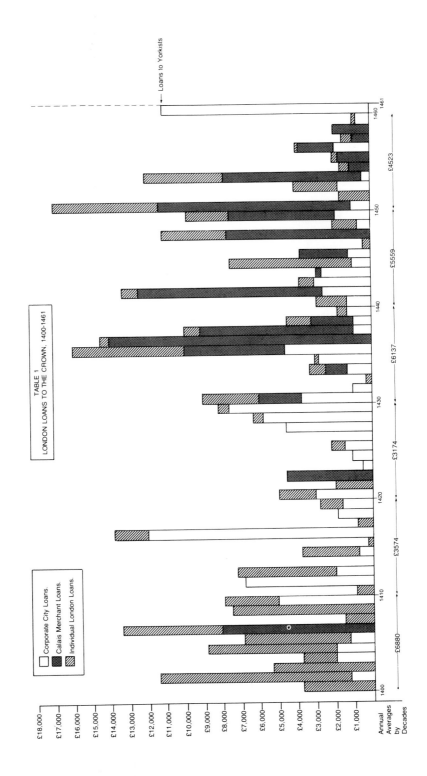

TABLE 1
LONDON LOANS TO THE CROWN, 1400-1461

Corporate City Loans.
Calais Merchant Loans.
Individual London Loans.

Loans to Yorkists

Annual
Averages
by
Decades

£18,000
£17,000
£16,000
£15,000
£14,000
£13,000
£12,000
£11,000
£10,000
£9,000
£8,000
£7,000
£6,000
£5,000
£4,000
£3,000
£2,000
£1,000

1400   £6880   1410   £3574   1420   £3174   1430   £6137   1440   £5559   1450   £4523   1460 1461

Table 2

Table of loans made by the citizens of London to the Yorkist Lords 1460-61

This list of loans is derived from the bill (E 404/72/1, no. 23) originally attached to Edward IV's warrant under the privy seal to the Treasurer, dated 24 July 1461, to make an assignment for the repayment of the loans (E 404/72/1, no. 22). It is supplemented with information from volume 6 of the City Journals.

4 July 1460	loan of £1,000	Journal 6, fo. 253
9 July 1460	loan of 500 marks	Journal 6, fo.251^v Notes that each alderman was to provide £10: John Wenlock to receive 100 marks for sailors and the rest of the money for city defences.
13 July 1460	loan of £1,000	Journal 6, fo. 255 Date of Common Council given, 14 July 1460.
8 December 1460	loan of 500 marks	Journal 6, fo. 280. Notes that it was agreed to lend 1,000 marks on certain conditions which were, presumably, not satisfactorily fulfilled.
5 January 1461	loan of 2,000 marks	Journal 6, fo. 285
11 February 1461	loan of £1,000	Journal 6, fo. 4^v Notes that the sum was to be made up of 500 marks still remaining from the levy of 8 December, together with a new levy of 1,000 marks.

13 February 1461   loan of 1,000 marks Journal 6, fo. 40
                                       Notes a further 500 marks agreed for
                                       'garnishing' the city.

[3] March 1461   loan of £2,000   Journal 6, fo. 36ᵛ

7 March 1461   loan of £2,000   Journal 6, fo. 14

7 April 1461   loan of 2,000 marks Journal 6, fo. 55

            TOTAL £11,000

A loan of £11,000 from the mayor, aldermen, and citizens of London is duly
recorded in the first Receipt roll of Edward IV's reign under the date 22
June 1461, P.R.O. E 401/877.

Notes

1. B. Wilkinson, *Constitutional History of England in the Fifteenth Century* (London, 1964), p.108; cf. the more cautious view of C.D. Ross *Edward IV* (1974), p.24.

2. E.g. Gregory's Chronicle printed in *Historical Collections of a Citizen of London*, ed. J. Gairdner (C.S., n.s. xxxii, 1876), p.215.

3. For the vexed topic of the population of medieval London see J.C. Russell, *British Medieval Population* (Albuquerque, 1948); Sylvia L. Thrupp, *The Merchant Class of Medieval London* (Michigan, 1948); and E. Ekwall, *Two Early London Subsidy Rolls* (Lund, 1951). I shall discuss it further in my introduction to the forthcoming volume of the *Historic Towns Atlas: Medieval London*.

4. A.H. Thomas (ed.), *Calendar of Plea and Memoranda Rolls 1364-81* (Cambridge, 1929), lxii. In 1538 there were 4,040 freemen householders (Thrupp, op.cit., p.51).

5. Mercers (36), Drapers (32), Grocers (28), Fishmongers (15), Skinners (13), Goldsmiths (12), Ironmongers (7), Vintners (2). Before 1461 only two aldermen belonged to artisan guilds: a tailor and a saddler. They were better represented between 1461 and 1485 by four tailors, three salters, and two haberdashers. The trades of three aldermen for the period 1400-85 are unknown.

6. Caroline M. Barron, 'Ralph Holland and the London Radicals 1438-44', in *Essays in Honour of the Golden Jubilee of the North London Branch of the Historical Association* (1970), pp. 60-80.

7. Sylvia L. Thrupp, 'Aliens in and around London in the fifteenth century' in *Studies in London History*, ed. A.E.J. Hollaender and W. Kellaway (London, 1969), pp. 251-72.

8. C(orporation of) L(ondon) R(ecord) O(ffice), Journal 6, original fo 10, (see notes to Table 1).

9. Gregory, op.cit., pp.214-15.

10. J.S. Davies (ed.), *An English Chronicle of the Reigns of Richard II, Henry IV, Henry V and Henry VI* (C.S., o.s. lxiv, 1855), 108-9.

11. *Historie of the Arrivall of Edward IV in England . . .* , ed. J. Bruce (C.S., o.s. i, 1838), p.34.

12. Caroline M. Barron, 'Richard II's quarrel with London 1392-7' in *The Reign of Richard II*, ed. F.R.H. Du Boulay and Caroline M. Barron (London, 1971), pp. 173-201.

13. *C.P.R., 1429-36*, p.248; and for further appointments, ibid., p.442; *C.P.R., 1436-41*, pp.40, 44. See A.L. Simon, *The History of the Wine Trade in England*, (London, 1906), i; pp.300-1. In the fourteenth century royal gaugers were frequently appointed in London, but the grant of 1432 is the first in the fifteenth century. Royal control of the office may have lapsed. The king's renewed interest in the office was certainly financial: the London gaugers' accounts survive intermittently from 1437 to 1457, P.R.O. E 364/75/13ᵈ; 81/2ᵈ; 91/7ᵈ. For London protests about the activities of the gaugers in the 1440s see *P.P.C.* vi. 50; C.L.R.O. Journal 4, fo. 36ᵛ; *Rot. Parl..* v. 113-15.

14. *C.P.R., 1436-41*, p.490; *Rot. Parl.* iii. 443-4; for London protests about the cloth-packers patent in the 1440s, see C.L.R.O., Journal 3, fos. 83-83ᵛ, 109ᵛ, 114ᵛ; Journal 4, fos. 32ᵛ, 36ᵛ, 53ᵛ, 60ᵈ; P.P.C. vi. 50.

15. *C.P.R., 1436-41*, p.485; C(alendar of) L(etter) B(ooks of the City of) L(ondon), ed. R.R. Sharpe (11 vols., London, 1899-1912), *K*, pp. 278-9.

16. *C.L.B.L., H*, p.424.

17. C.L.R.O. Journal 3, fo. 99. For protests about the wine-drawers' patent see Journal 3, fos. 103, 106ᵛ, 109ᵛ, 114ᵛ; Journal 4, fos. 18, 36ᵛ, 60ᵛ; *P.P.C.* vi. 50.

18. *C.P.R.*, *1441-46*, p.128.
19. *P.P.C.* vi. 50. For the city's resistance to royal patentees in the 1440s see *C(alendar) P(lea and) M(emoranda) R(olls) 1437-57*, ed. P.E. Jones, (Cambridge, 1954), pp. 60-61; C.L.R.O. Journal 4, fos. 22, 22^v,36^v. For the Grocers' activity see *Facsimile . . . of Archives of Grocers of London 1345-1463*, ed. J.A. Kingdon (London, 1886), ii. 43^v, 63, 94; Sylvia Thrupp, 'The Grocers of London', in *Studies in the History of English Trade in the Fifteenth Century*, ed M.M. Postan and E. Power (London, 1933), pp.247-92.
20. C.L.R.O. Journal 3, fos. 109^v, 114^v.
21. C.L.R.O. Journal 3, fo. 75. In 1444 the grocer Richard Hakeday who had accepted the office of garbeller by royal patent stood in danger of losing his citizenship, Journal 4, fos. 22, 22^v. Thomas Quyne who had a share in the wine-drawers' monopoly lost his citizenship on 20 February 1444, Journal 4, fo.18.
22. G.L. Harriss, 'Cardinal Beaufort — patriot or usurer?', *T.R.Hist. S.*, 5th series, xx (1970), 129-48.
23. E.g. February 1441, C.L.R.O. Journal 3, fo. 74^v.
24. *C.L.B.L.*, *I*, p.135; C.L.R.O. Journal 4, fo. 33^v.
25. *C.L.B.L.*, *K*, p.190; C.L.R.O. Journal 5, fos. 58^v, 100^v.
26. The only clear case between 1416 and 1448 of a complete refusal to lend was on 16 July 1426, C.L.R.O. Journal 2, fo. 80^v.
27. A. Steel, *The Receipt of the Exchequer 1377-1485* (Cambridge, 1954), p. xxxiii; G.L. Harriss, 'Fictitious loans', *Ec.H.R.*, 2nd series, viii (1955-6), 187-99.
28. C.L.R.O. Journal 3, fo. 9^v.
29. C.L.R.O. Journal 5, fos. 227-228^v, transcribed by E. Jeffries Davies and M.I. Peake, 'Loans from the City of London to Henry VI 1431-1449', *B.I.H.R.* iv (1926-7), 165-72.
30. The London assignments were usually drawn upon the revenues of parliamentary taxation or the proceeds of the wool subsidy in the port of London.
31. On four occasions the London support for the crown in the Lancastrian period took the form of goods or troops rather than a cash loan: for example, in 1418 for the siege of Rouen; and in 1436, 1449, and 1451 for the defence of Calais.
32. E.B. Fryde and M.M. Fryde 'Public credit, with special reference to north-western Europe', *The Cambridge Economic History of Europe*, ed. M.M. Postan, E.E. Rich, and Edward Miller, vol. viii (Cambridge 1962), p.470.
33. R.L. Storey, *The End of the House of Lancaster* (London, 1966), p.75. Cf. A.B. Steel, 'The financial background of the Wars of the Roses', *History*, n.s. xl (1955), 18-30.
34. On 10 September 1450, 2 May 1453, 1 August 1453, 8 August 1453, 7 December 1453, 13 May 1454, 9 August 1454, 13 May 1455, C.L.R.O. Journal 5, fos. 45^v, 100, 116^v, 117, 136, 184, 242.
35. See above Table 1, note 3.
36. P.R.O. Receipt Rolls of the Exchequer, E 401/813, 16 October 1449; E 401/829, 31 January 1453.
37. London also raised a contingent to help to defend Calais in 1449. The costs of providing 43 lancers and 319 archers were divided amongst the city companies and amounted to about £700, C.L.R.O. Journal 5, fos. 10^v-12^v, 105^v; Kingdon, op.cit., fos. 301. 307.
38. The amount of the loan was £1,766 6s 2½d; the king's council had refused a further £233 13s 9½d composed of unpaid royal tallies. The bill from John Poutrell was 'made after the use of the kinges rescette of the resceivyng to the behove of the kinge'. C.L.R.O. Journal 4, fos. 35, 39; Journal 5, fos. 227^v – 228.
39. C.L.R.O. Journal 5, fos. 43, 43^v, 49, 57.
40. *An English Chronicle*, ed. J.S. Davies, op.cit., pp.69-70. On 4 March 1452 the duke of Exeter brought news of the accord between the king and the duke of York, C.L.R.O. Journal 5, fo. 71.

41. 20 November 1453, C.L.R.O. Journal 5, fo. 132ᵛ.
42. 20 February 1454, C.L.R.O. Journal 5, fo. 150.
43. 20 May 1455, C.L.R.O. Journal 5, fo. 243ʳ.
44. During York's first protectorship in 1454 the Londoners made only a small loan in June, of £300, on the authority of parliament, C.L.R.O. Journal 5,, fos. 170, 171, 174. In August 1454 they refused York a loan for Calais,
45. R. Flenley, 'London and foreign merchants in the reign of Henry VI', *E.H.R.* xxv (1910), 644-55; 29 October 1456, C.L.R.O. Journal 6, fo. 85.
46. E.g. on 29 March 1457 the men of the city companies were enjoined not to meddle in affairs touching the king, queen, or prince, or any lords of the king and queen, but to hold their tongues and to refrain from speaking any scandalous, shameful or dishonest things, C.L.R.O. Journal 6, fo. 117ʳ.
47. 8, 25 February, 3 March 1458, C.L.R.O. Journal 6, fos. 191ᵛ, 192, 193ʳ, 194.
48. *An English Chronicle*, ed. J.S. Davies, op.cit. p.77.
49. C.L. Kingsford, 'Medieval London houses', *London Topographical Record*, x (1916), 59-64, 114-16; ibid. xii (1920), 52-55.
50. C.L.R.O. Journal 6, fos. 193, 193ʳ.
51. 26 September 1459, C.L.R.O. Journal 6, fo. 138.
52. 6 October 1459, C.L.R.O. Journal 6, fo. 143ᵛ.
53. 11 October 1459, C.L.R.O. Journal 6, fo. 145.
54. 13 October 1459, C.L.R.O. Journal 6, fo. 163.
55. 8 November 1459, C.L.R.O. Journal 6, fos. 166ᵛ, 168ᵛ.
56. C.L.R.O. Journal 6, fos. 224ᵛ, 225ᵛ, 227.
57. 5 February 1460, C.L.R.O. Journal 6, fo. 196ʳ; *C.L.B.L.*, *K*, pp.402-3; J.A.F. Thomson, 'Tithe disputes in later medieval London', *E.H.R.* lxxviii (1963), 1-17.
58. 28 February 1460, C.L.R.O. Journal 6, fo. 204.
59. Date between 9 and 14 June 1460, C.L.R.O. Journal 6, fo. 217ʳ.
60. 23, 26 June 1460, C.L.R.O. Journal 6, fos. 219-220ʳ.
61. 27 June 1460, C.L.R.O. Journal 6, fos. 237-237ʳ.
62. Ibid.
63. C.L.R.O. Journal 6, fo. 238ᵛ.
64. 1 July 1460, C.L.R.O. Journal 6, fo. 239ᵛ.
65. See Table 2.
66. I have traced the following loans: 5 December 1460 £200 from the Grocers; 27 January 1461 £200 from the Drapers; and £133 6s 8d from the Fishmongers (P.R.O., E 401/873). These companies received assignments for repayment recorded on 27 January, 3 and 9 February 1461 (E 403/820). On 8 March 1461 William Edward, grocer, lent £100; Hugh Wyche, alderman, £100; John Norman, alderman, £40; the prior of Christ Church, £333 6s 8d (E 401/873 and E 404/72/1, no. 16). On 16 March 1461 the Prior of St Bartholomew's, Smithfield, lent £40 (E 404/72/, no. 19). By July 1461 John Lambard, one of the sheriffs, had lent a total of £273 18s 8d (E 404/72/1, no. 24). It should be remembered that all dates given on the Receipt Rolls are notional and *ex post facto*.
67. On 8 August 1460 the aldermen provided £125 for the earl of March, and on 29 November 1460 500 marks for the earl of Salisbury (C.L.R.O. Journal 6, fos. 260, 278ʳ). On 13 December 1460 the wardens of the city companies were assembled to discuss the question of safeguarding the person of the king and the safety of the city (ibid., fo. 282ʳ). Perhaps as a result of this meeting the mercers agreed to lend 500 marks 'for the wele of oure sovereigne lorde the kyng and the comon wele of all the londe, to the hasty spede of the Erle of Warwick into the northcuntre'; 130 mercers contributed to this loan (*Acts of Court of the Mercers' Company 1453-1527*, ed. L. Lyell and F.D. Watney (Cambridge, 1936), pp.48, 54-58). The mercers provided a further

£100, lent by eighty-four individuals, for the earl of Warwick during the years 1460-1 (ibid., pp. 51-53).

68. In their accounts for 1460-61 the Pewterers recorded payments of 5d a day for two men 'watchynge att the Towre of London' for thirty days (C. Welch, *History of the Worshipful Company of Pewterers* (London, 1902), i. 427).

69. 6 July 1460, C.L.R.O. Journal 6, fo. 251.

70. 10 July 1460, ibid., fo. 250^v.

71. 16 July 1460, ibid., fo 256.

72. Royal proclamation, 21 July 1460 (C.L.R.O. Journal 6, fo. 257).

73. P.R.O., Exchequer Miscellanea, E 163/8/10; *Coram Rege* Roll KB 27/798, Michaelmas, 39 Henry VI, *Rex* m.^{v}; *John Benet's Chronicle for the years 1400 to 1462*, ed. G.L. and M.A. Harriss, *Camden Miscellany*, xxiv (1972), p.227; C.L. Scofield, *The Life and Reign of Edward IV* (1923), i. 92-93. I owe these references as well as the previous four sentences to Dr Robin Jeffs. He and I hope shortly to publish a full account of the earl of Warwick's *oyer* and *terminer* of July 1460. Warwick's commission was not enrolled on the Patent Roll. Nor can it be found in the surviving records of the sign manual, the signet and the privy seal.

74. 10 October 1460, C.L.R.O., fo. 271.

75. 2 December 1460, ibid., fo. 279.

76. 18, 19 December 1460, ibid., fo. 284.

77. John Harowe was a prominent mercer. As he was serving his apprenticeship by 1422-23, he would have been born about 1406. He was Warden of the Mercers' Company in 1443 and 1449. On occasion, however, he had himself fallen foul of the wardens; he was fined 'for words spoken in court' and 'for lying and uncorteous language'. Although a common councilman by 1444, he never attained the rank of alderman. He was three times M.P. for the city, and the chroniclers indicate that he was more markedly active in the Yorkist cause than most of his contemporaries in the city. He left no extant will. See J.C. Wedgwood, *The History of Parliament: Biographies of the Members of the Common House 1439-1509* (London; H.M.S.O. 1936) i, 429-30; unpublished information from the Mercers' Company records kindly supplied by Miss Jean Imray.

78. 5 January 1461, C.L.R.O. Journal 6 fo. 285.

79. At this time Queen Margaret addressed an undated letter to the citizens of London urging them to ignore Yorkist rumours that she intended 'to draw toward you with an unseen power of strangers, disposed to rob and despoil you of your goods and havings' *Letters of Royal and Illustrious Ladies of Great Britain* ed. M.A.E. Wood, (London, 1846), i, 95).

80. 11 February 1461, C.L.R.O. Journal 6, fo. 4^v.

81. See above p. 89. On 21 February 1461 Common Council sent a deputation to Barnet to meet the Queen's deputation headed by Sir Edmund Hampden, Sir John Heron, and Sir Robert Whityngham. A proclamation from the queen enjoining peace throughout the city was agreed to by the Common Council and published, C.L.R.O. Journal 6, fos. 10^v, 35^v.

82. On 24 February 1461 men were mustered in the city, and steps were taken to provision and garrison the Tower, ibid., fo. 35.

83. 26 February 1461, C.L.R.O. Journal 6, fo. 13.

84. C.A.J. Armstrong, 'The inauguration ceremonies of the Yorkist kings and their title to the throne', *T. R. Hist. S.*, 4th ser. xxx (1948), 51-68.

85. C.L.R.O. Journal 6, fo. 37^v.

86. 7 April 1461, ibid., fo. 55.

87. 22 April, 20 June 1461, ibid., fos. 56, 50.

88. June 1461, ibid., fo. 54. The Goldsmiths, Carpenters, and Pewterers all sent men to greet the new king, Welch, op. cit., p.27; W.S. Prideaux, *Memorials of the Goldsmiths' Company* (London, n.d.), p.24; *Records of the Worshipful Company of Carpenters*, ed. B. Marsh, ii (Oxford, 1914), 34. The Mercers sent twenty-four men who were to pay themselves for their own black hats and tippets, but who were to be provided with the green gowns at the company's expense, *Acts of Court*, op. cit. p.49.

89. 5 August 1461, C.L.R.O. Journal 6, fo. 46^v; cf. June 1461, ibid., fo.54. Lee reported that the date under which the loans were recorded was 4 July. The king's warrant to the Treasurer, to enter the Londoners' corporate loans amounting to £11,000 in the book of receipt under the date 7 April 1461 and to make an assignment to them, is dated 24 July 1461 (P.R.O. E 404/72/1, no. 22). The loan is, in fact, recorded under the date 22 June 1461 (E 401/877). There is no record of assignment. For the dates at which loans from individual Londoners were recorded at the Exchequer see above, n.66.

90. 6 July 1461, C.L.R.O. Journal 6, fo. 44.

91. 30 July 1461, ibid., fo. 45^v.

92. 14 August 1461, ibid., fo. 23^v; *C.P.R.*, *1461-67*, pp.69, 70; The original letters patent of 26 August, C.L.R.O. Charter 57.

93. Edward also, on the day after his Coronation, granted the Londoners the manor of Blancheappleton, see n. 96 below.

94. On 10 February 1462, the Recorder reported to Common Council that he had had a meeting with the king who had expressed the hope that the citizens were not wanting their money urgently but had instructed the lords of his council to make appropriate assignments (C.L.R.O. Journal 6, fo. 15^v). In March there were further negotiations about the repayment of 18,000 marks (i.e. £12,000) owed by the king to the citizens (ibid., fo. 16).

95. Francis Palgrave, *Antient Kalendars & Inventories of the Exchequer* (London, 1836), iii. 27; C.L. Scofield, op. cit. ii. 215 n.6.

96. 20 June 1478, Walter Birch, *The Historical Charters . . . of the City of London* (rev. edn, London, 1887), pp.87-89; C.L.R.O. Original Charter no. 63. In 1411 the citizens had obtained a royal grant to hold lands to the yearly value of £100, *C.L.B.L.*, *I*, p.92.

97. 20 June 1478, Birch, op. cit., pp.90-93; *C.P.R.*, *1476-85*, p.103. The citizens had been in dispute with Henry VI over the officer of Coroner in 1437, see W. Kellaway, 'The coroner in medieval London' in *Studies in London History*, op.cit., pp.75-91.

98. Blancheappleton was part of an ancient city soke which had passed from the Bohuns to Henry IV on his marriage to Mary de Bohun, co-heiress of Humphrey, earl of Hereford. Its privileged status and immunity from civic jurisdiction, which made it a haven for criminals and shoddy workmen, were a source of anxiety to London's rulers during the 1440s and 1450s. See C.L.R.O. Journal 4, fos. 86, 96, 102^v, 184, 187; Journal 6, fos. 236^v, 110,; *P.P.C.* vi. 50. *C.L.B.L.*, *K*, p.336. On 26 May 1462 the city was granted the lease of Blancheappleton and Stewards Inn at a farm of £20 (Journal 7, fos. 2, 107^v). In 1465 this rent was abrogated at the queen's request. In 1478 both the grant of the manor and the release from the annual farm were confirmed in perpetuity (Journal 8, fos. 145^v, 168^v, 169^v-70, 173^v). Two of Edward IV's letters patent to the mayor and citizens, dated 29 September 1465 and 18 June 1478 respectively, are not recorded on the Patent Roll. The originals are at Merchant Taylors' Hall, Miscellaneous Documents, Box 122, nos. 8a and 8b.

99. C.D. Ross, *Edward IV* (London, 1974), p.378.

100. 6 July 1460, C.L.R.O. Journal 6, fo. 251.

6

The *bonnes villes* and the King's Council in Fifteenth-Century France

B. Chevalier

When modern political concepts are used to analyse late medieval institutions, distortion often results. In France today the relations between the king and his *bonnes villes* in the fifteenth century are studied in terms which underline the differences between an all-powerful central administration and communities possessing neither power nor scope for manoeuvre. From this derives the traditional picture of free communities which were once endowed, according to the terms of their charters, with a very large measure of autonomy, but which were progressively stifled. An ambitious and wilful monarchy, we are told, was as resolute in its intentions as it was patient in achieving them;[1] like a boa-constrictor, it suffocated its prey before swallowing it. Often, however, the Crown's supposed victims were communities which lacked any real privileges, while communities of any status did not enjoy full liberty in matters of justice, public order, or finance. Thus they had little to lose. Yet the *bonnes villes* were a different matter. A *bonne ville* was a town which possessed not only a large population from which forced loans could be readily extracted, but also up-to-date walls and fortifications. Since *bonnes villes* enjoyed financial as well as military power, the Crown had to treat them with respect and consideration.

Though the Crown is normally regarded as having had a continuous policy towards local communities, it never tried during the fifteenth century to impose its will on them through specialized administrative organs. Since 'the need creates the means', there can have been little need for an office or department of the council to deal with affairs of the 'interior'. Yet such a step was not inconceivable. From 1372, for instance, special secretaries dealt with financial matters discussed in council or chancery, and, as a result, a complete administrative system came into being; by the reign of

Louis XI, at the latest, military affairs and matters of justice which were reserved for consideration by the council had followed similar lines of evolution. How could the king, in such circumstances, have followed a definite policy of bending the communities to the arbitrary demands of royal administration? Was the relationship between the Crown and communities not, in fact, personalized, and of a purely political nature? Yet the meagre sources which survive suggest that the council was always active, and that its activity had an administrative bias.[2] Only by examining the workings of the council can we discover whether, in this ambiguous situation, the relationship took the form of negotiation between equals or ever-increasingly became one of strict subordination.

1. *The Requests of the Towns*

As a close examination of the *Ordonnances des Roys de France*, volumes xii-xxi reveals, the urban communities often had reason to turn to the king and his council during the fifteenth century. 642 of the 2,818 documents collected in these volumes were issued at the request of towns: in other words, 22.78 per cent of the total, or, roughly speaking, one letter patent out of five.[3] This proportion varies very little throughout the century. If all the letters are enumerated reign by reign from 1422, the respective totals are 537 for Charles VII; 1,476 for Louis XI; and 754 for Charles VIII. But the percentage of letters granted to towns hardly changes: 23.7 per cent for Charles VII; 19.4 per cent for Louis XI; and 24.4 per cent for Charles VIII. Though for each reign the number of such letters appears to be fairly constant, the reasons for their issue did, in fact, vary. Sometimes the king was approached by a town as its overlord, or as the successor to an original overlord, about matters of status or the exercise of justice; sometimes as sovereign to whom certain regalian rights alone belonged.[4] On the other hand, he might be asked to grant or confirm municipal ordinances, or to authorise the building of a rampart, or the raising of a tax to pay for its upkeep. Finally, the king alone could impose financial burdens upon the kingdom, grant exemptions from them, and unite communities, in perpetuity, to the kingdom.[5] In every case the king acted either by virtue of his sovereign and/or seignurial rights, or because the need for proper order or reasons of state demanded that he do so. Indeed, he usually acted for all these reasons without making any distinction.

If the king's motives for granting letters patent to towns were confused, so, too, was his procedure. Any community which petitioned the king acted in the same way as an individual who addressed him personally.[6] No petition or complaint survives which can, by its nature, be equated with a declaration made in the name of some or all of the towns. Instead, petitions, whether made by an individual or by a community, took the form of a 'humble supplication'. Such supplications led neither to the issue of a general ordinance nor to the drafting of a private one. All that was being asked in either case was a simple grace.[7] Thus no office or organization for the receipt of petitions came into being, for none was needed. Petitioners were preoccupied by the necessity of getting their petitions into the hands of the king. He, by immemorable tradition, devoted his audiences on Friday mornings to receiving petitions. If, following the example of Charles V, fifteenth-century kings wanted it to be believed that they still maintained this paternalistic tradition, they no longer performed it themselves except on Good Fridays. Responsibility was delegated to the chancellor of the kingdom, aided by masters of requests attached to the royal household.[8]

The urban communities clearly understood what was happening. They may have put little faith in an administrative machine which could all too readily lose their letters. But they preferred to rely on an 'embassy' to introduce their requests. Yet they also knew that their 'embassies' had scant chance of being received by the king himself. Though he wanted to convey the opposite, Henri Baude, a poetaster who was also one of Charles VII's financial officers in Bas-Limousin, demonstrated the position of the *bonnes villes* only too well when he wrote: 'when requests were made to him (the king), he had them accepted and examined, and when their contents had been reported to him, he sent the supplicants home to where they lived'.[9] Thus the principal purpose of urban assemblies was not to obtain an audience with the king, but to find persons who would introduce their requests. Once their requests had been accepted, they would then be examined and allowed to follow their natural course.[10]

The important persons who had the king's ear were not only princes, especially those under whose authority the towns lived, but also members of the council whom the king knew well. Close relationships sometimes developed between influential councillors and the towns which became their clients. Such relationships, founded upon the exchange of services, gifts, and large rewards, are difficult to trace unless municipal accounts are fully analysed.[11] As a careful study of the letters patent granted to towns which are included in the volumes of the *Ordonnances* shows, the names of 'valued' patrons are not found among the signatories of letters sent as a result of their efforts. However, among the agents appointed and favoured by a town there would be one or more notaries and secretaries of chancery: men who played an indispensable part in sifting requests, and an even greater one in drafting the letters which resulted from them. In short, personal ties between the towns and their 'patrons' took the place of proper administrative links. At first, that was all that existed: certainly, there was no co-ordinated action on behalf of the towns, nor any systematic policy shown by the king about the granting of petitions.

Yet by the fifteenth century the paternalistic attitudes of the previous two centuries were becoming a thing of the past. It was rare for a request, once it had been submitted and considered, to be granted immediately.[12] All requests — and especially those from towns — were thoroughly investigated. Every request was referred to the council; and where the petitioners were their own advocates, the entire proceedings were recorded.[13] A reporter, more often than not a master of requests, was appointed to take charge, and, at the appropriate moment, the request in question was submitted to the higher financial officers for their advice in case they would be absent when the council came to deal with it. To make itself better informed the council did not hesitate to seek expert outside opinion;[14] neither did it fail to send commissioners to towns requesting letters patent;[15] nor did it omit to consult the *Chambre des Comptes*.[16] Only then did the council submit reasoned advice to the king, upon whom lay the final responsibility for granting or refusing letters. When the king finally approved letters, the chancery drafted them, using the texts of requests themselves; and letters patent were handed to petitioners on payment of a fee.[17] Yet this was not the final stage. However little the letters in question were concerned with the administration of the royal domain, they had, nevertheless, to be submitted to the *Chambre des Comptes* for confirmation. This was far from being a mere formality.[18] An administrative procedure of this kind was slow as well as cumbersome. Why, then, should the council have made practical advances in such matters? Why, on the other hand, did it not keep records, or develop its own legal precedents? Why did it not even attempt to create a department which might have specialized in the internal affairs of the realm?[19]

The answers to these questions can be found only in the contents of letters patent of the 596 letters sent to towns during the fifteenth century; 43 are directly concerned with political matters — for example, the general amnesties granted between 1449 and 1453 after the reconquests of Normandy and Gascony, or declarations of perpetual unity with the crown.[20] But 273 (or 49.36 per cent of the total) are confirmations of diverse privileges, some of them very ancient. Thus only 280 letters are concerned with new developments. If the chancery sent to a town five or six letters a year, most were concerned with matters of moment. Given the limitations of the source material, the subjects of the letters may broadly be tabulated as shown in Table 1.

Yet of the grants of letters patent intended to facilitate administrative action on the part of municipal authorities, exemptions from the *taille*, and the grant of fairs and markets consist of more than half — 53.92 per cent. More significant, however, for an over-all view is the predominance of confirmation; on every second occasion that a town made a request it was only going through a formality, the purpose of which was, for a payment, to obtain confirmation of rights which had normally been hallowed by time. This happened at every royal accession. During the fifteenth century this

Subject	Number of letters	%
Matters of finance and justice	72	25.71
Diverse exemptions	51	18.21
Exemptions from the *taille*	41	14.64
Fairs and markets	38	13.57
Individual rights	21	7.5
Creation of offices	18	6.42
New urban statutes	17	6.07
Miscellaneous	22	7.85
Total	280	99.97

Subject	Number of letters	%
Political information	129	28.22
Military affairs and demands for subsidies	69 / 46 — 115	25.15
Dispatch of commissioners and governors	68	14.87
Favours to individuals	60	13.12
Summons to estates	17	3.71
Commercial affairs		3.28
Miscellaneous	53	11.59
Total	447	99.98

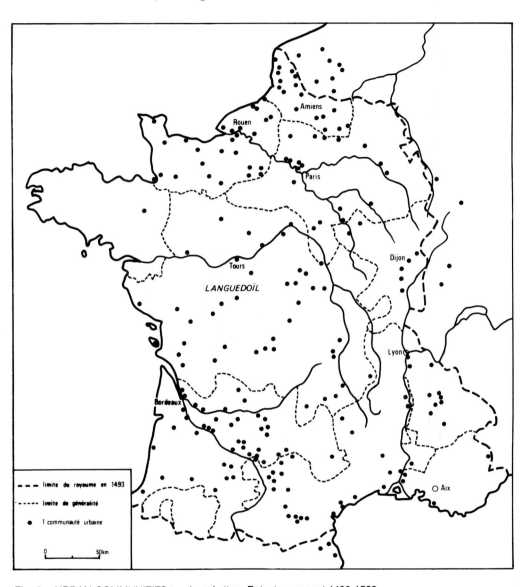

Fig. 1: URBAN COMMUNITIES to whom Letters Patent were sent 1400-1500

practice increased. For the accession of Louis XII in 1498 the relevant volume of the *Ordonnances* (xxi) contains little else than confirmations of urban privileges. As for the geographical distribution of the 256 communities receiving letters patent which are printed in the *Ordonnances*, it falls into two distinct zones. One zone is in the north, stretching from the Cotentin, in north-western Normandy, to the River Aisne; the second, in the south, lies between the Rhône in the south-east, and the Gironde in the south-west. This geographical distribution exactly represents the situation at the start of the fourteenth century, when communities and consulates were created and some were ordered to send representatives to meetings of estates.[21] Nevertheless, not all of these 256 communities can be defined, strictly speaking, as towns; many, especially in Languedoc, were little more than large rural villages.

This impression of the relationship between the King's Council and the towns is confirmed by evidence other than that of letters patent. In 1455 only twelve out of the forty-nine known meetings of the council had a petition from a town on their agenda; in 1484 there were also twelve petitions from towns, but the council in that year met (so far as we know) ninety-two times. Also in 1484 only fourteen recorded items of a total of 1,223 considered by the council concerned the towns. In both 1455 and 1484 such items can, in general, be divided into two categories: (1) the granting of municipal taxes; and (2) conflicts of jurisdiction with local royal officers. Thus the towns were increasingly faced with administrative problems which they could solve only with difficulty. The king and his council hoped to help them by granting their petitions; thus they would enjoy the widest possible scope for manoeuvre. But the statutes of towns not only needed to be clarified and made standard: the system of local finance also had to be reorganized. The council, however, was unaware of the urgency of these problems: it dealt only very occasionally with any aspect of them.

The council rarely asked for advice about petitions from towns. None the less, it considered, especially at the start of a reign, many files which should have been sent to the *Chambre des Comptes*. For such files largely consisted of documents relating to the administration of the royal domain. No doubt they contained information which the council might have used to formulate a policy for the interior. But the evidence for the possible existence of such an over-all administrative vision is insufficient, diverse, and confused. The origins of the 'council of despatches', the body which was created during the seventeenth century to deal with correspondence emanating from within France itself, must be sought elsewhere. If they are to be located and understood, then a reverse movement must be analysed: the motives as well as the methods of the king in council when he took it upon himself to deal with the towns.

2. *Royal and Conciliar Intervention*

Phillipe de Beaumanoir, the renowned feudal jurist of the early fourteenth century, wrote that the king should treat towns in the same way as he treated 'under age minors'.[22] But the king, in fact, had no wish to do that. He did not give his local officers instructions to exercise a form of tutelage; nor were local officers subordinates of the council; nor, indeed, did they have to transmit orders of the council, be responsible to it, and report back. They had, of course, to execute major decisions of general application: through the councils of the *bailliages* or *sénéchaussées* for matters of public order or justice; through the *élus* of the *aides* for extraordinary finances. But although all other measures were addressed to royal officers as *pro-forma* instructions, they saw these measures only when those whom they directly concerned presented them for confirmation.[23] For royal officers in the local-ities remained what they had always been: personal representatives of the king, appointed to maintain his rights and prerogatives and to protect his domain, rather than civil servants entrusted with the task of maintaining public order. They had to check the trustworthiness and the legality of the documents presented to them — not advise whether they be published. It is in this context that the general measure (which was extended even to the *Estates* of Languedoc in 1389)[24] obliging all communities to hold assemblies in the presence of royal representatives should be considered. This is also the proper context of that clause in financial grants which prescribed that account be finalized only under the presidency of a royal representative. Yet despite their duties in these respects, royal officers did not seek to control the affairs of towns. They were merely concerned to ensure their loyalty.

How could it have been otherwise? If an urban community enjoyed wide powers in matters of justice, public order, and finance, royal officers had therefore little scope for action. Moreover, the relations between communities and royal officers were either very limited or liable to give rise to conflict. When conflicts arose, the royal council did not intervene as a superior authority which had to support its subordinates; it acted, instead, as an administrative tribunal arbitrating between two local powers which appeared before it as equals.[25] It ignored the fact that because it was ulti-mately responsible for all decisions being opposed, it could, or ought to have been, a party to such suits.

If a town lacked a proper corporation and consisted, as was often the case, simply of a community of inhabitants, then the king's representatives — all of whom came from notable families in its neighbourhood — parti-cipated in its activities, deliberated constantly with its constituted represen-tatives, and acted as though they, too, were members of the citizen body. In such cases there could be no question of the Crown exercising control or tutelage. Powers in such towns were, in fact, mixed: Tours is a good example.[26] Even the king himself could not always penetrate the institutional 'fog' that resulted from this admixture of powers. Whenever he wished to exercise close control over a town and its affairs, he seldom, if ever, knew whom to contact. Thus when in 1439 Charles VII wanted to compel Rheims to fulfil its military obligations, he wrote to the official principal of the Archbishop rather than to the *échevins*.[27] Often the same royal orders were sent both to the *échevins* and to royal officials. It was as though their respective authorities overlapped. At the same time, however, the original royal letter was addressed to the town itself.[28]

Why did the king and his council act thus? The reason is that neither king nor council was ever particularly concerned with administrative problems. Their interest in the towns was political. *Bonnes villes* possessed ramparts, artillery, and a population capable of being called to arms. Their military power made them partners in government whose help the king had to beseech. They could not be treated as a subject to whom orders were dictated through the hierarchy of authority. The king sought their help and advice, gave them political information, and was anxious to obtain their consent to the measure he proposed. Thus he consulted them by means of general or local assemblies. He did so systematically until 1439; and thereafter, even in Languedoil, with greater frequency than historians usually admit.[29] More often still, he wrote to them. The form of his letters was simple: during the fifteenth century letters 'de par le roi' ('by the king') were signed by the king, countersigned by a secretary, and sealed with the privy seal.[30] A procedure of this kind was simple enough; it lacked the formality associated with the granting of letters patent; it could also create a relationship, almost bordering on confidence, between the king and his *bonnes villes*. Such a relationship could withstand the force of circumstances. Where correspondence between a king and a particular *bonne ville* survives, it reveals the broad outlines of his policy. The royal council usually furthered the king's policy; it also provided an element of continuity.

The main topics of the informal correspondence by letters close from king to his *bonnes villes* differ considerably in subject from those of letters patent. For the years 1461-98, 3,267 missives, or letters close, survive. Only 457, or 13.98 per cent, a small proportion of the total, were sent to towns. This small proportion corroborates the point I made earlier.[31] Allowing for some latitude in classification, and also for the fact that only one subject is allowed for in the classification of each letter, their subjects are as shown in Table 2.

Thus the king wrote, more often than not, to his *bonnes villes* to inform them of victories, to request their help in his military undertakings, or to ask them to receive his representatives. At least 66 per cent of letters close to towns deal with such matters. Royal intervention of this kind was already apparent during the reign of Charles VII;[32] it proceeded systematically thereafter. Its purpose was to give a special administrative status to some towns. The principal ones among them were singled out as being the king's *bonnes villes*.[33]

In provinces where meetings of the estates were regularly held, towns alone provided representatives for the third estate. The nobility, ecclesiastical or lay, alone represented rural France. But things began to change between 1435 and 1450. Charles VII inaugurated, for his army, a system of permanent taxation, based on *aides* and *tailles*. He also reformed the entire military organisation of the kingdom. Local assemblies were therefore rendered useless. Walled towns, the king's *bonnes villes*, had until then been differentiated, whatever their economic or demographic importance, from the countryside.[34] Charles VII gave some a special status. They might be exempted from the *taille* or from the obligation to billet soldiers.[35] Their inhabitants might also be exempted from the vestiges of military or feudal obligation (the *arrière ban*) if they held noble fiefs. At the same time, their *échevins* might, as frequently happened, be ennobled.

Research has yet to be done on such changes. But they appear to have been limited: individual measures were taken in isolated cases and they had no over-all political purpose. How valid is this? If extraordinary taxation and rarely repaid loans are taken as examples, then two points become clear: first, that the king's council decided to raise subsidies and loans only after lengthy deliberation; and, secondly, that it apportioned, among likely contributors, the sums it sought. The council, therefore, must have had a close knowledge not only of which towns were exempt from the *taille* (for these alone paid such taxes),[36] but also of their respective abilities to contribute. The same holds for the billeting of soldiers. The council had to consider which towns were exempt, so that they might be asked to accept, just for the occasion and without prejudice for the future, an abrogation of their privileges. The council also decided the text of circulars designed to provide an 'official' version of events, as well as the timing of their publication.[37] (Such frequent and well-arranged operations ought to have been the concern of a specialized department, which would have kept (as it were) an up-to-date card index of the *bonnes villes*, their particular franchises and attributions, the rates at which they might be taxed for forced loans, and — a fact of the greatest importance to Louis XI — the general state of their fortifications.) Furthermore, it seems clear — though not yet proved — that the Crown's financial officers possessed, for each region, lists of free towns and their financial liabilities. Likewise, the council could readily locate, when it so needed, towns which possessed mints.[38] Nor did the *Chambre des Comptes* lack records which the Crown might use to its advantage. Yet these diverse sources never appear to have been brought together. When the council deliberated about matters of general policy relating to the towns, it could not therefore rely on having full information at its call. It is doubtful whether research among administrative records would modify this peremptory judgement. Why should Pierre Amer, an officer of the *Chambre des Comptes*, have compiled, between 1439 and 1484, a small collection of extracts from its archives, and have thought it necessary to copy, with the greatest possible care, a list of towns which had been made for an assembly of estates held in 1316?[39] Was it because he found nothing more recent to transcribe? How should such a lacuna be interpreted? As I have already said, the routine character and domainial nature of petitions from towns may explain why a special office for their receipt was not created; the lack of administrative links between the council and royal officers in the *bailliages* and *sénéchaussées* may also have made the creation of a specialized secretariat unnecessary.[40] But how could a policy towards the towns, or at least towards some of them, which was so clear and so coherent, be applied without even a small administrative body?

Any attempt to answer this question involves having another look at the correspondence between the king and the towns for the period 1461-98. Two points emerge. First, the correspondence is concerned not with the 256 or so communities which are badly defined in the *Ordonnances*, but only with fifty-three towns, of which thirty-nine were episcopal sees. Secondly, the geographical distribution of their fifty-three towns is significant: the map (fig. 2) reveals a remarkable reversal of perspective, which is even more accentuated if account is taken of the number of letters received by regions.

Chevalier
Table 3

Region	Letters received	%
Lyons	101	22.69
Outre-Seine-et-Yonne, Picardy and Flanders	218	48.98
Languedoil, Burgundy, Normandy	87	19.32
Languedoc, Gascony, Provence	41	8.98
Total	457	99.94

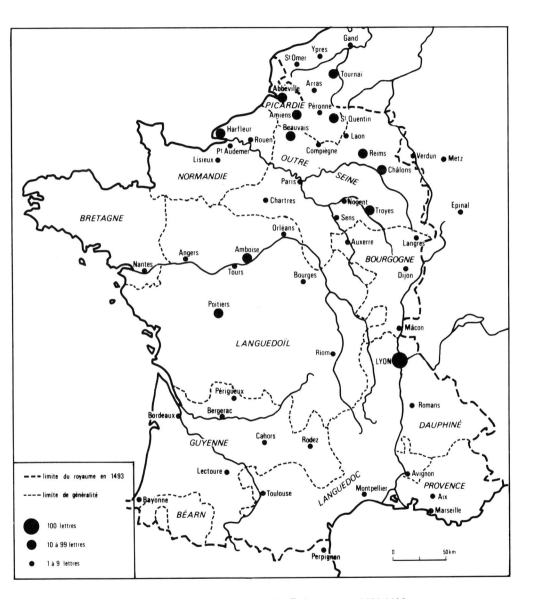

Fig. 2: THE 'BONNES VILLES' to whom letters 'De par le Roi' were sent 1461-1498.

Even allowing for elements of chance in the survival of documents, the result is so clear that the conclusions speak for themselves. Lyons alone received more than a fifth of the known royal letters; while almost half were sent to towns on or near the northern and the north-eastern frontiers. On the other hand, the king maintained little contact, at least by letter, with the south. This may be explained by the fact that estates met regularly in Languedoc, Dauphiné, and even Gascony. Such meetings resulted in a special, and therefore a privileged, means of communication between king and towns; they also provided an excellent way, which Louis XI would greatly have liked to extend, of allocating subsidies. But why did Toulouse preserve only three royal letters for a period of thirty-seven years, Montpellier four, and Bordeaux two? For Rheims preserved forty, Troyes twenty-seven, St Quentin and Tournai twenty-five each, and Amiens twenty-two.

This royal policy which appeared to favour certain *bonnes villes* was certainly not the result of haphazard initiatives designed either to please or to convey illegitimate favours. At the same time, however, royal policy, being the result of political and military needs, was inevitably concerned with events outside France. Its emphasis could not be purely administrative; for during this period the crown was always closely concerned with Picardy and Champagne and thus with the northern and eastern frontiers even when Charles VIII was preoccupied first with Breton, and then with Italian, affairs.

Some *bonnes villes*, however, did not support the Crown simply because they were afraid of external enemies. Their support was forthcoming whenever a coalition of princes jeopardized royal authority. This is a further context in which the letter-writing activities of the king and his council can be seen. Although letters sent to towns represent only about 14 per cent of all royal letters in print, the number of such letters rose sharply during each major political crisis: in 1465, 1477, 1486, and 1492. (It is, of course, difficult to distinguish between internal and external crises because of the anomalous position of the duchy of Burgundy.)

Decisive dramas between the monarchy and the princes were enacted in Languedoil, and more especially in the regions east of the Seine. These regions also experienced the full weight of Burgundian influence, under both Charles the Bold and Maximilian I. In the case of their *bonnes villes*, the Crown was less concerned about their administration than with exhorting them to be loyal, taking military precautions, and obtaining logistic support for its armies. Hence the council's empirical and pragmatic approach to administrations. Its approach matched the geographical divisions of the kingdom — with the exception of Lyons, because of its special political, commercial, and financial standing. The area south of a line running from Poitiers to Dijon contained urban communities as well as local assemblies; it received little attention. But in the area north of that line the council was ever vigilant. Not only did the king often intervene in its affairs. Because he was not hindered by the existence of assemblies, he could maintain a direct as well as a continuous relationship with its towns.

But should account be taken of geography to explain differences of policy? The size of France certainly did not allow for direct contacts readily to be made between the centre and the regions. Yet this point should not be too greatly stressed. During the fifteenth century the king and his council resided in Touraine. Therefore they were no further from Bordeaux or Cahors than from Amiens or Rheims. Likewise, they were no further from Toulouse or Montpellier than from Tournai or Ghent.

The differences between regions are, in fact, illusory. The relationships between the Crown and the *bonnes villes* were never constant, because they depended not only on geography, but on the internal and external crises which the crown faced from time to time. Yet throughout the fifteenth century the Crown made increasing use both of governors and temporary commissioners in the provinces. This made for unity. Royal letters to *bonnes villes* arose from the need of the Crown to support men who already possessed letters of credence. When Charles VII was appealing, with varying degrees of enthusiasm, to regional assemblies, he constantly sent commissioners to *bonnes villes*. His commissioners were responsible not only for steering public opinion and obtaining such help as he sought, but also for reporting on local situations. They were then subsumed into the development of an institution about which little is yet known: that of provincial governors. Heirs to the *lieutenants-généraux* who had been sent *ad hoc* to the provinces at various times during the fourteenth century, governors were first appointed as permanent officials in Languedoil by 1400. During the fifteenth century they progressively established themselves in regions with whose towns the king corresponded. Governors were concerned about exactly the same matters as the king in his letters: loyalty; maintainence of fortifications; logistical support for armies; and speedy payment of subsidies levied in place of the *taille*. Commissioners or governors were not appointed by chance; they were always members of the king's council — though not masters of requests, since the latter were already fully occupied with judicial and administrative routine. They were also men close to the king, and, on their appointment, held honorary posts such as that of royal chamberlain or master of the royal household. Although strictly enjoined to obey them, towns also found that commissioners and governors would speak, as members who possessed right of access, to the king's council on their behalf.[41] Commissioners and governors therefore played several diverse roles simultaneously: as representatives of the king; as privileged spokesmen for the *bonnes villes*; as royal agents more concerned with political than administrative matters. If ever during the fifteenth century the Crown exercised tutelage over the *bonnes villes*, evidence will have to be sought in the correspondence between commissioners and governors and the king and his council. This correspondence should also contain requests forwarded by *bonnes villes*; but such requests are known to have been made less frequently by the end of the fifteenth century.

What degree of control, then, did the king's council exercise over the *bonnes villes* during the fifteenth century? So far as the comings and goings of governors and commissioners were concerned, it was slight. So far as administration was concerned, the Crown allowed the *bonnes villes* increasing independence — independence which they achieved not under the control of local royal officials, but with their assistance. The requests and complaints which the *bonnes villes* forwarded to the Crown through its local officers became less and less concerned with new and embarrassing problems. The only important concern of the Crown was that governors should exercise political control whenever necessary. Specialist financial and military institutions, together with their respective personnel and archives, existed to provide governors with detailed information. Everything else depended on their personal initiative. Such was the system used by the Crown: a nascent centralizing power. The system itself was benevolent, flexible, and reasonably efficient. But it was open to risk, as the troubles of the late sixteenth century were to emphasize. The *bonnes villes* possessed freedom of administration; they also retained virtually all their military powers. Thus they could — and did — connive with provincial governors. As soon as the latter put down roots in the provinces which the Crown had entrusted to their care, they became formidable local potentates.

Notes

1. This pessimistic view stems from A. Luchaire (*Les Communes Françaises* (Paris, 1890)) and H. Sée (*Louis XI et les villes* (Paris, 1891)), but P. Viollet (*Histoire des institutions politiques et administratives de la France* (4 vols, Paris, 1890-1912)) had a clearer understanding of the problem. Yet the approach was only to change with F. Olivier-Martin (*Histoire du droit français des origines à la Révolution* (Paris, 1951), pp. 402-11), who wrote under the influence of 'corporatist' theories synthesized by E. Lousse (*La Société d'ancien régime. Organisation et représentation corporatives* (Paris-Louvain, 1943). More recently J.V. Lemarignier (*La France médiévale; institutions politiques* (Paris, 1970), who on this point rather too closely follows the ideas of Marguerite Boulet-Sautel (*Recueils de la Société Jean Bodin. vi. La Ville* (2 vols, Brussels, 1954-5), i. 371-406), has remarked (p. 305) that local liberties were given their full scope in the fifteenth century; he has also underlined the importance of the notion of the *bonne ville*; but the brevity of his treatment does not allow him fully to make his point. Chevalier, 'La Politique de Louis XI à l'égard des bonnes villes. Le cas de Tours', *M.A.* lxx (1964), 473-503; reprinted in *The Recovery of France in the Fifteenth Century*, ed. P.S. Lewis (London-New York, 1972), pp. 265-93) and *Tours, ville royale, 1356-1520* (Paris-Louvain, 1975) only partly treats of a subject which needs further attention.

2. The council was not a body of final appeal, nor did it keep records of its proceedings. Its work can be understood if the letters patent which it sent out are studied, or at least those brought together in the collections of the *Ordonnances des rois de France de la troisième race* (23 vols, Paris, 1723-1849). As for its proceedings only three fragments of incomplete memoranda survive; drawn up, for its own use, by a secretary who was present at its meetings, and took notes regarding letters which would have to be written. These three fragments cover the months 1 March – 14 June 1455 (fragment of a register of Charles VII's *grand conseil* in N. Valois, *Le Conseil du roi aux XIVe, XVe et XVIe siècles* (Paris, 1888)); 4 March – 24 July 1484 (Valois, 'Le Conseil du roi et le grand conseil pendant la première année du règne de Charles VIII', *B.E.C.* xliii (1882), 594-625; xliv (1883), 137-68, 419-44); and, finally, from early August 1484–24 January 1485 (*Procès-verbaux des séances du conseil de régence du roi Charles VIII pendant les mois d'août 1484 à janvier 1485*, ed. A. Bernier (Paris, 1836)).

3. These figures establish a relative scale: it should be remembered that the totals are only of those letters collected by the editors, and that there is no precise definition of what constituted a town.

4. Practice here had become fixed by the end of the thirteenth century (Viollet, *Histoires des institutions*, iii. 38-41). An example is the case of the count of Sancerre who asked the king to create a town council in his own chief town (*Ordonnances*, xviii. 598).

5. See below, p. 113, or n. 20.

6. The council took little notice of the nature of petitioning communities: for example, the matter-of-fact reference to the people of the lordship of Peyre-en-Gévaudan, in the confirmation of an accord made between them and their lord in 1466, 'as the so-called proctors and syndics of the remaining inhabitants of the said land' (*Ordonnances*, xvi. 501-2).

7. Towns possessed no unity of purpose. None the less they were the sole representatives of the third estate in the meetings of estates. It was in a more restricted regional framework that they showed solidarity of feeling even to the extent, as happened in Languedoc, of presenting grievances together. But P. Dognon (*Les Institutions politiques et administratives du pays de Languedoc du XIIIe siècle aux guerres de religion* (Toulouse, 1895),

pp. 270-83) made it clear that they were concerned almost entirely with the means of apportioning the royal tax. See also G. du Fresne de Beaucourt, *Histoire de Charles VII* (6 vols, Paris, 1881-91), v. 317-19.

8. F. Lot and R. Fawtier, *Histoire des institutions françaises au moyen âge* (3 vols, Paris, 1957-62), ii. 83: N. Valois, *Inventaire des arrêts du conseil d'état (règne de Henri IV)* (2 vols, Paris, 1886-93), i, pp. cxvi-cxvii.

9. 'Eloge de Charles VII' in *Chronique de Charles VII, roi de France, par Jean Chartier*, ed. V. de Viriville (3 vols, Paris, 1858), iii.132. Similarly Thomas Basin, *Histoire de Charles VII*, ed. C. Samaran (2 vols, 2nd edn, Paris, 1964-5) ii. 305-7. See also Beaucourt, *Histoire de Charles VII*, v. 336. For Baude, see M. G. A. Vale, *Charles VII* (London, 1974), p. 142.

10. The report of the representative of Lyons at the Court is particularly illuminating in this respect (Beaucourt, op.cit, iii. 501-9); cf. Lewis, above, p. 37 ff.

11. At Tours, for example (B. Chevalier, 'Pouvoir urbain et pouvoir royal à Tours pendant la guerre de cent ans,' *A. Bret.* lxxxi (1974), 698), help was sought from councillors with local links, as well as from the chancellor. By contrast, Jacques Coeur, who 'protected' Lyons and the big towns of Languedoc at such great cost, was never asked to assist. Albi sought the help of its bishop, Louis d'Amboise, the future cardinal, who was well regarded at the court of Charles VIII (M. Harsgov, 'Recherches sur le personnel du conseil du roi sous Charles VIII et Louis XII' (unpublished thesis, Paris, 1972), p. 951).

12. Letters patent granted 'par le roi', without other qualifications, and issued on the king's own orders without any intermediary, were largely sent to towns. They represent only 1-3 per cent of the total, with a slight increase between 1467 and 1481.

13. On 21 April 1455 the royal officers and the consuls of Montferrand in Auvergne, then in litigation, were heard (Valois, *Le Conseil du roi*, p. 274); so in 1484 were the representatives of Lyons and Bourges, who were then in dispute over the matter of fairs (*Procès-verbaux*, ed. Bernier, p. 155). In both cases, the parties were invited to present their cases in writing.

14. For example, the lord of Esquerdes, governor of Picardy, over Arras (*Procès-verbaux*, ed. Bernier, p. 168).

15. For example, to Montreuil-sur-Mer in 1464, with regard to the town's debts, its revenues, and its administration (*Ordonnances*, xvi. 234).

16. H. Jassemin, *La Chambre des Comptes de Paris au XVe siècle* (Paris, 1933), pp. 227-30.

17. There was no fixed scale of fees for the towns and the flagrant abuse of this system was vigorously denounced at the Estates General of Tours of 1484. A simple confirmation of privileges could be charged at 400 *écus*, of which at least 140 went into the pocket of the secretary; in addition, an equal sum would be payable to his clerk (Jean Masselin, *Journal des états-généraux tenus à Tours en 1484, sous le règne de Charles VIII*, ed. A. Bernier (Paris, 1835), pp. 684-5, 707). In addition, numerous gratuities were payable by delegations seeking to have their petitions presented; thus such proceedings at court could be very expensive.

18. This rule had been made in 1319 (O.Morel, *La Grande chancellerie royale et l'expedition des lettres royaux de l'avènement de Philippe de Valois à la fin du XIVe siècle (1328-1400)* (Paris, 1900), pp. 328-9), but had been so often ignored that a reminder of its existence had to be made as late as 1490 (*Ordonnances*, xx. 284-7).

19. An element of specialization was nevertheless being introduced into the meetings of the council. Thus, on 23 December 1484, nothing was done other than the granting of requests ('pou ledit jour rien ne fut fait que l'expedicion des requestes') since between 14 and 20 December none had been considered, because the council had then been preoccupied with military and financial affairs (*Procès-verbaux*, ed. Bernier, pp. 222, 227). For an example of documents being sent to the 'gens de finances' who were not present in the council, see Valois, *Le Conseil du roi*, p. 274 (10 May 1455).

20. When a town or a region declared that it was perpetually united with the Crown, this meant that henceforward it would recognize the sole authority of the king of France, and not that of any other prince.
21. See the maps published by J. le Goff, 'Ordres mendiants et urbanisation', *Annales E.S.C.* (1970), 933-5.
22. See C. Petit-Dutaillis, *Les Communes françaises. Caractères et évolution des origines au XVIIIe siècle* (Paris, 1947), p. 153.
23. Morel, *La Grande chancellerie royale*, p. 344.
24. Dognon, *Les Institutions politiques*, p. 473.
25. The affair in which the royal officers and the consuls of Montferrand were opposed (27-28 April 1455) is very revealing (Valois, *Le Conseil du roi*, pp. 241 and 263).
26. See, for instance, Chevalier, *Tours, ville royale*, p. 94.
27. Beaucourt, op.cit. iii. 524-5.
28. In 1465, Louis XI wrote 'A noz chierz et bien amez les esleus, maire, eschevins, bourgeois et habitans de nostre ville d'Amiens' (*Lettres de Louis XI, roi de France*, ed. J. Vaesen and E. Charavay (S.H.F., 11 vols, Paris, 1883-1909), ii. 240); and also 'A noz chiers et bien amez les clergie, bourgois et habitans de nostre ville de Troyes et aux lieutenant de nostre bailly, advocat, procureur et receveur de noz aides en ladicte ville' (ibid. ii. 339). A similar letter was sent to Lyons in 1480 (ibid. viii. 129). Charles VIII wrote to the town of Saint-Quentin and to the officers at the mint in 1483 (*Lettres de Charles VIII, roi de France*, ed. P. Pélicier (S.H.F., 5 vols, Paris, 1898-1905) to the lieutenant of the *bailli* and to the corporation of the same town in 1490 (ibid. iii. 104); and to the officials of the town of Troyes in 1494 (ibid. iv. 12).
29. J. Russell Major, *Representative institutions in Renaissance France, 1421-1559* (Madison, 1960), contains much useful information on this subject.
30. G. Tessier (*La Diplomatique royale française* (Paris, 1962), pp. 301-3), shows clearly that in the fifteenth century letters close were to be distinguished from letters missive by their 'mandatory' characteristics, although their outward forms were scarcely distinguishable. The editors of the letters of Louis XI and Charles VIII (see n.28) made no such distinction and called them 'missives', although it is clear that a number are, in fact, letters close. These two collections are an incomparable source of information; but two reservations, especially with regard to the towns, must be made about the way in which they were compiled. The state of preservation of municipal archives was one. Another rises from the method of search the editors adopted. On some occasions they limited themselves to the contents of bundles of letters, but on others extended their search to include registers of deliberations into which many letters had been copied. The results of these two different approaches can be quite considerable, because they give false impressions about the relative richness of particular collections. Unhappily, no such collection exists for the reign of Charles VII. We have to rely on the letters published by Beaucourt (*Histoire de Charles VII*, i. 437-471; iii. 497-537; iv. 444-51; v). 444-56.
31. See above p. 111.
32. An analysis of the letters published by Beaucourt gives a result which only slightly differs from those for the reigns of Louis XI and Charles VIII: demands for subsidies . . . 13 (26.53 per cent); political information . . . 12 (24.48 per cent); military affairs . . . 7 (14.28 per cent); despatch of commissioners . . . 6 (12.24 per cent); summons to estates . . . 5 (10.20 per cent); and miscellaneous . . . 6 (12.24 per cent).
33. In 1473 there appears for the first time in a letter 'de par le roi' the formula 'nostre bonne ville de . . .': 'a noz tres chierz et bien amez les eschevins, bourgois, mannans et habitans de nostre bonne ville et cité d'Amiens' (*Lettres de Louis XI*, v. 150). The use of this formula becomes much more common in 1477-8, the years of crisis over the succession to Burgundy.

34. Originally the term *bonne ville* had no other meaning (G. Mauduech, 'La "bonne" ville: origine et sens de l'expression', *Annales E.S.C.* (1972), 1441-8). Even at the end of the fifteenth century, the council could still use the phrase 'tant villes closes que villaiges' as a general description of such centres (*Procès-verbaux*, ed. Bernier, pp. 156-7).

35. R. Gandilhon, *La Politique économique de Louis XI* (Paris, 1941), p. 286; P. Contamine, *Guerre, état et société à la fin du moyen âge. Etudes sur les armées des rois de France, 1337-1494* (Paris-The Hague, 1972), p. 494.

36. 'Et pour ce que les habitans des villes, lieux et plat pais de nostre royaume, con-tribuables a noz tailles ont este et sont oppressez . . . nous avons, par l'advis et deliberacion des gens de nostre conseil et de noz finances, ordonne faire lever certaine grant somme, qu'il nous convient promptement recouvrer sur les bonnes villes . . .' (*Lettres de Louis XI*, vii. 155 (1478)). Charles VIII spoke of the 'taux' applied upon the *bonnes villes* (*Lettres de Charles VIII*, iii. 265). See also ibid. iv. 117; v. 25.

37. Fifteen of the 150 letters sent by Charles VIII to the towns were circulars. The same could almost certainly be said of those letters which were intended to carry news or to make demands of a fiscal nature on all the free *bonnes villes*. This is clearly reflected in the letters published in *Lettres de Louis XI*, x. 37-45. They concern a circular publicizing the peace of Arras of December 1482. Four versions are extant, sent respectively to Senlis (on 18 December), to Compiègne (on 22 December), to Chalon on 26 December), and to Lyons (on 27 December). The texts, however, are not absolutely identical. Secretaries perhaps noted the message to be conveyed in general terms, as well as those to whom the letters were to be sent: the work was then shared, but the variants in the respective texts suggest that each secretary enjoyed a certain liberty of action.

38. Twenty-four towns possessed mints in 1484 (*Procès-verbaux*, ed. Bernier, p. 211).

39. C.H. Taylor, 'Assemblies of French towns in 1316', *Speculum*, xiv (1939), 273-99.

40. See above, p. 112; also Lewis, above, p. 42.

41. Such interventions are difficult to trace because the proceedings of the council barely survive. But in 1471 the lord of Castelnau, who had been sent into Rouergue to counter the rebellion of the count of Armagnac, transmitted the complaints of Rodez to the Crown and added the full weight of his support to them (*Lettres de Louis XI*, x. 317-18; Sée, *Louis XI et les villes*, pièce justificative xiii, p. 395).

7

The Relations between the Towns of Burgundy and the French Crown in the Fifteenth Century

André Leguai

In the fifteenth century the duchy of Burgundy did not include the whole of Burgundy west of the river Saône, but only the Dijonnais, the Beaunois, the Chalonnais, the Autunois, the Auxois, and the *bailliage* of Châtillon (sur-Seine) which was then known as the region of 'La Montagne'. Other regions, such as the Charolais, the Mâconnais and the Auxerrois, although Burgundian, did not form part of the duchy. To the east of the Saône, on the other hand, with the lands of 'Outre-Saône' which came under the *bailliage* of Chalon, the borders of the duchy extended to those of the Empire. It is not easy to say exactly which centres, even within this well-defined territory, deserve to be called towns. An arbitrary, if not necessarily exclusive, list may include those places which regularly sent representatives to the meetings of the Estates of Burgundy: Dijon, Autun, Avallon, Beaune, Chalon, Châtillon, Montbard, and Semur.[1] To these, for purposes of this study, may be added Auxonne, a town situated geographically within the Empire but in fact part of a small *comté* which belonged to the duke of Burgundy, until at least 1477 when, according to a document of Charles VIII's reign, it became part of the duchy while preserving its own distinctive estates, before reverting to the status of a *comté* under Louis XII. Auxonne was to play an important role in the difficult period 1477-9.[2]

On the death of Philippe de Rouvres in 1361, the duchy of Burgundy ceased to be a patrimonial fief, and was attached once more to the royal domain. It became an 'apanage' of the French Crown when John II granted it to Philip the Bold, one of his younger sons, in 1363 — though the term 'apanage' was not used explicitly in documents until about fifteen years later.[3] When tracing the evolution of the relations between the towns of the duchy of Burgundy and the Crown in the fifteenth century, three periods may be distinguished: (1) the ducal period, which lasted until the

E

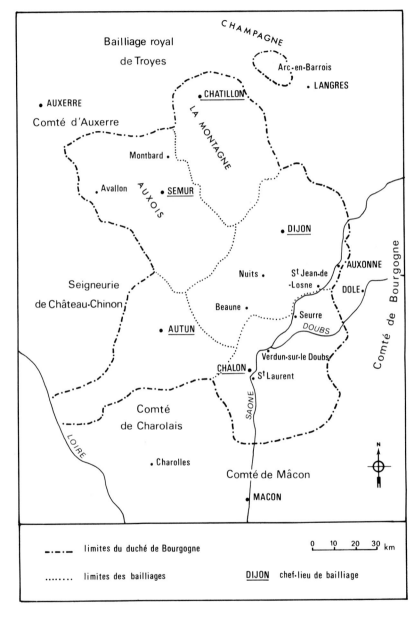

THE DUCHY OF BURGUNDY IN THE 15th CENTURY

death of Charles the Bold in 1477; (2) the period of the reunification of the duchy to the royal domain between 1477 and 1479; and (3) that of the duchy subjected to the king from 1479 onwards.

Before 1477, even during those periods when Philip the Good was allied to the king of England or Charles the Bold was in open conflict with Louis XI, the towns of the duchy never forgot that they were ultimately dependent on the Crown of France. Except for the brief period 1471-7, they recognized the reality of the duchy's subjection to the kingdom, even if many inhabitants were far from agreeing with a man from Dijon who in 1465 proclaimed publicly that the king had ultimate authority within all the lands of the duchy, and that the duke was more closely subject to the king than his own servants were to the duke himself.[4] This, however, did not prevent the Burgundians from showing mistrust and hostility towards those whom they called 'les Français', even during those periods when no cause for dissension existed between them. Thus, in 1424, four years after the treaty of Troyes, Odinette de Champdivers, a former mistress of Charles VI, who was then living in Dijon, was accused together with a Franciscan friar of providing Charles VII with information about the defences of the towns of Burgundy and the raising of forces within the duchy.[5] Later, in September 1434, only a year before the treaty of Arras, certain natives of Grancey and Langres, who were then in Dijon, were requested to leave the town ('vuider la ville') forthwith.[6] Even in March 1454, during a period of calm, one Jean le Paveur could say: 'I am not the first Frenchman to whom things have been done (here)', adding that although he himself had obviously not suffered in this way, 'men have been killed and drowned in this town', and concluding with a final 'You hate them, the French'.[7] In November 1468 one Catherine Vyon abused a man who, like her, was a subject of the duke by calling him a 'François' — 'François' in the context being clearly intended as an insult.[8]

Yet until 1471, when they took a sudden turn for the worse, the relations between Charles the Bold and Louis XI had been at least courteous. Thus the records of town council meetings at Dijon show that the mayor's clerk always referred to 'our lord the king';[9] the town's magistrates continued to observe the custom of making gifts to persons of royal blood, and of freeing criminals in their honour, on their first arrival in Dijon;[10] orders concerning Beaune were issued in the name of Charles VI;[11] and Monin d'Echenon and Jean Aubert represented Dijon at an assembly of notables, somewhat inappropriately termed an assembly of 'estates', held at the Hôtel Saint-Pol in Paris in April 1411, to suggest measures to put an effective end to the military preparations of the duke of Orléans and to force him to seek peace.[12] In the years which followed this assembly the Dauphin Louis, duke of Guyenne, and after him Charles VI, both wrote to the inhabitants of Dijon.[13] From these relatively insignificant facts two conclusions emerge.

First, in spite of the very independent policies pursued by the dukes of Burgundy themselves, not only did the royal administration regard the towns of Burgundy as part of the kingdom, but they, too, saw themselves as such. Indeed they never believed that they belonged to anybody outside the kingdom of France. Nor did the dukes, with the exception of Charles the Bold in the very last years of his rule, think otherwise. The fact that on several occasions they came to control the royal government, directly or indirectly, (something in which only Charles the Bold was never involved) confirmed this, both in their own minds and in those of their subjects within the duchy. Secondly, successive kings of France, and their councillors, always considered that the duchy of Burgundy was, in a phrase of Louis XI in 1477, part of 'la couronne de France', just as were, or had been, the lands held as 'apanages' by the dukes of Berry, Orléans, or Bourbon.

The relations between the Burgundian towns and the Crown would scarcely be worth studying on the basis of such facts. More fundamental is the question of the extent to which the royal administration interfered in the affairs of the towns of the duchy. With regard to financial matters, the reply is clear enough. Ever since the time of Philip the Bold, the towns had been exempted from royal taxation, which was raised only within the royal enclaves in the dioceses of Autun and Chalon, neither of which included any towns. Moreover after the treaty of Arras of 1435, these enclaves had only a theoretical existence and in 1476 were suppressed by Charles the Bold on his own authority.[14]

On the other hand, the towns of the duchy never ceased to be subject to royal justice except, for limited periods, on the unilateral initiative of the dukes of Burgundy, when the crown certainly made no renunciation of its sovereign rights.[15] According to the 'Coutume de Châtillon', drawn up by a *bailli* of La Montagne about 1371, appeals to the *Parlement* of Paris should only have been possible from judgements handed down by the *Grands Jours* of Beaune, which were regarded as a *Parlement*. Its author could state: 'Appeals in Burgundy procede by due order, namely from *prévôt* to *bailli*, from *bailli* to *auditeurs* at Beaune, from these *auditeurs* to the *Parlement* of Beaune, and there suits are terminated.'[16] The right to appeal was denied to criminals who had either confessed or had been caught red-handed, to heretics, and to those found guilty of rape or treason. In practice, however, certain litigants continued to appeal directly from the judgement of a *bailli* to the *Parlement* of Paris, thereby omitting the intervening procedures. At the end of the fourteenth century Philip the Bold tried, but without conspicuous success, to counter this tendency,[17] which was a cause of dissatisfaction to the towns since their officers were men of relatively low judicial rank. Litigants unwilling to accept their judgements should normally have appealed to the ducal *bailli* or to the court of appeal at

Beaune; but some chose to appeal directly to the *Parlement* of Paris. In their view, appeals made to France had the advantage of taking cases before judges foreign to the duchy who were likely to be more impartial than local magistrates. In addition, since it was possible to make several successive 'appelacions', valuable time could thus be won since an appeal had the effect of suspending a judgement. The *Parlement*, however, was encumbered by such appeals, and became dilatory in dealing with them.[18] Thus in 1464, a Dijon merchant, Jean Douhet, was able to delay for more than a year the application of a sentence made earlier against him, thereby saving his goods from confiscation. Accused of an 'outrage at night in the house' of a ducal secretary, he had, under a series of pretexts, made four such 'appelacions' to escape the vengeance of his victim and the rigours of the law applied by the municipal magistrates.[19] The municipality tried unsuccessfully to prevent appeals by various means,[20] including the proposal of an agreement to be made between the litigating parties.[21]

Normally, however, appellants did accept such measures. The towns could not prevent the intervention of the officers of the *Parlement* sent to Dijon to apply the judgements of the Parisian court. Sometimes such officers might be officers of the *Parlement* itself; but more often they were officers or *prévôts* from a neighbouring royal jurisdiction, like those of the *bailli* of Sens or of the *prévôt* of Villeneuve-le-Roy.[22] Royal representatives, who even had the right to execute distraints, not only came to bring and carry out the court's judgements: they also sometimes claimed prisoners who had lodged appeals and who were detained by the civil administration in the town's prisons, before taking them to the *Conciergerie* in Paris.[23]

The towns resigned themselves to royal interference. It appears to have been more frequent in Dijon than elsewhere, perhaps because it was the duchy's capital.[24] The civil administration did its best to provide royal representatives with conditions favourable for completing their work. In 1466 the deputy of the *procureur-syndic* initiated proceedings against persons unknown who had removed the royal arms attached to the door post of a house from which the royal officers had issued writs.[25] But the representatives of the crown could in no way prejudice the rights and privileges of a town. The officers of several royal jurisdictions — *Parlement* and *baillis* — who were obliged to discuss judgements always sought the cooperation of *serjents* of the town, or at least gave early assurance of their intention of respecting its prerogatives.[26]

Even those towns which saw, with a certain displeasure, their citizens having recourse to the justice of the *Parlement* of Paris were themselves sometimes obliged to seek its arbitration. In the course of conflicts between rival jurisdictions one party might decide to appeal to the king's justice rather than to that of the duke of Burgundy. At the beginning of the fifteenth century, for example, a suit was pending before the *Parlement* 'aux jours de Sens et de Champagne' to determine whether claimants from Dijon or from Talant should exercise jurisdiction over two mills located between the two towns.[27] In a similar way the royal court intervened in legal conflicts between Beaune and the house of the Hospitallers there;[28] between Beaune and the bishop of Autun;[29] between Dijon and the lord of Sombernon or the Sainte-Chapelle;[30] and, on occasion, even between Dijon and the duke of Burgundy himself.[31] Of the towns of the duchy, Dijon certainly found itself obliged to maintain paid advocates and proctors before the *Parlement*. At the beginning of Louis XI's reign the proctor was Michel de Pons, a man known to and well regarded by the king; he later became *procureur-général* in the *Parlement* of Paris.[32]

Yet the *Parlement* did not have a definite and consistent policy towards the towns of Burgundy. Nor was the court systematically hostile to them: rather the opposite.[33] Hostility is recorded only once: in the last years of the fourteenth century, at the very time when Philip the Bold, then in conflict with Dijon, was himself in control of royal policy.[34] But, in general, appeals to France annoyed the dukes, and their hostility increased as they came to act more and more independently of the Crown. On two occasions, indeed, they tried to put an end to appeals. The first occasion was in 1422, when the *Parlement* of Paris was an organ of the Lancastrian kingdom of France; it is likely to have been ineffective,[35] and, in any case, the treaty of Arras in 1435 restored the *status quo*. The second occasion was on 12 November 1471, when Charles the Bold reasserted Burgundian independence. A year earlier an assembly of nobles, meeting at Tours, had declared Louis XI to be freed ('quitte et délié') of the terms of the treaty of Péronne (1468). The duke fell back upon one of the clauses of the treaty which stated that both he and his subjects would be freed from dependence upon the king if its terms were not fully implemented; he therefore solemnly declared that all the inhabitants of the duchy should, in future, take their appeals before the ducal council in Dijon rather than before the *Parlement* of Paris.[36] This was an important decision, for between 1471 and 1478 the relations between the towns of Burgundy and the Crown of France were ruptured. In documents the title 'king of France' was no longer followed by the description 'notre sire';[37] royal officers living in Dijon either ceased to exercise their functions[38] or left; and the collector of the town's revenues no longer paid sums which had hitherto been made over to the proctor in the *Parlement* of Paris since the latter was regarded as being of 'le party contraire de monseigneur le duc'.[39]

This was rather an exceptional period in the history of the towns of Burgundy: one which coincided with the attempts of Charles the Bold to create from his possessions a unity outside, as well as foreign to, the kingdom of France. Yet Dijon, Châtillon, Semur, and Montbard continued to preserve their links with the kingdom. Unlike Chalon and Autun they were all situated in the diocese of Langres whose bishop was a peer ('pair') of France and a direct vassal of the Crown. Langres had been a royal bishopric since Carolingian times. In 1471 its bishop was Gui Bernard, a native of Touraine, a protégé of the king and, for the past two years, chancellor of the Order of St Michael, a man who was to play an important role at the time of the reunification of Burgundy to the kingdom. His representative in Dijon was his 'scelleur' who claimed jurisidiction over all cases involving clerks, and who also maintained that only the church court at Langres could initiate proceedings in cases of heresy and witchcraft.[40] Although in normal times neither the bishop nor his officers could be regarded as representatives of the French Crown, in difficult ones their position caused them to act, albeit unconsciously, as its agents. Furthermore any appeals stemming from disputes between the towns of the duchy and the official-principal of Langres had always been referred to the court of the archbishop of Lyons, itself within the kingdom. Thus all ecclesiastical cases concerning the Burgundian capital were settled in the kingdom and by subjects of the king.[41]

Even when relations between France and Burgundy were harmonious, the duke's subjects never completely trusted royalty — a long-term effect, perhaps, of King John II's attempt at annexation between 1361 and 1363. The towns, notably Dijon and Beaune, displayed their distrust in 1420-1, at the very time when the royal government, acting in the name of Charles VI, and Duke Philip the Good were acting in unison. In 1420, after the negotiations which led to the treaty of Troyes, Charles VI requested the towns of the duchy to undertake to obey his designated successor, Henry V of England, after his own death: 'You shall swear that the mighty and powerful prince Henry, king of England, is (truly) governor of the kingdom of France; . . . that you shall in all humility obey him in all matters; . . . you shall also swear that after the decease of Charles, your sovereign, you shall obey the king of England as true king of France and, after him, his heirs in perpetuity.' The oath was taken, but with reservations. 'It is determined', reads the register of deliberations of the corporation of Dijon, 'that among other things it shall not be agreed that the people of Dijon shall become liege men of the king of England as king of France, *nor of any others* except our said lord the duke and his successors as dukes of Burgundy.' The passage in my italics is of great importance, for it strongly suggests that it was not hostility towards the king of England as such which motivated the people of Dijon, but rather a fear of no longer being subjects of the king of France. It required a personal visit from Philip the Good before the towns would yield on this point.[42] Under the rule of Charles the Bold, without always approving or understanding his policies, and in spite of a general weariness, the towns of the duchy remained consistently faithful to him, took part, in spite of complaints, in the defence of the duchy, and energetically sought out the spies and secret agents of Louis XI.[43]

This explains why the towns of Burgundy were not enthusiastic about the presence of French soldiers in the duchy after the death of Charles the Bold. The soldiers were preceded by Charles d'Amboise, governor of Champagne, and Gui Bernard, the duke-bishop of Langres, who both made their entry into Dijon on 12 January 1477, only a week after the battle of Nancy. If, during this very early phase of the reunification, there were a few signs that some of the nobility were willing to resist, the towns, by contrast, followed the example of Dijon, led by the *chambre de ville* and the new mayor, Etienne Berbisey, and submitted quite readily.[44] The town's representatives took part in the meeting of the estates which began in Dijon on 25 January and culminated with the making of the treaty with the king's envoys. The towns, among others, received confirmation of their rights and privileges as they had existed at the time of Philip the Good. Symbolically, the president of the council of Burgundy[45] handed over to the royal commissioners the keys of the town of Dijon; these were returned to Mayor Berbisey who promised to keep the town faithful to the king against all-comers. Representatives of Dijon, bearing copies of the town's charters and written instructions 'concerning the increase of the rights and privileges of the town before the king', were among those who took part in the 'great embassy' sent to Louis XI. Then, on 1 February 1477, royal soldiers, who had until then been bivouacked outside the walls, entered Dijon.[46]

The estates of the county of Burgundy, in their turn, treated with the king's representatives on 18 February. Only the problem of Auxonne and of the lands of the duchy 'Outre-Saône' remained. Their estates, separate from the remainder of the duchy, met at Dôle in the county of Burgundy; the representatives of Auxonne took the lead. Those who came from 'Outre-Saône' recognized the king's sovereignty, but they sent envoys to Mary of Burgundy, the daughter and heiress of Charles the Bold.

At the beginning, therefore, the towns of the duchy presented a united front to the French Crown. They were ready to make a proper submission to the royal authority, but coupled it with a desire, perhaps sincere, to safeguard the rights of the Duchess Mary. Then, early in March, the situation changed. Auxonne and Saint-Jean-de-Losne, encouraged by the example of the neighbouring county, rebelled. In the eyes of Mary of Burgundy these lands could never be dependent upon the Crown of France, even if it should be admitted that the king possessed rights over the duchy, since they were situated outside the kingdom.[47] Thenceforward, the towns of Burgundy were to be divided.

The revolts which took place in the duchy need not be recorded in detail.[48] The role of the towns, however, is significant. Two points largely explain their attitude. First, in Dijon and Chalon, at least the 'menu peuple' were antagonistic towards the ruling oligarchies of merchants and lawyers. They did not perhaps feel any 'Burgundian sentiment', but they were none the less shocked by the rapid and self-seeking attachment of the bourgeois to the new rulers and the oligarchy of merchants and lawyers who controlled the towns. The oligarchies were anxious, above all, to preserve, even under new masters, the social position and privileges which they had previously enjoyed. Secondly, there was a rivalry between the three main towns of the duchy, Dijon, Beaune, and Chalon, especially between Beaune, where the ducal *Parlement* sat, and Dijon, where the council of Burgundy met. Their mayors and magistrates, especially in the early years of the reunification, did all that they could to seek royal favours for their respective towns. Although after the death of Charles the Bold contacts were established between the three towns, the magistrates of Beaune and Chalon were the victims of what J. R. de Chevanne has called an unworthy and surprising comedy. For they received from the mayor and *chambre de ville* of Dijon a copy of letters sent on behalf of Jean de Cleves and the prince of Orange, the leaders of the revolt in the county of Burgundy, inviting them also to rebel. At the same time, Dijon asked Beaune and Chalon to state their attitude to de Cleves and Orange's proposals, while warning George de la Trémoille, the governor of Burgundy, of the questions it had asked its neighbours. Chalon and Beaune fell into the trap when they received a letter from La Trémoille informing them of the negative response which Dijon had already conveyed to de Cleves and Orange. Their feelings must have been bitter.[49]

Thus if the towns of Burgundy reacted against the Crown, they did so without co-ordination. For two years Auxonne took part in the revolt in the county of Burgundy; its participation cost it dear, in payments made to the German mercenaries of the prince of Orange, in payments to the garrison of Dôle and the governor of Auxonne, Claude de Vaudrey, as well as in the cost of receiving many refugees from the neighbouring countryside.[50] The corporation and the large majority of the bourgeoisie of Dijon, on the other hand, remained faithful to the king.[51] In June 1477, however, there occurred an outbreak of popular violence (the 'mutemaque'). It lasted two days and cost the life of Jean Jouard, the president of the council of Burgundy, who had played a leading part in the submission of the duchy to the crown. Violent but badly managed, the 'mutemaque' caused alarm among the bourgeoisie, although order was restored by the *chambre de ville* with the help of soldiers sent at once by George de la Trémoille. Claude de Vaudrey, who had come from Auxonne to encourage and lend it practical assistance, was chased out of town.[52] The result at Chalon was, it seems, a token one: the inhabitants, and even the *échevins*, made contact with the supporters of Mary of Burgundy, but did no more. The violence at Dijon perhaps made the *échevins* of Chalon more wary. They may also have been more ready to maintain order because royal officers visited Chalon twice, and La Trémoille personally intervened.[53] Although incited to rebel and threatened by the king's enemies, both Beaune and Tournus remained faithful throughout 1477, as did the other towns of the duchy.

After 25 April 1478 Beaune, Châtillon, Semur, Seurre, Verdun-sur-le-Doubs, and other towns actively participated in a revolt which affected a large part of the duchy:[54] the Auxois, the Châtillonais, the Morvan, the Beaunois, and part of the Val de Saône. This revolt clearly had something in common with events which had occurred in the county of Burgundy; but it did not possess the characteristics of the 'mutemaque' in Dijon, noble leadership, or even noble participation as had the revolt in the county and in the Charolais. It was largely a revolt of the urban bourgeoisie, a class which not only adhered to the notion of an independent Burgundy, but which was influenced, in all probability, by self-interest. This was almost certainly the case at Beaune. Its participation in the wine trade had suffered from Louis XI's policy of advancing the interests of the fairs at Lyons.[55] Beaune, indeed, was in difficulty, and the failure of the revolt was to accelerate its decline.[56] But Chalon, Autun and Nuits, all close to Beaune, remained quiet. Dijon even contributed to the collapse of the revolt. The king's men held it well. The most active participants of the Burgundian cause had either been exiled or had gone, indeed, had been executed after the 'mutemaque'. The *chambre de ville* therefore supported the new régime — that of the Crown — as also did the officers of the *Chambre des Comptes* and the council of Burgundy. Dijon thus did not support towns in revolt: it was also a base from which the royal army could operate. Its foundries busily produced munitions; it also provided conscripted pioneers to help when the king's forces besieged Beaune.[57]

The towns of the duchy in revolt were obliged to capitulate one after the other. They had enjoyed little support from the county of Burgundy as a whole; they had also been left to their own devices by Maximilian of Austria, the husband of Mary of Burgundy. The fall of Semur in June 1478, followed by that of Châtillon, led to the surrender of the smaller towns of the Auxois, the Châtillonnais, and those on the border of the Morvan. Verdun-sur-le-Doubs surrendered shortly afterwards; and Beaune, on 2 July.[58] But Auxonne held out until June 1479; it capitulated only when no help was forthcoming after a siege of ten days.[59] The king's army destroyed Dôle; this example was not lost on other towns. The whole of the duchy of Burgundy thus became subject to the Crown of France.

Thenceforward the Crown took the initiative in its relations with the towns of the duchy. The towns themselves had to take stock of their new situation. But they still found it possible on occasion to resist the royal will. Louis XI tried to reward the towns of Burgundy which had served him best at the expense of those which had rebelled. His policy could only exacerbate jealousies and increase resentment, thereby further aggravating existing divisions. He may have wanted to achieve this. The case of Beaune and Dijon is a typical example. The *Parlement* of Beaune was abolished in 1480 when a royal *Parlement* of Burgundy was established at Dijon. Thus, at a stroke, everyone's motives for making appeals to France were ended. Burgundian particularism was satisfied, but without prejudice to the king's justice.[60] At the same time, Beaune was deprived of its court of appeal; its powers were given to *baillis*, now royal officers.[61]

Louis XI's policy was not only variable, but also at times contradictory. He was influenced by two considerations: first, by a wish to rally the towns around the Crown; and secondly, by fear of seeing new troubles arise. He therefore wanted to be benevolent, but at the same time he was self-seeking and vigilant. He showed his benevolence as early as August 1477, only two months after the failure of the 'mutemaque', in Dijon when he confirmed the town's privileges. Not only did he confirm the privileges of Dijon: he also freed its inhabitants from all conditions and restrictions which had earlier been imposed by the dukes of Burgundy.[62] Two years later, in July 1479, in answer to an invitation extended to him by the *chambre de ville*, he visited Dijon; he received a warm welcome, and yet again confirmed the town's privileges. For their part the mayor and *chambre de ville* swore to be the king's good, loyal, and obedient subjects, and to defend his rights against all.[63] But on this occasion there was a minimum of ceremony. The king chose to stay in a private house near the town wall which, it was said, had a postern giving access to the countryside.[64] Although Dijon had shown him loyalty in times of difficulty, it had nevertheless witnessed a popular rebellion. Furthermore, it had been the capital of the dukes of Burgundy. Why should he not have been suspicious?

Louis XI was certainly vigilant. In 1480, for instance he learned that Autun, which remained neutral during the reunification, had appointed François Rolin as its captain. Rolin, as a document emanating from Autun itself shows, was a member of the king's household and was in receipt of a royal pension; he was also a nephew of Cardinal Rolin who had once enjoyed the favour of the dukes of Burgundy. Louis XI therefore despatched to Autun a master of requests, Philippe Baudot, a Burgundian who was full of zeal for his new master. The people of Autun, surprised and annoyed by this move, were obliged to accept a new captain, Antoine de Lamet, *bailli* of Autun and Montcénis, and the town's apologies had to be conveyed to the king's representatives.[65] However, when, in 1482, the corporation of Dijon wished to appoint as captain of their town Robert Vyon, whose brother, Chrétiennot, had been one of the leaders of the 'mutemaque', Jean Baudricourt, governor of Burgundy, and Jean d'Amboise, the duke-bishop of Langres, imposed a veto.[66] Following the same policy the king ordered costly castles to be built in Dijon, Beaune, and Auxonne.[67] Although, from the time of the treaty of Arras (1482) onwards, the duchy of Burgundy became a frontier region and Auxonne, in particular, was called upon to play an important part in withstanding any attack which the Imperialists might launch, the building of these castles, which continued after Louis XI's death, had been decided on beforehand. Their chief *raison d'être* was, therefore, as much to oversee the towns and to resist any threat of rebellion as to assure the defence of the duchy.[68] The danger against which the king was trying to guard by such measures was indeed present even if his naturally suspicious temperament tended to exaggerate it. For there existed in the duchy's towns a hard core of unyielding opposition. It was founded upon nostalgia for the past, fanned by the victims of purges and repression which had followed the revolts, and aided by those whose material interests had been affected by the presence of French administrators and French soldiers. If, out of self-interest and in appreciation of reality, rather than out of conviction, civic notables had, more often than not, rallied to the new régime, their actions had been neither approved nor shared by all town dwellers.[69] This situation was to develop beyond the reign of Louis XI: during that of Charles VIII some of the bourgeoisie of Dijon were to become involved in a plot inspired by Jean de Jaucourt, lord of Villarnoul who, in 1478, had led the revolt in Auxois.[70]

The efforts and hopes of the opposition were, however, destined to fail. The end of an era had been reached, and the towns of Burgundy were to follow a destiny common to all the towns of the kingdom. Some sent representatives to the assemblies of the *bonnes villes* which Louis XI liked to consult;[71] both Dijon and Beaune were represented at the *Estates* of Tours in 1484, the first such meeting in the history of the kingdom to deserve the name of 'Estates General'.[72] Both Charles VIII and Louis XII made solemn entries into Dijon, Chalon and Auxonne, confirming the privileges of each as Louis XI had already done for Dijon in 1479.[73] In 1501 Louis XII even restored to the *vicomté* of Auxonne its former title of *comté*.[74] But the coinage of Burgundy, from the time of Louis XI onwards, was modelled upon the royal coinage.[75] At the beginning of 1481 a regular system of messengers was organized at Dijon to establish a direct link with Plessis-les-Tours where the king resided.[76] The towns paid the royal taxes and billeted soldiers, especially during the Italian wars.[77] Above all, they had constantly to watch against the encroachments of royal officers; their only hope was in the arbitration of the king himself whose personal authority was bound to grow the more often he intervened. Once again the evidence for Dijon is very clear. Under Louis XI, the governor of Burgundy claimed to try cases of treason; the soldiery became accustomed to arrest suspects with no proper regard for municipal jurisdictions;[78] and both the royal *bailli* and *procureur-général* attempted to limit the extent of such jurisdictions. As early as 1478, Guillaume Cheval, formerly *procureur* to the duke and now in the service of the Crown, announced publicly ('a haulte voix' and 'tant qu'il pouvoit parler') that the town was no longer its own mistress, that the king was sovereign, and that the town did not possess the powers which it thought it did.[79] All the Crown's agents, from the governor of Burgundy to the most humble officer, strove to reduce the effective powers of the municipality.

At the beginning of Charles VIII's reign a'more serious threat arose. It was to the very existence of the *Parlement* of Burgundy whose creation had only just been properly recognized by the *Parlement* of Paris. Once more the old rivalry between Dijon and Beaune was to be important. At first the king agreed to give the *Parlement* back to Beaune, and its first session was held there on 2 January 1485. In the following year, however, he abolished it, a decision which caused the *estates* of Burgundy to agitate for its re-establishment. This was achieved when the *Parlement* was set up, yet again in Beaune, only for it to be transferred three years later to Dijon where it survived until the Revolution.[80] As a result Dijon gained a supremacy over her rivals, especially Beaune, which she had never enjoyed under the dukes. Endowed with the *Chambre des Comptes* and playing host to the *Estates* of Burgundy which the Crown had confirmed and regularized, Dijon assumed the position of the capital of Burgundy, coming to dominate, both socially and administratively, what was to become a 'province'. Following the lead of Dijon, the towns of Burgundy, in spite of some bitterness and regrets as well as not infrequent minor brushes with the royal administration, were thenceforward to remain faithful to the Crown just as, before 1477, they had been faithful to their dukes.

Notes

1. J.-C. Chaton, 'Le Personnel administratif et l'entourage ducal sous Philippe le Hardi duc de Bourgogne, 1363-1404' (unpublished thesis, Dijon, 1975), p. 125. All these cited by me can be consulted at the University Library, Dijon. On the towns under the Capetian dukes, see J. Richard, *Les Ducs de Bourgogne et la formation du duché, du XIème au XIVème siècle* (Paris, 1954), p. 340.

2. See P. Camp, *Histoire d'Auxonne au moyen âge* (Dijon, 1961), p. 78. In letters dated 17 December 1495, Charles VIII claimed that Auxonne was 'de notre duché de Bourgogne et en icelui ressortissant' (Arch. Mun. Auxonne, *liasse* 37).

3. See A. Leguai, 'A Propos de la succession de Bourgogne en 1361', *A.B.* xl (1968), 67-69 (with bibliography).

4. '. . . le Roy avoit à cognoistre par tout le pais de Monseigneur de Bourgogne, et que mondit seigneur de Bourgogne estoit plus subject du Roy' (Arch. Dép. Côte d'Or, B.II 360/9 (Inquiry of 11 June 1465)).

5. C. Joly, 'Dijon sous le principat de Philippe le Bon' (unpublished thesis, Dijon, 1974), pp. 28-29.

6. Ibid., p. 28, citing Arch. Mun. Dijon, B 154, fo. 52ᵛ (17 September 1434). Langres, which supported the Burgundians from 1417 until 1434, then went over to Charles VII under the influence of the lord of Châteauvillain (M. Guyard, 'Langres pendant la Guerre de Cent Ans (1417-1435). Les Langrois "Bourguignons" ou "Armagnacs"?', *Les Cahiers Haut-Marnais*, no. 80 (1965), 1-26).

7. Joly, 'Dijon sous . . . Philippe le Bon', p. 28, citing Arch. Dép. Côte d'Or, B.II 360/6, fo. 679 (3 March 1454): 'vous les haissez bien les François'.

8. Arch. Dép. Côte d'Or, BII 360/11 (Inquiry of 4 November 1468).

9. E.g., Arch. Mun. Dijon, B. 163, fo. 28; B. 164, fo. 86.

10. E.g., Arch. Mun. Dijon, B. 161, fo. 147ᵛ; B. 162, fo. 32. Cf. A. Voisin, 'Autour d'une election de maire à Dijon sous Philippe le Bon', *A.B.* xiii (1941), 104-8.

11. Arch. Mun. Beaune, *Carton* 51, *parchemin* 49, and C. 94, fo. 25. See R. Peuvot, 'La Commune de Beaune de 1202 à 1478' (unpublished thesis, Dijon, 1970), p. 145.

12. *Correspondance de la Mairie de Dijon*, ed. J. Garnier (Dijon 1868), i, doc. 7, pp. 10-11.

13. Ibid., doc. 10, pp. 16-17 and doc. 19, pp. 28-29.

14. On these enclaves, see P. Gras, 'L'Election de Chalon-sur-Saône du XIVème au XVIème siècle', *A.B.* xviii (1946), 89-110; J. Richard, 'L'Election financière d'Autun, du XIVème au XVIème siècle, *Mémoires de la Société Eduenne*, l, (1947), 1-17; '"Enclaves" royales et limites des provinces. Les élections bourguignonnes', *A.B.* xx (1948), 89-113.

15. P. Gubian, 'Le Parlement de Bourgogne et la cour d'appeaux avant 1476', *Revue bourguignonne de l'enseignement supérieur*, xi (1901), 282.

16. Ibid. 281: 'L'ordre des appeaux en Bourgogne va par ordre, c'est assavoir de prevost à bailli, de bailli aux auditeurs de Beaune, des auditeurs au Parlement de Beaune et la se prend la fin des causes.'

17. Chaton, 'Le Personnel administratif', p. 104.

18. On this problem, in addition to the works of Chaton and Gubian previously cited, see E. Champeaux, *Les Ordonnances des ducs de Bourgogne sur l'administration de la justice du duché* (Dijon, 1907), pp. ccxc-ccxci; C. Bertucat, 'La Juridiction municipale de Dijon. Son étendue', *Revue bourguignonne publiée par l'Université de Dijon*, xxi (1911), 89-235; A. Leguai, *Dijon et Louis XI* (Dijon, 1947), pp. 10-11 (originally published in *A.B.* xvii (1945), 26-37, 103-15, 145-69 and 229-63, and xix (1947), 40-41).

19. On this episode, see A. Voisin, 'Un Problème criminel à Dijon au XVème siècle: l'appel direct au Parlement de Paris', *Mémoires de la Société pour l'histoire du droit et des institutions des anciens pays bourguignons, comtois et romands*, fasc. 3 (1936), 230-1; *Correspondance de la Mairie de Dijon*, i, pp xlix ff.; Arch. Mun. Dijon, B. 162, fos. 4, 5ᵛ, 6, 8, 9ᵛ, 10ᵛ, 12ᵛ, 13, 14, 15, 21, 22-22ᵛ, 30.

20. In the case of Jean Douhet, for instance, attempts were made to bring into play a case of rape in which he had been involved five years previously. As has been stated, no man found guilty of rape could make an appeal.

21. E.g., the trial of the bastard of Thoisy and of Jean Gorgias *(Correspondance de la Mairie de Dijon*, i, pp. xxxviii-xlviii).

22. E.g., Arch. Mun. Dijon, M.71, fos. 12, 36ᵛ; B. 38 *bis* (16 January 1469); B. 68 *bis* (6 July 1468); B. 449, fo. 128.

23. Arch. Mun. Dijon, M.71, fos. 36ᵛ-37; B. 161, fos. 146ᵛ-7ᵛ; B. 449, fo. 128; Arch. Dép. Côte d'Or, B.II 360/10 (Inquiry of 27 August 1466).

24. This may be an optical illusion. The surviving archives of Dijon are more full than those of the other towns of the duchy. These archives are being fully exploited in a number of theses which have been, or are being written under my supervision at the University of Dijon.

25. Arch. Dép. Côte d'Or B.II 360/11 (Inquiry of 12 November 1466).

26. Bertucat, 'La Juridiction municipale de Dijon', 138-40; Arch. Mun. Dijon, C.5.

27. Bertucat, ibid., 131, citing Arch. Mun. Dijon, B. 151 and C. 18.

28. Arch. Mun. Beaune, *carton* 51; Peuvot, *La Commune de Beaune*, p. 141.

29. Arch. Mun. Beaune, *carton* 51, fo. 49.

30. Arch. Mun. Dijon, B. 161, fo. 189ᵛ; Bertucat, 'La Juridiction municipale de Dijon', 126; Arch. Mun. Dijon, B. 163, fos. 3, 6, 10, 13, 15, 16, 39.

31. There were conflicts with Philip the Bold at the end of the fourteenth century (Arch. Mun. Dijon, Trésor des Chartes, *layette* 4, *cote* 5; C. Breton-Sbihi, 'Dijon sous Philippe le Hardi' (unpublished thesis, Dijon, 1975) pp. 100-3; *Correspondance de la Mairie de Dijon*, i, doc. 66, pp. 78-86); with John the Fearless (ibid. i, doc. 72, pp. 92-94); and with Philip the Good (Bertucat, 'La Juridiction municipale de Dijon', 152-4).

32. Leguai, *Dijon et Louis XI*, pp. 14-15.

33. Ibid., p. 14.

34. This year, 1386, witnessed a general hardening in the attitude of the royal administration towards the towns; it was caused by the often violent opposition which the crown last experienced from towns during the preceding years in several parts of Languedoil, Languedoc, and Flanders.

35. Gubian, 'Le Parlement de Bourgogne', 282; Plancher, *Histoire générale et particulière de Bourgogne*, iv, p.j. xviii. The task of the 'Chambre du Conseil' at Dijon was to hand down definitive sentences and to hear appeals from the *Parlements* of Dôle, Beaune and Saint Laurent.

36. Champeaux, *Ordonnances des ducs de Bourgogne*, pp. ccciii-ccciv, 194-6.

37. E.g., Arch. Mun. Dijon, M. 76, fo. 43ᵛ.

38. Arch. Mun. Dijon, M. 74, fo. 20.

39. Ibid., fo. 62.

40. Leguai, *Dijon et Louis XI*, pp. 15-16; M. Roussel. *Le Diocèse de Langres* (3 vols, Langres, 1873-8), vols. i and iii.

41. The municipality of Dijon employed agents at Lyons [to see to its affairs] (Arch. Mun. Dijon, B. 162, fo. 13; B. 481, fos. 33 and 34).

42. M. Rossignol, *Histoire de Beaune* (Beaune, 1854), p. 272; M. Chaume, 'Le Sentiment national bourguignon, de Gondebaud à Charles le Téméraire. Essai de synthèse sur l'histoire de la Bourgogne. Royaumes, duchés et comtés', *Mémoires de l'Académie des Sciences, Arts et Belles-Lettres*, 5ème série, iv (1922), 254. The text cited is to be found in Arch. Mun. Dijon, B. 150, fos. 91-91ᵛ. The italics are mine.

43. Leguai, *Dijon et Louis XI*, pp. 29-35, and 'Espions et propagandistes de Louis XI arrêtes à Dijon, *A.B.* xxiii, (1951), 50-55.

44. A general study on the reunification of Burgundy with France still remains to be written. Reference thus has to be made to the now dated study of C. Rossignol, *Histoire de la Bourgogne pendant la période monarchique. Conquête de la Bourgogne après Charles le Téméraire* (Dijon, 1853) and to J.R. de Chevanne's more limited 'Les Etats de Bourgogne et la réunion du duché à la France', *Mémoires de la Société d'Archéologie de Beaune*, (1930), 195-245.

45. The text of the treaty is printed in Plancher, *Bourgogne*, iv p.j. cclxx. The council of 'Burgundy' concerned itself only with the administration of the duchy and the county. It should not be confused with the ducal 'grand conseil' which, under the chairman-ship of the duke or of the chancellor of Burgundy, dealt with political and administrative matters concerning the whole Burgundian state.

46. Leguai, *Dijon et Louis XI*, p. 45.

47. On this, see Camp, *Histoire d'Auxonne*, pp. 70-71 (with references).

48. For a general study of this see A. Leguai 'Troubles et révoltes sous le règne de Louis XI: les résistances des particularismes', *Rev. Hist.* ccxlix (1973), 285-324.

49. Arch. Mun. Dijon, B. 164, fo. 89^v; J.R. de Chevanne, 'Chalon et Louis XI', *Mémoires de la Société d'Histoire de Chalon*, xxiv (1932-3), 25.

50. Camp, *Histoire d'Auxonne*, pp. 72-73.

51. There were a few exceptions, especially among the young.

52. For this episode see, A. Voisin, 'La "Mutemaque" du 26 juin 1477. Notes sur l'opinion à Dijon au lendemain de la Rèunion', *A.B.* vii (1935), 337-56.

53. See the article by Chevanne, 'Chalon et Louis XI'.

54. J. R. de Chevanne, 'Les Débuts de la campagne de 1478 en Bourgogne', *Mémoires de la Société d'Archéologie de Beaune* (1931-2), 289-306. It is not certain whether Avallon took part in this revolt.

55. J. Billioud, *Les Etats de Bourgogne aux quatorzième et quinzième siècles* (Dijon, 1922), p.315. On the revolt at Beaune, see Rossignol, *Histoire de Beaune*, pp. 218 ff.

56. Peuvot, *La Commune de Beaune*, p. 172.

57. Leguai, *Dijon et Louis XI*, p. 66.

58. Rossignol, *Histoire de Beaune*, pp. 222-4.

59. Camp, *Histoire d'Auxonne*, pp. 74-77.

60. Rossignol, *Histoire de Beaune*, pp. 356-7. On the foundation and organization of the new *Parlement*, see G. Chevrier, 'Les Débuts du Parlement de Dijon (1477-1487)', *A.B.* xv (1943), 93-124.

61. Rossignol, *Histoire de Beaune*, p. 357.

62. *Chartes de communes et d'affranchissement en Bourgogne*, ed. J. Garnier (Dijon, 1867), no. lxxix, pp. 109-11, citing Arch. Mun. Dijon, B. 2.

63. E. Perard, *Recueil de plusieurs pièces curieuses servant à l'histoire de Bourgogne* (Paris, 1664), p. 590; *Chartes de communes*, no. lxxxii, pp. 114-15.

64. H. Drouot and J. Calmette, *Histoire de Bourgogne* (Paris, 1928), p. 198.

65. See Rossignol, *Histoire de Bourgogne pendant la période monarchique*, pp. 328-31. The account is based largely on a document in the archives of Autun.

66. Arch. Mun. Dijon, B. 165, fos. 100^v-1.

67. The problem of the cost of castle-building is insoluble: figures for Dijon, almost certainly exaggerated, were put forward by Rossignol (*Histoire de Bourgogne pendant la période monarchique*, pp. 297-300), but these probably were for the cost of the three castles (see Billioud, *États de Bourgogne*, pp. 137-8). It is clear that part of the moneys raised were used for other expenses.

68. Leguai, *Dijon et Louis XI*, pp. 67-71; Rossignol, *Histoire de Beaune*, p. 349; Camp, *Histoire d'Auxonne*, pp. 77-78.

69. Arch. Mun. Dijon, B. 165, fos. 61-62^v, 88, 98.
70. On resistance under Charles VIII, see M. Rossignol, *La Bourgogne sous Charles VIII* (Paris-Dijon, 1862), pp. 122, 140-1; M.J. Meyer, 'Dijon sous Charles VIII' (unpublished thesis, Dijon, 1973), pp. 45-46; *Correspondance de la Mairie de Dijon*, i, doc. 146, pp. 236-7; doc. 149, p. 241.
71. Ibid. i, doc. 142, pp. 230-1; Arch. Mun. Dijon, B. 165, fo. 110.
72. Meyer, 'Dijon sous Charles VIII', p. 27.
73. Ibid., p. 39; Camp, *Histoire d'Auxonne*, p. 78. Several towns had their privileges confirmed (*Chartes de communes*, no. lxxxiii, pp. 116-17: no. lxxxiv, pp. 118-20: no. lxxxviii, pp. 125-7: no. xc, pp. 128-9).
74. Camp *Histoire d'Auxonne*, p. 78.
75. R. Gandilhon, *Politique économique de Louis XI* (Paris, 1941), p. 336.
76. Ibid., pp. 213-14.
77. Meyer, 'Dijon sous Charles VIII', pp. 42, 51-52, 55, 64-65.
78. Arch. Dép. Côte d'Or, B. II 360/13 (Inquiry of 12 August 1477).
79. On Cheval's attitude and the reactions of the municipality, see Arch. Dép. Côte d'Or, B. II 360/13 (Inquiry of 1 March 1478) and Arch. Mun. Dijon, B. 165, fos. 15^v, 80^r, 82, and 89. The conflicts between royal and municipal jurisdictions are described by Bertucat, 'La Juridiction municipale de Dijon', pp. 167-8.
80. See Chevrier, 'Les Débuts du Parlement de Dijon'; Rossignol, *La Bourgogne sous Charles VIII*, pp. 61-67 and *Histoire de Beaune*, p. 557; *Correspondance de la Mairie de Dijon*, p. ci.

8

Local Reaction to the French Reconquest of Normandy: The Case of Rouen

C.T. Allmand

That in the year between July 1449 and August 1450 the French won two victories, one military, the other moral, against the English was recognized by most contemporaries, and has been accepted by historians, indeed eagerly by French historians, ever since. None would dispute the truth of the first statement; at first, slow to gather momentum, the final expulsion of the English from northern France (Calais excepted), although greatly assisted by a lack of opposition on the part of the people of Normandy, was carried out, in the last analysis, by force of arms. More open to discussion, however, was the reaction to events in those areas newly recovered during the course of these decisive months. Was opinion always as whole-heartedly in favour of what had recently been done as men, both at the time and since, have seemed to think?[1]

Every attempt was made to show contemporaries the significance of what was being achieved at this time. Documents emanating from Valois sources referred to the period of English rule in northern France as an occupation,[2] necessarily implying usurpation,[3] which has lasted over thirty years. Behind the use of such words lay the assumption that Normandy was French and that, in expelling the English, Charles *le Trèsvictorieux* was bringing back under his effective control an area of the kingdom which was rightfully and naturally his. Hence the interest which lies in the choice of words and phrases used not only by those who wrote the king's official letters,[4] but also by chroniclers who wrote of the 'reduction' or 'recovery'[5] of territory held under 'detention'[6] by the English, and of the desire of Normans to return to their 'natural and ancient . . . rule'.[7] These were the words which Thomas Basin used to express not only what had happened but also why it had happened. As the French herald pointed out, it was the intention of the people to show that Charles of Valois rather than Henry of Lancaster was their natural lord: this made it possible for Charles VII to achieve in one year what two kings of England had signally failed to do in the space of thirty-three years.[8] The point was to be further emphasized by a show of majesty, which, as Dr Vale has recently demonstrated, was an important element in the public manifestation of authority exercised by the French king.[9] On 10 November 1449 Charles, both to reward the people of Rouen for their seemingly decisive efforts in bringing their city under Valois rule and to assert in person his claim over them, entered the capital of Normandy. His well-managed state entry is recorded in several contemporary chronicles and also in an eye-witness account; the main purpose of their retrospective authors was to recall an event of extraordinary importance, the final return into French hands of one of the kingdom's richest provinces, now (in November 1449) in the process of being recovered, by force and with the assistance of the people themselves, from the usurping English.[10]

For reasons which scarcely need explanation, the chroniclers were emphatic about the willingness of the Normans to become French again. The *Chroniques de Normandie* recalled how Charles VII was received with great joy by the people of Pont-de-l'Arche, the town, as Basin recounted with some satisfaction, having been captured by a ruse.[11] From here, only a few miles upstream from Rouen, the French armies made sorties to the very walls of the Norman capital. Before long an agreement was reached that the citizens would give the king's forces every help, the official-principal of Rouen, followed soon afterwards by the archbishop, playing an important intermediary role in the negotiations. On Sunday, 19 October, the people rose against the English whose garrison at the Mont-Sainte-Catherine, just outside the city, quickly surrendered 'when they realised that the city was against them and they felt the king of France approaching'. Shortly afterwards the count of Dunois, acting upon the request of the clergy, nobility, and bourgeois that he should take possession, entered the city, his entry being 'very fine to observe'. By the evening, the white cross was everywhere to be seen.[12] 'The honour which the churchmen, nobility and people of Rouen showed towards the crown and the fleur de lys of France' had ensured that Rouen was once again French.[13]

The people had to wait some three weeks before the king graced their streets with his presence.[14] The event was intended to celebrate the recovery of Rouen, although military operations against the English in Normandy were to continue for at least another nine months. If the events of these weeks were of the greatest political significance to the crown, for the people of Rouen themselves they marked a change of allegiance which, they hoped, would improve their lot. All classes seemed ready to welcome the king. The clergy, led by the metropolitan chapter, displayed their best relics and sang the *Te Deum*; the people put out decorations in the royal colours and exhibited the royal arms; bonfires were lighted in the streets and tables were covered with wines and meats, made freely available to all. The king was requested that, in spite of the lateness of the season, he should not abandon his war since places in English hands, such as Harfleur and Honfleur at the mouth of the Seine, could still do much material damage to all their interests.[15] The city promised to help with men and money in the pursuit of this end. The king's reply to this request, conveyed through his chancellor, Guillaume Jouvenel des Ursins, was such that the people 'were well satisfied'.[16]

Historians today have normally described the events and feelings of the time as these were recorded by the chroniclers. Understandably enough, their accounts and commentaries have tended to favour the monarchy of Charles VII. The English, cast in the role of usurpers, were obliged to yield before the patriotic sentiments of the people of Rouen who rallied to the emotive influence of the national colours worn by the king's heralds.[17] The moderation of the French king, rather than his desire for vengeance, has received emphasis. Thus his repeated pleas for reconciliation; thus, too, his recognition of the Church's privileges, his maintenance of the Norman *Echiquier*, and his confirmation of local custom enshrined in that great symbol of local autonomy, the *Charte aux Normands*.[18] The conditions and circumstances under which Rouen returned to the French fold were made to contrast strikingly with those which had witnessed the capture of the city by the English, after a prolonged siege, in 1419 a generation before.

Thus far chronicles and record sources are in broad agreement. From this moment onwards, however, the records assume greater importance since they provide testimony of a story which the chroniclers could not, or would not, tell in full. Just as the Bourgeois de Paris reported that a certain disillusionment set in soon after the fall of Paris in April 1436 (the king did not appear in person, and captains acting in his name continued to rob and pillage as before, so that there was little to choose between a French and an English soldier);[19] just as, too, the inhabitants of Bordeaux were shortly to react against Valois fiscal measures,[20] so in Rouen there are indications that doubts about the future under French rule existed from the very first moments. Too much might be read into the statement, made by Basin immediately following his account of the surrender of Rouen, that French officers accepted bribes from high-born English prisoners who were thereby allowed to depart without paying their debts,[21] were it not that the records of both the city council and the cathedral chapter in some measure reflect his unease. Neither set of records which report, albeit briefly, the discussions among the city's civil and spiritual leaders, tells of the change of government effected in the autumn of 1449, although it may readily be admitted that the chapter's record for 1419 had made no reference to the fall of Rouen to the English army, either.[22] Clearly, however, a need was felt to keep on the side of those who represented the French king. On 20

November 1449 a grant (or bribe?) of 1,000 *livres tournois* a year was made by the city to its newly appointed captain, Pierre de Brézé, 'as a matter of courtesy . . . in order that the city shall not be subject to the captain except by its own choice',[23] while a few months later, on 20 March 1450, the chapter, in an effort to please him, presented the Treasurer of France with a volume of chronicles belonging to the cathedral.[24] Coupled with Basin's comments, such evidence suggests misgivings on the part of the corporations of Rouen. The celebrations over, men were beginning to see more realistically what the future held in store.

In this respect, the chapter's act book is most informative. As an influential ecclesiastical body whose wealth had been much reduced by the ravages of war, the chapter, on 20 November 1449, at first expressed itself unwilling to give financial support towards the recovery of Harfleur which the king, at the behest of the city which had requested its capture, was soon to invest.[25] The reason for this opposition and unwillingness to co-operate, which in the long term would seem to have been against the chapter's interests since the economic prosperity of Rouen depended so much upon easy access to the sea by river,[26] appears to have been that the contribution was to be raised without proper consultation ('sine expresso consensu eorum'). However, discussions between representatives of the chapter, of the archbishop, of the abbots and royal officers took place a few days later, and on 1 December the king obtained an agreement that the clergy of the city and diocese of Rouen would contribute 4,000 *livres tournois* towards the costs of the recovery of Harfleur.[27] Within a few days collectors of the tax had been appointed, and the processions were soon to be held and Masses said for the success of the undertaking.[28]

The episode suggests that the metropolitan chapter was less concerned with the change of allegiance and administration than with the due recognition and preservation of ecclesiastical privileges, which it saw being further threatened by two consequences of the reconquest. The first concerned the terms accorded to Rouen at the time of its surrender. Had these terms affected the rights of individual clergy to be maintained in their benefices? Were the corporate rights of the cathedral chapter to be in any way limited? Was the reconquest to lead to a change of personnel among the cathedral clergy who had held their positions under the English, and perhaps specifically by English favour? As the chapter record clearly shows, many outsiders hoped to take advantage of the uncertainty and confusion current at the time to further their own ambitions. On 8 November 1449, two days before the king's formal entry into Rouen, Guillaume Morin appeared before the chapter to claim a canonry and prebend for which, he claimed, he had royal letters of presentation dated 1437. The members of the chapter, plainly unhappy at such developments, were determined enough to inform Morin that the offices which he was claiming had been occupied by the present incumbent for the past twenty-eight years and that, by the terms of surrender granted to Rouen, clergy, whether living in the kingdom of France or in the duchy of Normandy, were generally to remain possessed of their benefices. Morin appears to have accepted this decision for the time being, although he reiterated his claim in the following April, only to be told again that he could not be admitted under the terms of surrender of the previous autumn.[29]

Time was to show that many claimants, by trying every legal trick of the trade, would harass the chapter in the hope of ecclesiastical advancement; might well the canons come to fear this unwelcome consequence of the reconquest.[30] On 10 November, two days after hearing Morin and on the very day of Charles VII's entry into Rouen, members of the chapter went before the royal lieutenant to remind him of the king's expressed intention that those in possession of benefices should have peaceful use of them; two days later some canons discussed with Pierre de la Hazardière, one of their most senior colleagues and himself a man who had accepted ecclesiastical advancement from the English, the content of a sermon in which Hazardière expressly intended to recall to the king that he had promised to maintain all clergy in their benefices.[31] The need for a preacher to remind the king of his policy and of his undertaking (and, by implication, that neither was being fulfilled) stemmed from the state of uncertainty in which members of the chapter found themselves at this moment. It comes as a surprise to learn that the complete terms of surrender made between the city and the royal captain appear not to have been fully publicized or understood for some time after the actual day of surrender. At first only their general intent appears to have been known, and each seems to have been at liberty to interpret them as he wished. Therein lay the danger for the chapter, and from it stemmed the need to recall, for the benefit of the king and his officers, that churchmen had a special place in the terms accorded to the city, a place which effectively prevented the chapter from accepting too many new members into its ranks too readily. When, on 20 November, the canons refused to admit one Jean Dubec, in spite of the physical presence of Jean Havart, *bailli* of Caux, in his support, they did so by reference to the terms of surrender which were still unpublished;[32] a month after the surrender, on 11 December, the chapter still claimed that it did not know how long the terms accorded to the city would allow those absent on the day of surrender to return to claim their benefices before an automatic deprivation would apply.[33] The inescapable conclusion conveyed to the reader of the chapter's record is that the canons, fearing for their rights, were very soon on the defensive.

The months which followed the reconquest of Rouen witnessed the emergence of another problem which was to be of concern to the chapter; the possible application of the terms of the Pragmatic Sanction to

Normandy, a region which, under English rule, had lived subject to a rather different régime regarding appointments to benefices. Within days of the city's capitulation, in a case over a disputed prebend in the cathedral, there was the possibility that the Pragmatic Sanction would be invoked as the result of the threat of one claimant to have the dispute referred to Rome and the angry assertion, made in reply, that it should be heard before the *Parlement* in Paris. On 30 July 1450, the royal authority and that of the *Parlement* were again invoked in another long drawn-out dispute over a canonry and prebend, a case in which the opponent of the chapter sought the support of the *Parlement* in an attempt to have the affair resolved in his favour. The fact that a fortnight earlier the canons had forbidden a claimant to an ecclesiastical office from taking his case outside the boundaries of the duchy of Normandy underlines how strongly and how soon the chapter was coming to fear the new legal influences to which it was having to submit.[34]

If the Church in Rouen very soon came to doubt some of the consequences of the city's recovery by Charles VII, the secular authority appears to have been immediately less affected by these same events. The record of the council's deliberations suggests that steps were taken to please the king, even to curry favour with him. By May 1450 some 30,000 *livres tournois* had been lent to the Crown, chiefly as a contribution towards the recapture of Harfleur, and in that month it was agreed that, in spite of difficult financial conditions and of some apparent criticism of the way the campaign had been managed, a force of 200 men, all wearing a cap or jerkin with the town's colours ('huque ou hoqueton dune livree de la ville') should be sent to assist at the siege of Caen.[35]

It was not until the early months of 1451, with Normandy now completely recovered, that signs of opposition began to show themselves. On 1 March it was announced that Charles VII had, on the previous 28 October, reissued the terms of an earlier order, the so-called Edict of Compiègne first promulgated in 1429, regarding the settlement of property in the newly recovered areas, and that the terms appeared to be incompatible with those granted to the city at the time of its capitulation, to the detriment of many inhabitants.[36] The importance of this edict was that it attempted, in general terms which did not always take into account particular local problems or conditions, to restore men deprived of their estates and property as a result of the English invasion, and that it did so having in mind principally the interests of those who had left Normandy rather than those who had remained behind, a decision which was bound to affect the people of Rouen, who had never been outstanding in their anti-English attitudes, more than many. The very next day it was decided to send spokesmen, armed with the text of the edict and its confirmation (criticized as being obscure and cryptic in meaning) to the king at Tours to seek elucidation and guidance over this complicated problem. On 6 April the spokesmen reported to the city's council on a number of important matters regarding Normandy and, more particularly, on the royal confirmation of the Edict of Compiègne. Whether, and how, the problem had been resolved is not known, the records being regrettably silent on this point. The feeling, however, which the negotiations provoked in the city is hinted at by the fact that on 8 April the spokesmen reported directly to a meeting of churchmen, nobility, and bourgeois of Rouen which was attended by large numbers. The delegates were then thanked for their work.[37]

Reluctance to go along with such royal measures might have only a limited interest and little significance were it not that these complaints formed the essential background to demands which were to be put forward, within about two years of the recovery of Normandy, for the formal recognition of the duchy's liberties. Both the spirtual and the civil power in Rouen, as on more than one occasion in times past, were to take an active lead in the making of such demands. In the autumn of 1450 the chapter and the archbishop entered into discussions with royal officers regarding the terms of surrender ('de materia composicionis') and the *Charte aux Normands*; the chapter agreed to lend its original of the *Charte* to an assembly of the provincial estates meeting in Rouen so that its text could, if necessary, be compared with others.[38] If, before long, the canons were joined by the civil authority it was partly because of the unsatisfactory manner in which the terms of surrender had been made known, and also partly because, even when they had become known, the king had maladroitly appeared to nullify their effect by confirming an old order, made some twenty years earlier, which seemed to give undue advantage to those who had abandoned their lands out of loyalty to the Valois cause. It was the dismay and uncertainty provoked by this step, and a fear that the king was avenging himself on those who had remained in Normandy during the period of English rule, which brought civil and ecclesiastical leaders together in opposition to the king and to the authority of Paris.

The *Charte* was soon to be the focal point of a wider appeal to Norman separation inspired and led by Rouen.[39] On 25 June 1451 the city's council decided to make a stand for the rights and privileges of Rouen and Normandy against the pretensions of Paris; a demand was to be made for the renewal, in its entirety, of the *Charte aux Normands*, as well as for a confirmation of the validity of the duchy's customs. The all too brief record refers to a meeting which was to take place with royal commissioners on 1 August at Vernon (almost on the frontier between Normandy and France) for which the men of Paris were said to be making elaborate preparations, the Normans being urged to do likewise.[40] Some while later it was reported that the *Parlement* was trying to have cases referred to itself, and that its officers *(huissiers)* had been active in Gisors, in eastern Normandy, and elsewhere contrary to the terms of the *Charte*. A decision was taken to send complaints to the king; the *bailliage* of Gisors was to be encouraged to do the same.[41]

The spirit of opposition of the immediate post-war period seems to have come to a head in the autumn of 1452. Some important formal demands were formulated. On 7 October the city's council decided to consult with the king's advocates regarding a number of cases pending in the courts, including the *Echiquier* and elsewhere, concerning the rights and liberties of Rouen. Further, in accordance with the wishes of the Norman estates, it was decided to ask the king for the confirmation of the *Charte aux Normands*; for the restoration of the *Chambre des Comptes* and the *Cour des Aides* at Rouen, for the establishment of a chancellery ('le seel du roy') there; and for the re-establishment of the university of Caen.[42]

A more comprehensive document survives which fully indicates what demands Rouen was making on the Crown. Although it is dated 22 November 1452, it was directly based on demands drawn up for a meeting of 7 October, or perhaps much earlier; it is included at the end of a volume containing contemporary records of the deliberations of the chapter.[43] Headed 'the articles regarding which it seems reasonable that the three estates of the duchy of Normandy should petition our lord the king', the document summarizes many earlier complaints. The effect of war upon the ability of the population to pay what was regarded as excessively high taxation was emphasized, accompanied with the threat that unless taxes were lowered, people would be forced to leave the duchy to seek homes elsewhere;[44] the *Charte aux Normands* should be confirmed and renewed as the last king, Charles VI, had done; a university, with a complete range of faculties, should be founded at Caen, and be given privileges;[45] legal and financial institutions should be established in Rouen; and, in an important reference to a matter which had already given rise to the expression of considerable feeling, the king should be requested to confirm the terms of surrender granted to individual towns, and to allow all disputed cases arising from these to be heard in Normandy under the jurisdiction of the sovereign *Echiquier*, without interference from the *Parlement* or justices from outside the duchy, especially in cases which might be summoned to Paris by virtue of the privileges of its ancient university.[46]

It may be readily understood why the Normans were anxious to rid themselves of English rule, and why, as at Rouen in November 1449, they cheered the arrival of Charles VII and displayed on their balconies hangings bearing the fleurs de lys. But they did not regard themselves as unquestioning subjects of the king of France.[47] They reacted strongly to domination by Paris or at least to domination by some royal officers. Ironically their questioning, as the records show, was prompted by the acts and attitudes of the king and his officers. It consisted of legal and institutional demands which reflected developments that had been attempted, though they may not always have been achieved, during English rule. Such were the moral and practical assistance given to those who had challenged the authority of the *Parlement* of Paris to judge Norman cases, supported by the encouragement given to the hearing of appeals, and certain types of disputes, such as those arising out of royal land grants, by the council in Rouen, as well as by the revival of the Norman *Echiquier* as a sovereign court ('cour souveraine') on four occasions, in 1423, 1424, 1426 and, more recently, in 1448;[48] Similar developments were the reintroduction of the office of seneschal which had been abolished by Philip-Augustus;[49] the creation, between 1429 and 1449, of a *Cour des Aides* at Rouen, an institution closely linked with the *Chambre des Comptes* which, itself, had been established in the Norman capital after the fall of Paris in 1436;[50] and finally, the foundation, in the 1430s, of a university at Caen whose very existence had been vigorously challenged by that of Paris which saw the new *studium*, endowed with many privileges and liberties, as a rival to its political, social, and intellectual hegemony in northern France.[51]

The period of the English occupation is so frequently regarded as negative and unproductive, especially by French historians, that it may come as something of a surprise to learn that the period left a legacy which was promptly put to good political use by the Normans themselves. The English, under the Lancastrians, had always based their claim to the duchy upon the past; they had had a practical interest in reviving 'old' institutions — but they had done more, for the *Cour des Aides*, for example, was an institution of the 'new' type. Thus the measure of the influence of the English occupation may, to some extent, be reflected in the future history of institutions, legal, financial, and educational, revived or founded under their rule, which were sought in the demands of the estates of 1452. On 30 October 1452 the king authorized the foundation of an enlarged university at Caen although proper recognition was not given, perhaps deliberately, to the part which the English had played in founding the *studium* almost twenty years earlier.[52] Similarly, the *Cour des Aides*, although abolished by Charles VII, was re-established (although not with sovereign rights) some time between 1453 and 1455, largely as a result of the demands of the estates of 1453; only in 1462, having first been abolished and then restored by Louis XI, was it to be given existence as a sovereign body.[53] As for the *Echiquier*, it was to serve the future by providing the basis for the *Parlement* founded by Louis XII in 1499, which in turn was to become the *Parlement de Rouen* under Francis I. Only the legal existence of the duchy itself, to some extent encouraged by the English (Henry V had styled himself duke of Normandy and had appeared as such in Rouen wearing ceremonial robes) had a limited future. For although given a duke in the person of Charles de France, the king's brother, in 1465, Normandy became an inalienable part of the French king's domain by agreement reached with the *Estates General* meeting at Tours in 1468, and on 9 November 1469 the ducal seal was formally broken at a sitting of the *Echiquier*. By this act the duchy of Normandy ceased to exist.[54]

The demands of 1452 form a remarkable comment upon the previous thirty or forty years of Norman history. They suggest that historians have too readily interpreted the recovery of the duchy and the short-term enthusiasm of its people, as recorded by contemporary chronicles, as a necessary part of Normandy's predetermined movement along the road to assimilation into the French kingdom a generation later. What emerges from the evidence here presented is that the demands of 1452, which led to the concessions made by Charles VII later in the 1450s, far from being the romantic expression of a provincialism which would soon no longer have proper legal foundation, in fact formed a protest against maladroit attempts to impose measures which appeared to act contrary to both the immediate material interests of many Normans, laymen as well as clergy, and to the duchy's historical tradition of independence, this protest being expressed in terms of what was clearly regarded as having been best, most useful and most likely to be lasting in the legacy which the English had left behind them. What the Valois monarchy lacked most of all was tact; this, perhaps more than anything, as the events described above show us, turned people against it. Ironical as it may seem, it was the lead provided by their erstwhile political masters whom they themselves had so recently helped to expel, which showed the Normans how best to assert their self-respect and their independence of their new, French, masters.

The Articles

Articles containing requests to be made to the king on behalf of the *Estates* of Normandy, approved by the chapter of Rouen cathedral on 22 November 1452 (Archives de la Seine-Maritime, Rouen, G.2134, fos. 277ᵛ-8).
Sensuient les articles qui semblent estre raisonnables a requerir au roy nostre seigneur par les troiz estas du pays et duchie de Normendie.

Premierement, que en consideracion a ce que ses treshumbles subgiez de Normendie ont continuelment este en guerre depuis plus de xxxij ans enca audevant de la reduction de ce pais de Normendie et par ce a este et encores est ledit pais depopule et evacue de peuple, biens et chevance, et aussi que depuis icelle reduction ont este et sont de jour en jour cueillies en icelui pais tresgrans et excessives finances, tant par moien de tailles, impositions, iiijᵉˢ,[55] gabelles et autres aides plus grans et excessives que oncques ne furent de memoire de homme, et lesquelles sont importables audit pais a soustenir et continuer, il plaise au roy nostredit seigneur, en aiant regard a leurs bonnes loyautez, sur ce pourveoir a sesdiz treshumbles subgiez de Normendie et faire cesser lesdictes charges ou au moins les moderer tellement que ilz puissent vivre et passer le demourant de leurs jours en paix soubz sa tresnoble seigneurie et royal maieste. Car autrement sesdis treshumbles subgiez, qui lesdictes charges ne peuent plus porter ne soustenir, seroient en necessite de wider et aler ailleurs demourer pour icelles charges eschiver et trouver moyen de vivre plus paisiblement et a mendre charge, ainsi que desia sen est parti et encore fait chacun jour dudit pais grant nombre et quantite, et encore plus feroit se de sa tresnoble grace ny estoit remedie et pourveu en brief.

Item, que les loys, coustumes et usages dudit pais de Normendie et la chartre aux normans soient confermez, ainsi quilz furent par le roy Charles derrain trespasse selon sa chartre sur ce faicte.

Item, quil plaise au roy nostredit seigneur creer et erigier universite en la ville de Caen en toutes facultez, et la douer a son bon plaisir des privileges qui par les estas dudit pais de Normendie lui seront baillez par supplicacion.

Item, quil plaise au roy nostredit seigneur ordonner en la ville de Rouen seel de chancellerie, chambre de comptes et de generaulx sur le fait de la justice des aides pour le bien dudit pais de Normendie.

Item, que les composicions et concessions octroiees par le roy nostredit seigneur aux citez, villes, forteresses et pais de Normendie en faisant ou par le moien de ladicte reduction dicelles en lobaissance du roy nostredit seigneur soient aussi par lui auctorisees, confermees, entretenues et gardees selon leur fourme et teneur, et que se aucuns debatz et proces se [fo.278] meuvent touchant lesdictes composicions et concessions ou les deppendences dicelles, les juges ordinaires, tant ecclesiastiques que seculiers, dudit pais de Normendie, chacun en son regart, en aient la congnoissance et decision soubz le ressort, cestassavoir de leschiquier, court souveraine en Normendie, quant aux juges seculiers, et au regart des juges ecclesiastiques, soubz le ressort des greigneurs ou souverains juges a qui ordinairement il appartient, sans ce que la court de parlement ne autres juges en aient la congnoissance, ne que, par quelxconques previlleges de universitez ou autrement, puissent les habitans dudit pais estre ailleurs convenus es cas dessusdis et leurs deppendences. Et se aucunes causes en estoient ja meues et pendentes devant aucuns juges, quilz soient renvoiees devant lesdis juges ordinaires de Normendie pour en congnoistre et decider, comme dit est.

Chapitre de Rouen donne adhesion aux estas de Normendie a poursuir devers le roy nostre seigneur les articles dessusdis, et sont dacort que len y envoie de par lestat de leglise ung, deux ou troiz clers notables pour les poursuir, desquelz clers ils commettent lelection a maistres Gullaume Dudesert et Jehan de Gouvys, chanoines dicelle eglise, selon ce quilz verront estre a faire par ladviz et opinion des autres prelas et seigneurs deglise de Normendie qui sur ce seront assemblez. Ce fu fait et passe en chapitre lan mil iiij^c lij, le xxij jour de novembre.

J. Des Essars

Notes

1. Among the many accounts of the events of these months the following may be noted: those of Robert Blondel and of Berry le Héraut (*Narratives of the expulsion of the English from Normandy MCCCCXLIX — MCCCCL*, ed. J. Stevenson, R.S. (London, 1863), pp. 120-42, 144-50 and 296-324); that of Thomas Basin (*Histoire de Charles VII*, ed. and trans. C. Samaran, (2nd edn, 2 vols, Paris, 1965), ii 115-31); that of Jean Chartier (*Chronique de Charles VII*, ed. V. de Viriville, (3 vols, Paris, 1858), ii. 137-72); and that of *Les Cronicques de Normendie 1223-1453* (ed. A. Hellot, (Rouen, 1881), pp. 123-39).

2. For example, *Ordonnances des rois de France de la troisième race* (23 vols., Paris, 1733-1847), xiv, 59, 60, 75; B.N., Ms. fr. 5350, p. 44; Arch. Dép., Calvados, D.27; B.L., Add. Ch.4069.

3. *Ordonnances*, xiv. 65.

4. For example, 'recouvrement de nostre Seigneurie'; 'remectre & redduire en nostre bonne & vraye obéissance comme à celle de leur Souverain naturel & droicturier Seigneur' (*Ordonnances*, xiv. 60).

5. 'Reductio' and 'recouvrement' were used by Blondel and Berry le Héraut.

6. 'Detencion' (*Ordonnances*, xiv. 60).

7. '. . . naturale et vetustissimum . . . regale' (Basin, *Histoire de Charles VII*, ii. 107). The whole page merits close study.

8. *Le débat des hérauts d'armes de France et d'Angleterre, suivi de The debate between the heralds of England and France, by J. Coke*, ed. L. Pannier (S.A.T.F. Paris, 1877), p. 24.

9. M.G.A. Vale, *Charles VII* (London, 1974), ch.7 and especially pp. 202-4.

10. See the narratives in the chronicles: Blondel, *De reductione Normanniae*, pp. 144-50; *Cronicques de Normendie*, pp. 136-9. The eye-witness account is printed in B. Guenée and F. Lehoux, *Les entrées royales françaises de 1328 à 1515* (Paris, 1968), pp. 160-2, in which a miniature depicting the scene, taken from a manuscript of Monstrelet, appears as a frontispiece.

11. *Cronicques de Normendie*, p. 123; Basin, *Histoire de Charles VII*, ii. 79-83; Chartier, *Chronique de Charles VII*, ii. 137.

12. *Cronicques de Normendie*, pp. 123-31; Chartier, *Chronique de Charles VII*, ii. 154.

13. 'Par la bonne affection des gens deglise et des nobles et bourgeois dicelle et pour lhonneur que ils vouloient a la couronne et aux fleurs de lys de France' (*Journal parisien de Jean Maupoint, prieur de Sainte-Catherine-de-la-Couture, 1437-1469*, ed. G. Fagniez (Soc. de l'Hist. de Paris, 1878), p. 37.

14. The national importance of these events is emphasized by the brief references made to them not only in the work cited in n. 13 but also by the compiler of the *Journal d'un Bourgeois de Paris, 1405-1449*, ed. A. Tuetey (Soc. de l'Hist. de Paris, 1881), p. 392; *A. Parisian Journal, 1405-1449*, trans. J. Shirley (Oxford, 1968), pp. 371-2.

15. Basin, *Histoire de Charles VII*, ii. 131; Chartier, *Chronique de Charles VII*, ii. 170-1.

16. *Cronicques de Normendie*, p. 139.

17. V. de Viriville, *Histoire de Charles VII, roi de France, et de son époque* (3 vols, Paris, 1862-5), iii. 159.

18. Ibid. iii. 160; G. du Fresne de Beaucourt, *Histoire de Charles VII* (6 vols, Paris, 1881-91), v. 12.

19. *Journal d'un Bourgeois de Paris*, p. 327; *Parisian Journal*, p. 312.

20. M.G.A. Vale, *English Gascony, 1399-1453* (Oxford, 1970), p. 142.

21. Basin, *Histoire de Charles VII*, ii. 129.

22. Contrast with this the record of the deliberations of the cathedral chapter of Saint-André, Bordeaux, for 29 June 1451: 'Civitas Burdegale est regni Francie' (Cited in Y. Renouard, *Bordeaux sous les rois d'Angleterre* (Bordeaux, 1965), p. 513).

23. '. . . par courtoisie . . . non pas que la ville soit subiecte au capitaine si non de voulente' (Bibl. Mun., Rouen, A.7 (Délibérations de la ville, 1447-53), fo. 60).

24. Arch. Dép., Seine-Maritime, G. 2134, fo. 42^v.

25. Ibid., fo. 20. The siege of Harfleur lasted from 8 December 1449 until 1 January 1450.

26. M. Mollat, *Le Commerce maritime normand à la fin du moyen âge* (Paris, 1952), pp. 9, 12 ff, 44.

27. Arch. Dép., Seine-Maritime, G.2134, fos. 20^v, 21, 21^v.

28. Ibid., fos. 23^v, 27^v, 28^v, 36^v. When, on 18 April 1450, it was learnt that the French had defeated the English at Formigny three days earlier, the chapter ordered processions to be held to thank God for the victory which he had granted (fo. 46).

29. Ibid., fos. 18 and 45^v. See L. Fallue, *Histoire politique et religieuse de l'église métropolitaine de Rouen* (4 vols, Rouen, 1850-1), ii. 478-9.

30. In the fifteen months or so following the recovery of Rouen, the chapter was kept busy considering the claims of many who hoped, by legal means or otherwise, to gain positions within the cathedral. The canons, who did not wish to admit most of them, used every means available to them to keep such suppliants out, in spite of sometimes heavy pressure from royal officers (Arch.Dép., Seine-Maritime, G. 2134, fos. 19-100^v).

31. Ibid., fos. 18, 18^v.

32. 'Cui Dubec fuit responsum quod domini de capitulo non poterant sibi dare responsum quousque litera composicionis ville Rotomag. super facto beneficiorum sit sigillata' (ibid., fo. 20).

33. Ibid., fo. 23^v. The period granted to Rouen was 'dedans six mois', or three if the person lived in the English obedience (*Ordonnances*, xiv. 77). At Lisieux the period was three months for everybody (ibid. xiv. 62). Consistency was clearly not regarded as a virtue.

34. Arch. Dép., Seine-Maritime, G.2134, fos. 22^v, 63^v, 61^v. For the comparable situation in Gascony, see G. Hubrecht, 'Juridictions et compétences en Guyenne recouvrée', *Annales de la Faculté de droit de l'université de Bordeaux*, série juridique, iii (1952), 63-79; trans. in *The recovery of France in the fifteenth century*, ed. P.S. Lewis (London, New York, Toronto, 1971), pp. 82-101.

35. Bibl. Mun., Rouen, A.7, fos. 77^v-78.

36. 'Pour ce que len avoit eu en congnoissance que aujourdui matin, en lassise de Rouen, len avoit publie et leu certaines lettres roiaulx, donnees le xxviij jour doctobre derrain passe, de confirmacion dautres lettres roiaux de certain edit, loy et ordonnances pieca faictes et donne a Compiengne ou moiz daoust, le xxij jour mil iiij^c xxix, par le roy nostreseigneur, qui sembloient grandement preiudicier pluseurs de ceste ville, et quilz estoient directement contre aucunes choses accordees par ledit seigneur par le traictie, composicion [et] abolicion de ceste dicte ville de Rouen puis naguere fait et donne par icellui seigneur' [It is decided that it is important to obtain the king's opinion about this; spokesmen are sent to the king at Tours] 'obtenir de par ceste dicte ville du roy nostredit seigneur ses lettres pour adnuler les autres dessusdictes dont cy dessus est faicte mention, se cestoit le bon plaisir dicellui seigneur, ou au moins obtenir lettres dudit seigneur comme il nentend les lettres dessusdictes preiudicier ou deroguer les lettres dabolicion ou composicion par lui naguere donnees a ceste dicte ville. Et se ainsi lesdis ambassadeurs ne povoient obtenir ce que dit est, requerir devers le roy nostredit seigneur son interpretacion desdictes lettres de confirmacion et mesmes linterpretacion de celles dudit edit, loy et ordonnance donne a Compiegne, pource que lesdis leurs semblent bien obscures et criptueuses en ce quelles contiennent' (ibid., fo. 90^v).

37. Ibid., fos. 91 and 114; H. Prentout, *Les Etats provinciaux de Normandie* (3 vols, Caen, 1925-6), i. 158. On this general problem see C.T. Allmand, 'The aftermath of war in fifteenth-century France', *History*, lxi (1976), 344-57.

38. Arch. Dép., Seine-Maritime, G.2134, fos. 74 and 88.

39. 'La grande préoccupation de la province était de se faire confirmer toutes ses anciennes institutions' (Prentout, *Etats provinciaux*, i. 161). See also A. Chéruel, *Histoire de Rouen sous la domination anglaise au quinzième siècle* (Rouen, 1840), ch. viii and 'Remonstrance des habitants de Rouen contre l'université de Paris' (pp. 167-84). Aspects of Breton separatism of a slightly earlier period are discussed by Michael Jones, '"Mon Pais et ma Nation": Breton identity in the fourteenth century', *War, Literature, and Politics in the Late Middle Ages. Essays in honour of G.W. Coopland*, ed. C.T. Allmand (Liverpool, 1976), pp. 144-68.

40. Bibl. Mun., Rouen, A.7, fos. 95-95ᵛ. 'Il sera question plus tard de l'appointement de Vernon' (Prentout, *Etats provinciaux*, i. 193-4).

41. Bibl. Mun., Rouen, A.7, fo. 110ᵛ.

42. Ibid., fo. 134ᵛ; Prentout, *Etats provinciaux*, i. 160-2.

43. The date of the document suggests that a meeting of the estates took place in November 1452; on this matter I am more convinced by the positive reasoning of C. Robillard de Beaurepaire ('Les Etats de Normandie sous le règne de Charles VII', *Précis des travaux de l'académie des sciences, belles-lettres et arts de Rouen* (1874-5), pp. 273-7) than by the rather too cautious point of view presented by Prentout (*États provinciaux*, iii. 24-25). The demands which the document contains had, in all likelihood, been considered as early as December 1451, when they received the chapter's approval (ibid. iii. 24 and 91). Prentout suggested that the history of these demands may have gone back to 1450 (Ibid. i. 162, n.3)

44. Taxation under the Valois soon became almost as high as it had been under the English, without the excuse of a local war to justify it (Mollat, *Commerce maritime normand*, p. 74).

45. Charles VII had not originally confirmed the existence of the faculty of law, and was not to do so until 30 October 1452 (A. de Bourmont, *La Fondation de l'université de Caen et son organisation au XVe siècle* (Caen, 1883), pp. 54 and 265-9).

46. Arch. Dép., Seine-Maritime, G.2134, fos. 277ᵛ-8. The text, a version of which was published by Beaurepaire ('Les Etats de Normandie sous le règne de Charles VII', pp. 274-6) is printed here at the end of the chapter.

47. See the text of the 'Remonstrance' cited in n. 39. For reaction to not dissimilar events in the early thirteenth century, cf. M. Nortier, 'Le Rattachement de la Normandie à la couronne de France', *Positions des thèses de l'Ecole des Chartes* (1951), pp. 121-6. For the effects of the French reconquest of the Bordelais in these very same years, cf. A. Peyrègne, 'La Pénétration du régime français en Bordelais de 1453 à 1461', ibid. (1951), pp. 127-32; *Bordeaux sous les rois d'Angleterre*, ed. Renouard, pp. 505 ff.

48. Records for the *Échiquier* are to be found at the Archives Départementales de la Seine-Maritime at Rouen.

49. See R.A. Newhall, *The English Conquest of Normandy, 1416-1424* (Yale, 1924), pp. 244-6; R.N. Sauvage, 'Une Procédure devant la sénéchaussée de Normandie en 1423', *Mémoires de l'académie nationale des sciences, arts et belles-lettres de Caen* (1910), pp. 139-57; Prentout, *États provinciaux*, i. 160-1.

50. M. Le Pesant, 'La Cour des Aides de Normandie, des origines à 1552', *Positions des thèses de l'Ecole des Chartes* (1936), pp. 107-15.

51. Bourmont described the history of the university up to 1452 as 'la période la plus brillante de notre université' (*La Fondation de l'université de Caen*, p. 55).

52. Arch. Dép., Calvados, D.28. 'Ipse rex Karolus septimus eamdem Universitatem novam fecit, eamque de novo erexit atque creavit, non habendo respectum ad gesta per

Anglos, multisque privilegiis eam dotavit' (Caen, Musée des Beaux-Arts, Coll. Mancel 68, fo. 9; formerly Arch. Dép., Calvados, D.64). No modern historian has denied the lasting importance, for Normandy, of the contribution of this 'English' foundation; Prentout, himself a teacher there, could write of 'la création de l'université de Caen, voilà donc le seul bienfait de la domination anglaise en Normandie' (*États provinciaux*, i. 153).

53. Le Pesant, 'La Cour des Aides', pp. 107-8.
54. Prentout, *États provinciaux*, i. 197-8.
55. I.e. 'quatrièmes'.

F

Appendix

Dissension in the Provinces under Henry III, 1574-85[1]

Mark Greengrass

My aim is to discuss not only open rebellion in the provinces during the reign of Henry III, but also organized dissension. During the wars of religion this was endemic. As the English ambassador, Sir Amyas Poulet, remarked in January 1578, 'All things continue here after the French fashion; we can abide neither heat nor cold; war is too sharp and peace too sweet'.[2] Yet if the government of Henry III is fully investigated, it can be shown how resilient it was to the challenges it faced. The reign falls into four distinct periods. The first was one of open warfare between Catholics and Huguenots. It dated back to the reign of Charles IX, and was ended by the Peace of the King in September 1577. The second, which lasted until the spring of 1579, was one of conflict between the Crown and constituted bodies in the provinces, especially provincial estates; it coincided with sporadic Protestant resentment. During the third period, there were a number of rebellions which, though organized, had little to do with constituted bodies. In some provinces peasants revolted; in others brigandage was rife, and the nobility was factious. Furthermore, town councils disobeyed the Crown from time to time, and royal officers were guilty of turpitude. The fourth period began in 1584. Dissension within France rapidly escalated, coalesced, and found allies outside France.

The revolt of the Huguenots was dangerous to the monarchy. It was idealistic and sectarian, provincial and highly militarized, self-defensive and extra-national. Huguenot ideology was exclusive. It flourished not only in times of war but also in the brief periods of peace. By 1574 the heroic age of the Huguenots was over. No longer did pastors trained in Geneva roam the country under cover of darkness and in disguise. The Huguenot churches were fully established, and their pastors were more often trained in France.[3] Congregationalism was ended and presbyterianism confirmed. The consistories firmly established moral discipline.[4]

The Crown was certainly aware of the political threat being presented by the Huguenots. In 1570 it reluctantly accepted, after being forced to the peace table, their power in the provinces. Henry III was quickly made aware of their provincial strength when he returned from Poland in 1574 by the secretary of the governor of Languedoc. He provided a detailed list, province by province, of the military strength, main strongholds and morale of the Huguenots. He estimated their army to be 40,000 strong (excluding the province around La Rochelle).[5]

How did the Huguenots fare between 1574 and 1577? They became less of a political danger to the monarchy, a fact which can be measured in several ways. The Peace of the King in 1577 brought them few concrete advantages which they had not already gained in 1570. The brief truce of 1576 had been much more favourable, but had caused an instant Catholic reaction. In 1577 they were offered no revenge for the massacre of St Bartholomew; no help for their Dutch co-religionists who were then in revolt; only a paper guarantee that the troops of their ally Duke Casimir of the Palatinate would be fully paid; and, above all, no direct influence upon the royal council.[6]

Their strength in the provinces had become deceptive by 1577. It may have been a good basis for guerilla activities, but it prevented them from acting nationally. Thus they held fewer national and more provincial synods, and their provincial connections became ends in themselves.[7] The peace edict skilfully exploited their weakness to the Crown's advantage.

Furthermore, the Huguenots were limited by their militarism as well as by their need to defend themselves. Local communities became exhausted by war, especially in La Rochelle and Nîmes. Rentiers in the towns were the first to be caught; they were unable to collect their rents from scattered and sometimes devastated areas outside town walls. The tax-burden on the rest of the community therefore grew. The ability of the Huguenots to finance warfare from the sales of Catholic property grew less as the market for such property contracted and as military demands became more imperative. The need of their army for supplies at first masked the decline in trade; but eventually purchases at below market price, shortage of money, and the blockade of trade routes all created cumulative pressures within the Huguenot towns for peace.[8]

Nor did the Huguenots make long-lasting or beneficial alliances. Francis, duke of Anjou, the king's brother, deserted the Huguenots when it suited him.[9] Henri de Montmorency-Damville, the leader of the so-called 'politiques' in the south, joined the Huguenots because he was weak and the Crown was about to depose him from the lieutenant-generalcy of his province. During the Huguenot revolt he had maintained his own army, his own administration, and selected officials in the towns under his control.

His alliance with the Huguenots lasted less than three years; for the king eventually removed him from the towns in his tutelage.[10] His propaganda was, however, popular outside the Huguenot cause. Though his remonstrance to the Crown of November 1574 expressed loyalty, it spoke bitterly about the 'foreigners' at court who had displaced native French-born gentlemen. He blamed foreigners for the subversion of French fundamental law, venality, legal malversation, and the miseries of the common people. He advocated 'the re-establishment of everything in its original condition by the advice and deliberation of an assembly of states-general, as the only way of pacifying the troubles and maintaining France'.[11] But when he deserted the Huguenots, he did so with a confirmed suspicion that they were dreadful 'republicans'. The Huguenots, in their turn, suspected that he was a grand seigneur who could play the 'roulette' of court politics better than they.[12]

The Huguenots counted on less support from outside France than contemporaries believed. Beza in Geneva became more interested in the Netherlands than in France; England offered little practical assistance; and German princes drove hard bargains with the result that the promises the Huguenots had made to them for reimbursement were difficult to satisfy.[13] The lesser nobility turned to brigandage in the aftermath of peace; smaller towns such as Millau suffered at the hands of brutal captains. In the Vivarais, the Auvergne, and in lower Normandy brigandage was serious. In Dauphiné, lower Languedoc, and Poitou there were threats to the authority of Henry of Navarre (the future Henry IV) as a result of disputes between minor Huguenot captains.[14] All this worked to the advantage of the Crown. Dangerous though the Huguenot menace had been in 1574, it was contained by the peace of 1577. The peace would be broken and patched up time and time again until 1585. In the provinces, however, no break could be final: Huguenots and Catholics were equally balanced.

After the Edict of Pacification in 1577, there were many revolts in largely Catholic estates. But these revolts had antecedents in Paris, Champagne, Picardy, and Provence. In 1575 the *prévôt des marchands* of Paris protested personally to Henry III about taxation.[15] Champagne did likewise. The bad winter of 1574 had improverished those living on its poor soils. Although the remonstrances of Champagne — in the copy which survives — are not very constructive, they nevertheless reveal deep-rooted opposition to the Crown.[16] Champagne would pay neither its share of the war-costs nor the *taillon*. It also protested about the raising of troops in the villages. Its situation in 1575 was, according to the Venetian ambassador, Lippomano, appalling. Villagers sheltered in churches, once prosperous towns were half tumbled-down, and bourgeois frequently had to ransom themselves once they left the security of their town walls.[17]

In July 1576 the so-called League of Picardy was formed, mainly amongst the nobility. They were discontented by the calling of the *ban* and the *arrière ban*, and also by a truce. Some found their estates devastated. Even more to their distress, they discovered that their erstwhile enemy, the Protestant prince of Condé, had been appointed governor of Picardy. They adopted a national programme, but its bias was strongly provincial. The war against the Protestants was to be continued until victory was achieved; peace and Protestantism represented dangers to the frontiers of France.[18] The strength and appeal of the Picardy League cannot readily be assessed, because it was overtaken by events. Henry III declared himself sympathetic, but at the same time ordered the lieutenants of the provinces affected by the League to outlaw illegal assemblies, and also to keep a watch on illegal recruitment as well as on the movement of spies and messengers from grandees.[19] Whatever the appeal of the League of Picardy it was diminished by the calling of the *Estates-General* of Blois in November 1576 and the renewal of war shortly afterwards.

What can be learned from the *Estates-General* of Blois about the opposition in the provinces? It is clearly difficult to indicate a political climate from the composition of a representative assembly, for an assembly is a political event in its own right. Only a handful of *cahiers* from the provinces have been published, although many more probably survive. The Crown insisted that elections be held at the seneschalcy level; this enabled loyal seneschals to make sure that the nobility elected — and sometimes even the clergy — were either Crown nominees or reasonably sympathetic to the Crown.[20] As a result there was a solid block of *chevaliers du roi*, gentlemen of the king's chamber, captains, and budding seneschals. In the third estate, however, office-holders seem to have been predominant, particularly those from the lesser court, the *présidiaux* and *bailliages*. Indeed, some third estates submitted *cahiers* to the Crown complaining that they were unrepresented, such as the bourgeois of Troyes;

> particularly since five sixths of all deputies from our province are *gens de justice* and the other sixth are merchants and from the short robe, with the result that the majority opinion has been gained and is dominated by *gens de justice*.[21]

Troyes went on to demand that judges be appointed for three years; that the *présidiaux* be suppressed; and that judges be required to give a sentence in a case, at the most, six months after it had been initiated. It also remonstrated against abuses in ecclesiastical justice and, as an afterthought, suggested that justice in the towns be handled entirely by the *maire* and *échevins*. Similar sentiments were expressed in placards fixed to the gates of the *hôtel de ville* in Paris early in 1577; they also seem to have been well-echoed elsewhere.[22]

Perhaps as a result of the concentration of lesser magistrates in its ranks, the estates as a whole were divided when they suggested remedies to the king. On the reform of the Church, or a working alternative to venality, the orders could not agree. The delegates were united only about the need to dismantle Crown authority. Every estate disliked royal commissions, whether on fiscal or legal matters, the enforcement of a peace edict, or the ferreting out of provincial corruption. The proposals of the states — if they can be called such — for aiding Crown finances demanded the resignation of all financial officers, the institution of a commission of thirty-six deputies chosen by the king to investigate the finances of the previous reign, together with a suggestion that the *bailliages* levy royal finances in the place of *élections*.[23] Early in December the *Estates* asked Henry III to send all the proposals contained in the *cahiers* to a tribunal of judges, some of whom would be nominated by the king and some by the provinces. They put forward these proposals again in February 1577, just before the *Estates* were dismissed.[24] Since the proposals came from the third estate alone, they give some idea of the hostility of minor royal administrative officials in the provinces to the régime. They also indicate why the crown could not possibly have granted them, and why the *Estates* of Blois were a complete failure.

In 1578 the provincial assemblies again provided a focus for opposition. Burgundy gave the lead. As de Thou remarked:

> The Estates of Burgundy were the first who thought to remedy their ill, or at least to alleviate it. The nobility of this province, accustomed to liberty, carried impatiently the yoke of new taxes, and saw with horror young men without merit in the important posts.[25]

By May there were local but vigorous complaints concerning the refusal of the Crown to give concrete answers to the *cahiers des doléances* of the previous year. That session was not a success; in June it was reconvened. The abbot of Cîteaux, Nicholas Boucherat, then produced a remonstrance, supposedly from all the estates, which was printed and received considerable publicity throughout France.[26] In October the *Estates* of Burgundy met again. Instead of granting the Crown the cash it demanded, they made a bold request that the king be held accountable for his debts to the province. Only when his account had been satisfactorily rendered would they agree to pay more. Again their demands were printed. They ended:

> The only true remedy is that His Majesty take the common advice from all the provinces of the realm on the means of his acquittal (from debt). The true debts must be reorganised and separated from the false ones, and the amount levied in the least painful way, with the cash handled by receivers who will account for all. The reformation of the kingdom must also be seen to, following from the general *cahiers* of all the provinces.[27]

Other provinces echoed these demands. From 1577 to 1579 the Reformation of the State was a common theme.

The *Estates* of Auvergne also met in October 1578; they agreed to send deputies to court who would protest about new imposts.[28] In November it was the turn of Normandy. Normandy was important to the Crown in the sixteenth century because its taxable revenue was the highest of all the provinces. Rouen was second only to Lyons as a financial centre; it had been carefully groomed and then exploited by the Valois.[29] The Norman *Estates* also violently questioned royal authority. They threw out the *trésoriers généraux* who had been introduced in 1569 to represent the Crown. A representative of the clergy insulted the *premier président* of the *Parlement* of Rouen, turned to the governor and asked: 'When, Monseigneur, when will our afflictions come to an end? When will we see an end to the violent seizure of our goods and belongings by the sergeants?[30] The Estates refused the tax the Crown demanded, but themselves demanded a return to the levels of taxation of the good King Louis XII (not to mention Clovis) and also that the Crown reissue the Norman charter of 1314 and abolish the fiscal officers.[31]

The Crown also experienced difficulties in other provinces, though not to such a great extent as in Normandy. Guyenne did not possess unified *Estates* but a variety of regional assemblies. Those of Agenais, Condomois, and Gascony refused to pay their *taille*. They were aggrieved not only by the failure of the Crown to transform the demands of the *Estates-General* of Blois into an edict, but also by the fact that, owing to the ravages of the disavowed captains as well as a number of sectarian murders, the Edict of Pacification had not brought them complete peace.[32]

In 1579 the situation in the provinces became more grave. Both Normandy and Burgundy sat in emergency sessions in March; and both had deputies permanently at court pressing for its redress of their respective grievances. Normandy proved more intractable. The king's necessity was great, yet the necessity of Normandy, its *Estates* said, was greater. The only solution was 'a general assembly in which the acquittal of our debts would be dealt with and would satisfy present abuses — and those to come . . .'. They insisted that their *cahiers des doléances* be approved before they granted any taxation. They also demanded the reform of the Church, schools, hospitals, and the council of state; the removal of extraordinary commissioners — the suppression of royal officers; a temporary commission to replace the recently established *Parlement* of Rouen; the establishment of a chamber to investigate the 'officiers malversateurs' in finance; the suppression of the *trésoriers* and their *bureaux* as well as the *élections*; and, above all, the return of the Estates to their primary condition and importance. Henry III gave his verbal assent to these demands in April 1579. When asked to put his consent in writing, he told the deputies angrily: 'that they ought to content themselves that the king has given them his word concerning that assembly, which is more to be valued than any written guarantee which might be given to them'.[33] By 1583 the deputies of the *Estates* of Normandy, like others, may have believed that Henry's words belied his heart. Their delegates at court had been arrested and imprisoned.

How great was the opposition to Henry III? Did it openly attack the authority of the Crown? A few pamphlets published in Paris do not provide evidence for the existence of a coherent opposition. Nor should opposition to royal demands be immediately regarded as deep-rooted because it emanated from provincial Estates. The records of *bonnes villes* suggest otherwise. Thus in Toulouse there was more hatred of the Huguenots, who almost surrounded the city, than there were grievances against the Crown.[34] But demands of the provincial estates, taken as a whole, were broad-ranging, and, in economic matters, more impressive than those of the *Estates-General* of Blois. In some areas, of course, Estates were not active. In others there was little sympathy for the plans put forward by Normandy and Burgundy. In Dauphiné, for example, the nobility had been able, during the civil wars, to usurp yet more privileges, while some towns had bought privileges at the expense of the villages. The nobility and the third estate were, therefore, fighting a running battle. The third estate and a group of delegates who were known as coming from the 'villages' fought a similar battle. The demands made in the *cahiers* of Dauphiné reflected local rather than national problems.[35]

Was the opposition in the provinces the result of a plot? The English ambassador, Sir Amyas Poulet, thought so. He reported that the Guises held a secret family conference at Dijon on 31 May 1578, and that members of the Estates were present.[36] This meeting certainly took place. Yet as the brother of the governor there, the duke of Guise handled Burgundy diplomatically throughout 1579; he did no more than might have been expected of a governor who pursued the interests of his province. He was, of course, aware of provincial obstinacy, but he was also involved with his Lorraine relatives in plans for the invasion of England.[37]

The Crown worried lest the duke of Anjou, the king's younger brother, was encouraging provincial opposition. Anjou had lent support to the Huguenots in 1575 and 1576. In March 1579 Bellièvre, the *surintendant des finances*, was sent to investigate Anjou's behaviour, and to negotiate with the *Estates* of Holland. Bellièvre wrote to the Crown warning of rumours that Anjou was trying to create a league against it in the provinces.[38] Anjou denied the charge, although he admitted that he wanted to protect the 40,000 gentlemen who had accompanied him to Flanders from being prosecuted for *lèse-majesté*. This is the only mention of Anjou's involvement with the internal opposition in France before 1582. For most of the period from 1577 to 1582, he was kept well-occupied by his negotiations to marry Elizabeth of England, by his plans for Flemish expeditions, and by his dreams of winning kingdoms for himself in northern Italy.[39]

The clergy played a more important part in uniting provincial resistance to the Crown. Their general assembly met in 1578. Though many of its discussions were self-centred, it spoke not only for the clergy but for the nobility and the third estate when it denounced the despoliation of the Church, the rapacity of the Crown, and the flagrant disregard shown to old corporations by the monarchy. Its debates were well-publicized. Several provincial meetings of the clergy were told to repartition the *décimes*. Moreover, the clergy was often the most constructive and cohesive group amongst the provincial estates.[40]

How damaging to the Crown were the demands of the provincial Estates? Some demands, such as those for schools, hospitals, and better police, the Crown could satisfy in its own interest as well as in that of the estates. Yet there were other demands which the Crown could satisfy only by offending the other interests. Thus it could not legislate against *épices* (the tips permitted to office-holders in the law-courts) without causing protests from the legal profession. Nor could it attempt to reform the Church without arousing opposition from within the Gallican clergy and at Rome. If it attempted to reform the abbeys, the nobility would be offended. The Crown was expected to maintain the abbeys to provide indoor relief for indigent nobles. There were other demands which the Crown could not satisfy; time alone could remedy the ravages of civil war upon the economy about which the provincial Estates were so eloquent. When making their demands, provincial estates were also concerned to defend their own privileges. This is made plain not so much by their *cahiers* but by their *procès-verbaux*. Yet in their debates, as well as in their complaints to the Crown, they expressed views which came to be widely held about the nature of the state.

Although the opposition to Henry III appeared to be strong, it collapsed between 1579 and 1583. The first reason for this collapse was that Henry III aligned himself with the opposition in much the same way as he had done in 1576. He signed the Ordinance of Blois in 1579; this was substantially the *cahier* of protests which the *Estates-General* of Blois had presented three years earlier.[41] He thus promised a major reformation in the state which would be sufficiently substantial to encompass all the varying demands of the provincial Estates. But there were other changes which also defused the provincial opposition from within the 'constituted bodies'. One was the Huguenot revolt of 1580-1 in Gascony, a revolt which not only revealed all the paralysing weaknesses of the Huguenots, but one which made it difficult for the various *parlements* to pursue their dissent. The arrival of a new lieutenant-general, Jacques de Matignon, ended friction with the Crown in Gascony for the time being.[42] In other provinces there were noble revolts. One such revolt threatened Normandy in November 1579. Little is known about it save that it had some support from Picardy and upper Anjou and included several of the duke of Anjou's captains.[43]

Nevertheless, this revolt made the *Parlement* of Rouen nervous and split the unity of the provincial estates. In Provence the struggle between factions of the nobility grew worse with the reinstatement of the Grand Prior in 1581 as lieutenant-general.[44] Dauphiné was buffeted by a peasant 'league' which had been growing in the late 1570s; it spilled over into neighbouring provinces, and was put down with considerable violence, for it had manifested disturbing signs of class-conflicts, and had mocked ecclesiastical authority.[45] Rumours of Spanish interference kept some provinces loyal. Huguenots, peasants, disruptive seigneurs, Spain — these were the skeletons rattled before the provincial Estates by Crown deputies in 1580 and 1581, and they were sufficient to keep them loyal. For Henry III fulfilled few, if any, of the promises he had given in 1579.

In 1582 the provincial movement began to regroup. In June, Dieppe revolted against tax-farmers. A little later a tax-farmer at Beauvais was besieged by a mob.[46] Towns such as Amiens wrote to the Crown and sent recalcitrant deputies to court. The *Estates* of Champagne, Picardy, and Normandy, feeling the ground-swell, also sent deputies to court, particularly to remonstrate against the tax on cloth. Troyes sent merchants and artisans; it claimed that unemployment was the result of the Crown's actions.[47] The king refused to see them. The Midi, Provence, Dauphiné, Gascony, and the Lyonnais were aroused by new salt taxes and sent letters to the duke of Anjou, asking him to be their protector and protesting about the oppressions of the Crown. Anjou showed their letters to Henry III and warned of the 'effervescence' in the area.[48] For the first time the *Estates* of Brittany joined in the complaints. In December 1582 there were again demands for an *Estates-General*.[49]

Henry III responded with attempts to buy off the opposition yet again. He would summon an Assembly of Notables. Commissioners toured the provinces during the autumn and winter of 1582 with detailed instructions to visit all the main towns to hear complaints — and also to stop every seven leagues to listen to villagers.[50] Provincial governors were asked to assist them. Their range of inquiry was wide. They worked with a series of questions formulated by the Crown; those questioned had to swear to the accuracy of their replies.

1. Are the clergy hindered in the exercise of their ministry and by whom?
2. Is there anyone in your *bailliage* treating people with violence and extorting taxes, money and service from them?
3. How is justice administered?
4. Draw up a list of the most trustworthy men who are best fitted to hold office, including office-holders and private individuals.
5. Make the *vis-baillis* appear with their *procès-verbaux* of the arrests of criminals.

No government of the sixteenth century conducted so rigorous an examination of its own inadequacies, or so invited the opprobrium of its subjects. Some provinces hardly welcomed the commissioners. Lyons gave them a rough ride. So did the *Estates* of Picardy.[51] The latter said that they were delighted that the king wanted to remedy abuses, 'although very late'. But they ignored his questionnaire; instead they gave their own views of the ills in the body politic. During twenty years of civil war they had seen:

> So many fine assemblies, so many fine ordinances, the Estates (General) so solemnly convoked and held at Orleans and then at Blois, the colloquies and assemblies at Poissy, Moulins, Paris and elsewhere, all of them full of great hopes for the relief of the people; we see, however, that all this has achieved nothing.[52]

They claimed not only that the bureaucracy was too large, but that two-thirds of its members were useless. The bourgeois found that trade, especially in wine and salt, was 'taxed five or six times over'. The peasantry 'groaned'. The gendarmerie 'pillaged, raped and tortured'. A silent war was taking place in which the towns exploited the countryside. Many said: 'Let us make our homes in the forests, abandon our houses, live in other places where misery is not so great, where the sergeants and soldiers will not pester us.'[53] Knowledgeable contemporaries, like Estoile, the Parisian diarist, the English ambassador, Cobham, or the historian Jacques-Auguste de Thou, thought that the king was indulging in a propaganda exercise in order to buy time.[54] But they were perhaps mistaken. From May 1582 there were several rumours that the king had been converted to the need for better government: and numerous edicts and ordinances were issued to begin the reform of the royal court, to streamline the council's procedures, and to curtail pensions.[55]

After several delays the Assembly of Notables met in December 1583 and sat for two months. It was attended by the king's closest advisers as well as by the Masters of Requests who possessed specialist knowledge about trade, currency, and law. Anjou was invited but refused to come. The Queen Mother, Catherine de Medici, was delegated to go to Château Thierry to discover what he was plotting.[56] The King of Navarre (the future Henry IV) was also invited, but he declined, saying that it was not his business to tell the king how he should rule the kingdom.[57] Some ambassadors and some provincial lieutenants also attended. The debates and the resolutions of the assembly were realistic. They well describe the problems which faced the provinces of France under Henry III. They also indicate the extent to which the Crown, albeit in the short-term, could hope to solve them. But the assembly had little time to translate its conclusions into action. In May 1584 the king's brother died. Anjou alive had been a nuisance; Anjou dead was a disaster. His death meant that outsiders could begin to play on provincial discontent. Philip II of Spain had the most speculative eye as well as the most ready cash. In 1583 he had meddled in the Midi, by offering the governor of Languedoc, Henri de Montmorency-Damville, a substantial pension.[58] In 1584 the duke of Guise obtained a similar pension.[59] The 'bonne ligue' of the provinces against Crown exactions began to turn into the 'bonne et sainte ligue' of 1585.

Why did these great proposals for reform in 1576, 1579, and 1583, together with a number of piecemeal attempts, all fail? Was the Crown so financially in debt that, like a cat climbing a tree, it found that it could not move backwards? Or did it lack political will? Or would the provinces not accept reform at the hand of Henry III, even when he sincerely wanted to promulgate it?

First it is clear that piecemeal attempts to find solutions did not suffice. In 1577, and again in 1578, there were attempts to deal with monetary and currency problems caused by inflation and poor-quality coinage.[60] Also in 1577, attempts were made to stimulate industry by reorganizing the taxes on various products, particularly wool, iron, and textiles.[61] Early in 1578, yet other attempts apparently sponsored by the *prevôt des marchands* of Paris were made to repurchase areas of the royal domain.[62] Some *Grands-Jours* (sovereign courts on assize) were held in the provinces to suppress disorder, and also to investigate false titles of nobility.[63] According to the English ambassador, they were reasonably successful.[64] But the problems which these efforts attempted to solve would not be dealt with separately; they were too interconnected. Currency reform, for instance, implied a reform of the customs in order to deal with an adverse balance of payments. A customs reform meant, in its turn, dealing with the question of tax-farming which would strike at the heart of the bureaucracy. Domain repurchase and redemption of mortgages were vital issues to contemporaries; but they led to forest surveys, investigations of illegal usurpations, and to the need to find alternative sources of revenue to finance fiscal exactions. Thus the reform of the artisan corporations in December 1581 had much to commend it. The corporations were to be made less exclusive by extending them to every principle city throughout France; they were also to be made less corrupt by systematizing their rules of entry. Though the results might have been beneficial, the reform itself nevertheless provided a new tax for the Crown.[65] Reaction in the provinces to some of these projected reforms was luke-warm. Burgundy refused to have anything to do with the currency reform for years, while the *Parlement* of Paris refused the relevant edict, and remonstrated with the Crown that it was against the fundamental law of the kingdom — not to mention customs going back to Hebrew times.[66]

The second disadvantage of piecemeal reform was a fiscal one. To what extent could the Crown institute reforms without prejudicing its own treasury? In theory it should have been able to do what it liked. The Assembly of Notables was provided with financial details for the years from

1576, together with summaries of budgets going back much further, and also, for purposes of comparison, everything that could be discovered about royal finances in Spain.[67] The revenue for 1582, it was calculated, was about 23.5 million *livres*, excluding income from the creation of new offices, extraordinary levies upon towns, pensions to governors, and taxes imposed by provincial estates for their own purposes.[68] This was a huge sum by English standards of the day — and huge even by French standards.[69] The assembly was also told that the royal revenue in 1576 had been about 13 million *livres*, and was given full details of the increases in taxation during the intervening years. Royal receipts had, therefore, almost doubled within a decade. Not even Richelieu, in a time of war, was able to manage such a proportionate increase.[70] It is hardly surprising that Henry III should have encountered resistance in the provinces.

Henry III should have been free enough financially to buy off dissension. In fact, he was powerless to do so. Priuli, the Venetian ambassador, said that the Crown was isolated from the kingdom as a result of the 'malissima intelligenza' between the nobility and the people. The Crown, however, far outspent its income. The Assembly of Notables was again given details of the extent of its indebtedness. 114 million *livres* was the figure arrived at.[71] The assembly found it difficult to investigate the details of expenses. They were aware, of course, that the wars had been costly. Disbanding the German ritters in 1576 had cost nearly 6 million *livres*. Servicing the Crown debt in Paris in 1577 was already a major drain upon its resources. Because the clergy refused to continue their obligation to pay the interest on this debt in 1577, the receiver attempted resignation and flight. In Rouen Crown debts were also substantial, and its repayments were 89,000 *livres* in arrears.[72]

To many, though, it was self-evident that the Crown was an expensive luxury. In 1579, Priuli found it distasteful that amidst the 'gran necessita' of the realm the king 'spendi profusamente'.[73] According to Estoile, in the early months of 1580 Paris was in a fury over the king's largesse.[74] The Court tended to convince those deputies who came from the provinces of its prodigality rather than its desperate need. Thus a deputy from Metz reported to his constituency in 1581:

> The king easily found two hundred thousand *livres* to give to certain of his gentlemen favourites to be spent on clothes and decorations for Twelfth Night, which was celebrated in this court with as much magnificence, and luxury as had been seen for a long time, which makes me suspect that the Treasury is not yet exhausted . . . But I fear that I have come too late and this generosity will not extend to me.[75]

The Assembly of Notables found it impossible to put a price on the king's pleasures. Early in his reign Henry III had created a privy purse which was not audited by the *Epargne* (Treasury) or the *Chambre des Comptes* (Chamber of Accounts).[76] The miscellaneous quittances which survive can give spicy examples of court expenditure, but cannot provide the total picture. On closer inspection, many gifts prove to be pounds of flesh demanded by debtors and financiers. The Italians gained houses in Paris, substantial bishoprics, peerages, new tax-farms at a discount, and building contracts at inflated prices.[77] With them, enjoying the fruits of their posts, were the *intendants des finances*. Their rapid rise to political importance from their creation in 1556 was signalled by their entry to the council in 1583. Their purpose, initially, was to prevent corruption, and to keep the system running; but they had become corrupt as well. Only Claude Marcel, a former *prévôt des marchands* in Paris, enjoyed a reputation for honesty. The rest were to various degrees suspect, the most notorious being Benoît Milon, sieur de Videville, the son of a locksmith, who rose (as Estoile said) 'comme les champignons, dans une nuit'. He controlled a network which was only temporarily crushed by the establishment of a *Chambre de Justice* (a royal commission with judicial authority) by the advice of the Assembly of Notables. This commission sent Milon in flight to the Netherlands in autumn 1584.[78]

The court underwent successive and paralysing crises of liquidity in March 1574, July 1576, 1581, and July 1582.[79] This was despite attempts to obtain ready cash by such expedients as repudiating the debt to the German ritters and raising loans from the *conseillers* in the *Parlement* of Paris as well as from Crown servants.[80] The problem was caused by a combination of circumstances. The income of the Crown was, in theory, high, but its expenditure was also enormous. Yet its income was increasingly drained away by a 'leaky pipe' of financial maladministration in the provinces, as well as by the refusal of the provinces to pay taxes.

The Assembly of Notables was not entirely pessimistic. If the series of measures which they proposed were adopted, then over a period of ten years the Crown would be on the way to recovery. Offices would not be repurchased immediately; they would be left to fall vacant upon death. Domain inquiries would discover fraud. Chambers of Justice and commissioners investigating *taille* registers (*commissaires pour le régalement de taille*) would somewhat close the leaky pipe. The Assembly seemed to have accepted that Henry III would maintain his reformed attitude and keep pensions down to a minimum; not give places in the Church to those that were not fully qualified; maintain a smaller court; and account for all his expenditure in the Treasury. Although it accepted the Crown's goodwill, it asked much of the Crown. Not only did Henry III's *mignons* enjoy an entrenched position, but also the financiers were their allies, and they alone could provide the Crown with its short-term credit. Nor could any government in the sixteenth century be expected to forgo its ecclesiastical patronage. The provinces were sceptical. 'So many fine ordinances, so many fine assemblies', the *estates* of Picardy had said, yet nothing had been achieved. Why should the provinces have been more hopeful in 1583? The Crown possessed such crude and unreliable means for enforcing its political decisions that it could hardly have undertaken the schemes proposed by the Assembly. Royal governors and lieutenants were connected in the provincial mind with the infernal war-machines of previous decades. If aristocrats such as the duke of Anjou or the duke of Guise sought to exert influence on the provinces, the Crown could not thwart them. Some lieutenants were hard-working, and gained reputations for 'prudence' or political shrewdness; d'Inteville in Picardy and Matignon in Gascony are examples. But such men were not to be found everywhere.[81] The provincial *parlements* exercised themselves as best they could, but they could not repress disorder. They tended to be hidebound by tradition and were aroused only by issues like Gallicanism, or by taxes which affected them directly. They were divided from the Estates in their provinces. Moreover, some *parlements*, like that of Bordeaux, were split into factions. The lesser courts, particularly the *présidiaux*, were even more unreceptive to reform. They were staffed by the 'poor relations' of the office-holding world, men who had seen their differentials of pay eroded by inflation. Estoile referred to them thus:

> But as soon as His Majesty has thought of creating an office, no matter how small, there are disputes about who shall have it, and he is importuned about the reversion of the office; for there is no officer so poor that he does not wish to secure his estates and cannot find the ready cash to buy rights of reversion, and yet (there is no officer) who does not criticize the king, and blame him for the multiplication and sale of offices of which he is the first and prime cause.[82]

The Assembly's proposals for reform offered such officers nothing. In the short term, they might have to face vigorous judicial inquiries about their own irregularities. In the long term, they might be deprived not only of their offices which they had purchased, but also of their right to sell them in reversion.[83]

The Crown had one sure hold over the provinces. It could deploy Masters of Requests who served the Royal Council to inquire into local abuses. Yet they could hardly be expected to remedy the abuses they uncovered. Their experiences in the execution of the Edict of Pacification in 1577 suggest that there was a long, hard struggle ahead for them to impose their will throughout the provinces of France. By 1583 it was too late. The Crown had lost the confidence of the provinces.

Henry III himself perhaps realized this. Towards the end of his reign he wrote several personal letters to his secretary, Villeroy, in his characteristic spidery, almost illegible hand. Their tone is pessimistic. On 14 August 1584 he wrote about the former greatness of France and the impossibility of combatting sectarian disorder; of the lack of ready cash; and the 'evil spirits' whom he, as king, could not prevent joining the 'turbulents'. 'It has been in our power', he said, 'not to fall to the position we are now in, where I see no way out.' But he was not to be blamed for the machinations of either Philip II or his brother Anjou:

> I have not written you this letter hoping for any practical effect (No. I am not so mistaken as that); but simply to unburden my overcharged heart . . . I know well that we are without resources and I know that we are going to be worse off . . . We can only deal with things as they come (and I think that there is nothing else to be done at the moment). We must clutch at some straw.[84]

Notes

1. I am grateful to Dr J.M. Davies of the University of Essex for helpful comments and suggestions. I acknowledge the financial assistance of the Research Fund of the University of Sheffield towards the preparation of this paper.

2. *Calendar of State Papers Foreign* (1558-91), ed. J. Stevenson *et.al.* (28 vols, London, 1868-1969), *1577-78*, p. 448 (9 January 1578) hereafter (*C.S.P. For.*)

3. R. Kingdon, *The Consolidation of the French Huguenot Movement* (Geneva, 1967), cc. 2 and 3.

4. J. Estèbe and B. Vögler, 'La Genèse d'une société protestante: étude comparée de quelques registres consistoriaux languedociens et palatins vers 1600', *Annales E.S.C.* xxxi (1976), 362-88; see also J. Estèbe, 'Les Délibérations du consistoire de Montauban', *Montauban et Bas-Quercy* (Actes, 27e Congrès de la fédération de la Société Languedoc-Pyrénées-Gascogne et 24e Congrès de la Fédération historique du Sud-Oest) (Montauban, 1974), pp. 345-56.

5. Bibliothèque Publique et Universitaire, Geneva; Archives Tronchin MS. 149, fos. 66-79 ('Advertissement donné au Roy pour son service par Mathurin Charretier secretaire de monseigneur le mareschal de dampville, sa majeste estant dans Thurin au mois d'aoust 1574').

6. The Edict of Poitiers, September 1574, is to be found in Fontanon, *Les Edicts et ordonnances des rois de France* (Paris, 1611) iv. 460 ff. The edict of 1570 is reprinted in J.D. Laborde, *Gaspard de Coligny, Amiral de France* (3 vols, Paris, 1879-82), iii. 569-78. A discussion of the relative merits of the edicts is to be found in F. Garrison, *Essai sur les commissaires de l'Edict de Nantes* (Montpellier, 1905), pp. 15 ff.

7. There were eight national synods before the massacre of St Bartholomew in 1572, two in the following decade, and only one from 1582 to 1592 (J. Quick, *Synodicon in Gallia Reformata* (London, 1692), vol. 1). There were, of course, numerous political assemblies of the Huguenots in the 1560s and 1570s. An incomplete list is given in G. Griffiths, *Representative Government in the Sixteenth Century* (Oxford, 1968), pp. 161-2.

8. Though no study exists of the effect of the religious wars upon any Huguenot city the pressure of war on Nîmes can be gauged from the diocesan *assiette* (or tax-distributing assembly) in October 1575 in Arch. Dép. Gard C 845. For la Rochelle see L. de Voisin, sieur de la Popelinière, *Histoire de France* (n.p., 1581), Bk. 40, pp. 290, 317, 324ᵛ-6, 364-6.

9. G. Esquer, 'Le Rôle politique de François de Valois, duc d'Alençon et d'Anjou', *Positions de l'Ecole des Chartes* (Paris, 1903), pp. 67-73. See also H.C. Davila, trans. Aylesbury and Cotterell, *The Historie of the Civill Warres of France* (London, 1647), pp. 437-43.

10. F.C. Palm, in *Politics and Religion in Sixteenth-Century France* (New York, 1927), pp. 100-1, 104, regards Damville as 'an advocate of religious toleration' and 'a Politique leader', but he overestimates the strength of Damville and underplays the tenuous alliance with the protestants. Catholic and Huguenot alliances in other provinces enjoyed a brief existence. In Provence, for example, the alliance quickly collapsed because its nobility was divided (E. Arnaud, *Histoire des protestants de Provence, du comtat Venaissin et de la principauté d'Orange* (2 vols, Paris, 1884), i. 221-7.

11. The 'Declaration et protestation faicte par monsieur le mareschal de Dampville sur l'occasion pour laquelle il prit les armes pendant l'union' is dated 13 November 1574 in C.D. De Vic and J.J. Vaissète, *Histoire Générale du Languedoc* (16 vols, Toulouse,

1872-1905), xii (1891), col. llll. Some versions are dated 3 November. In 1575 it was published twice in Strasbourg and was also published in English (from an unknown provenance) and in German (from Basel).

12. De Vic and Vaissète, op. cit. (one word missing, supplied from the printed French edition).

13. Palm, op.cit., p. 121.

14. In Languedoc, Navarre had to work through his wayward supporter, François de Coligny, comte de Châtillon (Haag, *La France Protestante* (Geneva, 9 vols, reprint, 1966), iii. 405-7). Around la Rochelle, La Noue had problems (Haag, ibid. vi. 291). For Dauphiné see C. Dufayard, *Le Connétable des Diguières* (Paris, 1894), pp. 65 ff.

15. The *prévôt des marchands* told the king that since 1560 Paris had provided 36 million *livres* in taxation and the clergy of France a total of 60 million *livres*. But he estimated that the king's gifts for the previous four years had totalled 57 million *livres*. His sums are notional, but his substantive point is strong. Other nations enjoyed the benefit of peace, 'profitting to our disadvantage', while God's wrath afflicted France because of the 'universal corruption of all the estates and orders of your realm'. He also reminded the king of the teachings of St Louis (*Registres de délibérations de la ville de Paris*, ed. F. Bonnardot, A. Tuetey, and P. Guérin (Paris, 9 vols, 1866-), vii. 313-17).

16. 'Remonstrances au Roi de Troyes, Châlons, Guise, Laon, Langres, Chaumont et Bar-sur-Aube' in B.N. MS. Dupuy, vol. 87, fos. 39-43.

17. Haton, Claude, *Mémoires*, ed. F. Bourquelot (2 vols, Paris, 1857), ii. 797.

18. P-V. Palma Cayet, *Chronologie Novenaire* in *Collection des Mémoires*, ed. C.B. Petitot (52 vols, Paris, 1824-6), xxxviii (1823), 254-7.

19. *Lettres de Henri III*, ed. M. François (3 vols, in progress Paris, 1972), iii. 85-138.

20. E. Charleville, *Les Etats généraux de 1576; le Fonctionnement d'une tenue d'états* (Paris, 1901), pp. 43-69. Although the Protestant-dominated areas did not all submit *cahiers*, many still survive (cf. Drouot, *Notes sur la Bourgogne et son Esprit Public* (Dijon, 1937), pp. 94-95).

21. 'Remonstrances tres humbles extraictes du cahyer de Troyes qui ne sont comprinses au cayer general de la province' in B.N. MS. 500 Colbert 8, fos. 366-7.

22. P. de l'Estoile, *Le Journal . . . pour le règne de Henri III, 1574-1589*, ed. L.-R. Lefèvre (Paris, 1943), p. 143.

23. E. Picot, *Histoire des états généraux* (Paris, 1872), pp. 5-6.

24. C. Mayer, *Des Etats Généraux* (Paris, 1789), xiii, pp. 230-1, 256-9.

25. J.-A. de Thou, *Histoire Universelle* (London, 16 vols, 1734), vii. 717-31.

26. 'Remonstrances faicte au Roy le 18 Juin 1578 en la ville de Rouen par frère Nicolas Boucherat, abbé de Cisteaux, pour et au nom des estats de Bourgogne ensemble la response de S.M.' s.l.1578. It was printed in Dijon in 1579. The grievances which Boucherat made were derived from those of Blois: (i) abuses in the sale of ecclesiastical benefices, church property and wealth, and of the taxation of the clergy; (ii) sale of offices; and (iii) the reduction in the fiscal charges, renouncing 'tant de noveautes qui s'inventent tous les jours a la foule du peuple'.

27. 'Memoire trouvé clos sur la table de la salle des Estats tenus en Bourgogne 1 novembre 1578' in B.N. MS. fr. 7742 and afterwards in Drouot, *Notes sur la Bourgogne*, pp. 141-3.

28. Despatch of October 1578, Lippomano to the Doge, B.N. MS. It. 1730, fo. 470.

29. *Histoire de la Normandie (Univers de la France)*, ed. M. de Boüard (1970), pp. 273-4.

30. C.-M. de Robillard de Beaurepaire, *Cahiers des états de Normandie sous le règne de Henri III. Documents . . .* (Rouen, 1891), p. 324.

31. De Beaurepaire, pp. 5-13. Neither the king's secretary, Brûlart, nor the *surintendant des finances*, Bellièvre, knew what the Norman Charter was. Brûlart's reply to Bellièvre's enquiry briskly told him to ask the *parlement* of Rouen; 'Vous estes sur le lieu pour vous informer de la verite' (B.N. MS. fr. 15905 fo. 42, 19 March 1579). This is an

interesting sidelight on the attitude of the Crown to provincial liberties. Henry III regarded Normandy as the seed-bed of discord in other provinces ('Mémoire sur les états de Normandie', B.N. MS. fr. 15905, fo. 15). For a similar appeal to the remote past, made by Jean-Jouvenal des Ursins, see J.-P. Genet, above, p. 37.

32. The queen-mother's letters reveal the position as she saw it herself in Guyenne (*Lettres de Cathérine de Médicis*, ed. H. de la Ferrière and G. Baguenault de Puchesse, (10 vols, Paris, 1880, 1907), vi. 124, 177-8, 202). She advised her son, Henry III, to give way as much as possible 'et principallement de tant de petites parties', and rebuked him for having delayed so long; 'Cela les eust aucunement contentez . . . encores vaut-il mieulx tard que jamais' (ibid., pp. 202-3).

33. De Beaurepaire, *Cahier des états* . . . , pp. 16 ff.

34. 'Délibérations des capitouls', Archives municipales de Toulouse, BB 13, 1572-8.

35. L. Scott von Doren, 'Revolt and reaction in the city of Romans, Dauphiné, 1579-80', *Sixteenth-Century Journal*, v (1974), 71-100; A. Dussert, *Les Etats de Dauphiné de la guerre de cent ans aux guerres de religion* (Grenoble, 1923).

36. A. Paulet to Elizabeth I (*C.S.P. For.*, 1575-7 (1880), p.15).

37. A.L. Martin, *Henry III and the Jesuits* (Geneva, 1973), ch. iv; P-0 de Törne, 'Philippe II et Henri de Guise, le début de leurs relations (1578)', *Rev. Hist.* clxvii (1931), 323-35; Drouot, *Notes sur la Bourgogne*, pp. 133-4.

38. Instructions for Bellièvre before leaving to visit Anjou, 3 March 1579, reminded him that there were those who desired to 'troubler les aff(ai)res de ce Roy(aum)e pour mieux exercer leurs passions'. The king had heard 'de plusieurs endroicts Quil y en a quelques uns de sa maison qui soubz son nom taschent de f(air)e entrer ses subjects a une certaine ligue ou association et de les y obliger par promesses et signatures qu'ils leur font . . .'. Bellièvre's trip was to gain assurance of Anjou's loyalty (B.N. MS. fr. 15905, fos. 4 ff.).

39. P.L. Müller and A. Diegerick, *Documents concernant les relations entre le duc d'Anjou et les Pays Bas, 1576-1583* (5 vols, Utrecht, 1889-99), iii. 92-101, 122-6, 128-32, 156-9, etc.; B.N. MS. fr. 15573 (Henry III to Bellièvre, 7 March 1583), fo. 24 (déchiffré fo. 34); G. Esquer, op.cit., p. 72; N. Sutherland, *The French Secretaries of State in the age of Catherine de Medici*(London, 1962), pp. 225-9; 238-40.

40. L. Serbat, *Les Assemblées du clergé de France, 1561-1615* (Paris, 1906), pp. 89-108. The archbishop of Lyons, Pierre d'Epinac, had to defend himself against the charge of having 'intelligence' with 'ceux des estatz de bourgongne' see P. Richard, *La Papauté et la Ligue Française* (Paris, 1901), pp. 101-2.

41. F.A. Isambert *et al.*, *Recueil général des anciennes lois françaises, 420-1789* (28 vols, Paris, 1822-33), xiv, 380-463.

42. *The Letters and Documents of Armand de Gontaut, Baron de Biron*, ed. S.H. Ehrman (2 vols, New York, 1936), ii. 600-41, present the troubled picture of Guyenne in 1580-1 during the course of a war which the king's lieutenant Biron had a part in causing. Biron was recalcitrant too in undertaking the peace (see, for instance, De Neufville to Bellièvre, 3 February 1581, Saint André de Cuzac, B.N. MS. fr. 15906, fo. 174). The *pouvoir* given to the Marshal de Matignon, his successor, is in ibid., fos. 482 ff. (Paris, 28 August 1581, a copy). With the help of an army Matignon managed to hold the ring in this difficult province (J. de Callières, *Histoire du Maréchal de Matignon* (Paris, 1661), pp. 149 ff.).

43. M. Foisil, 'Harangue et rapport d'Antoine Séguier, commissaire pour le Roi en Basse-Normandie, 1579-80', *Annales de Normandie*, xxvi (1976), 25-40, and correspondence to and from Bellièvre in the course of 1579 in B.N. MS. fr. 15905, fo. 199 (Matignon — Bellièvre, 26 November 1579), etc.

44. E. Arnaud, op.cit., pp. 242 ff.

45. Crown mediation — forcefully attempted by Catherine de Medici — failed in Provence (A. Dussert, 'Cathérine de Médicis et les états de Dauphiné, préludes du procès des tailles et arbitrage de la reine mère en 1579', *Bulletin de l'Académie delphinale*, 6 série, ii (1931), 123-89). See also L. Scott Van Doren, op.cit., and E. Le Roy Ladurie, *Les Paysans de Languedoc, XVIe — XVIIe siècles* (Paris, 1966), pp. 394-6. The revolt spread to the Vivarais; in March 1579 the rebels there sent a petition to the Crown entitled 'La Requeste des ligues du Vivarais' which purported to come from the 'pauvres gens de nostres pauvre et desole plat pays de Vivaretz'. In 1579 and 1580 they refused to pay taxes (A. Mazon (pseud. Dr Francus), *Notes et documents historiques sur les huguenots en Vivarais* (4 vols, Privas, 1904), ii. 55-78).

46. The tax upon cloth, the *sol pour livre*, particularly harshly affected those provinces. The trouble continued into 1583 when a tax-farmer was killed (*C.S.P.For., Jan.-June 1583* (1913), p.110, Cobham to Walsingham, 5 February 1583).

47. B.N. MS. It. 1732, pp. 203-25 (L. Priuli to the Doge).

48. For the complaints of the estates of Brittany see Morice, *Histoire de Bretagne*, iii. 1445; Henri Sée, 'Les Etats de Bretagne, au xvie siècle', *A. Bret.* x (1894), 19, 128-9, B.N. MS. fr. 22314 (registres of the *greffier* of the Estates of Brittany). The *remonstrances* for 1578 and 1579 are published in I. Luchitsky, *Katolicheskaya Liga i Kalvinistî vo Frantsii* (Kiev, 1877), vol. 1, Appendix, pp. 40-57.

49. A. Karcher, 'L'Assemblée des Notables de Saint-Germain-en-Laye' in *B.E.C.* cxiv (1956), 115-62.

50. G. Hanotaux, *Origine de l'institution des intendants de province* (Paris, 1884), pp. 187-218.

51. E. Pallasse, *La Sénéchaussée et siège présidial de Lyon pendant les guerres de religion* (Lyons, 1943), pp. 364-9; *La Remonstrance faicte pour le tiers estat a la convocation des trois estats du bailliage de Chaumont en la salle du siege au chastel et donjon dudict Chaumont* (s.p., 1583) . . . , in Karcher, op. cit., p. 121). The meeting is referred to in *C.S.P. For., Jan.-June 1583* (1913), p. 373 (Cobham to Walsingham, 31 May 1583).

52. *La Remonstrance* (s.p., 1583).

53. Ibid.

54. L'Estoile, *Le Journal*, pp. 306-7; de Thou, *Histoire Universelle*, ix. 81-82.

55. After returning from a long fast, Henry III reorganized his council to reduce its numbers, and he ordered windows with glass to be cut into the council chambers in his châteaux, so that he could attend debates (*C.S.P. For., May-Dec. 1582* (1909), p. 112, Cobham to Walsingham, 27 June 1582). He held a large meeting of the council in June 1582 at Fontainebleau where the major problems of state were aired. Throughout 1582 and into the following year a stream of reforming ordinances was issued (Karcher, op.cit., p. 123).

56. Ibid. p. 129.

57. Ibid. p. 133.

58. A draft version of a proposed treaty between Damville and Spain is to be found in Archivo General de Simancas, Papeles de Estado. Milan y Saboya leg. 1258, fo. 160. Eventually, the arrangements for the payments of the pension were made through the duke of Savoy. Philip II approved of this arrangement (ibid., leg. 1259, fo. 74 (12 May 1584)). I am grateful to Mr C. Riley for these references, and to Dr N.H. Griffin for obtaining a microfilm of them for me.

59. J. de Croze, *Les Guises, les Valois et Philippe II* (2 vols, Paris, 1868), i. 300-1.

60. J. Lafourne and P. Prieur, *Les Monnaies des rois de France: François I — Henri IV* (Paris, n.d.), pp. 97-98. The economic and monetary background to the government reform is discussed by F.C. Spooner, *L'Economie mondiale et les frappes monétaires en France, 1493-1680* (Paris, 1956), pp. 90-92.

61. The *prévôt des marchands* wanted to repurchase the *rentes* on the *greniers à sel* in the ten *généralités* of France. The king was interested and ordered an investigation of all the

rentes on salt. But the inquiry was subsequently dropped because under the threat of an inquiry the farmer of the *gabelle* refused to take on the tax-farming. A promise to resume the royal domain was made again in the edict of Blois in May 1579 (Isambert, *Recueil*, xiv. 452-554), and again in 1582 (Karcher, op.cit., p.120).

63. Article 206 of the Ordonnance of Blois promised some *Grands Jours* (Isambert, *Recueil*, xiv. 429). In April 1581 the sessions began in Berry, Auvergne, Orléannais, Nivernais, Bourbonnais, Beaujolais, Lyonnais, Marche. In 1583 an important but long-delayed, *chambre de justice* was held in Gascony (R. Brives-Cazes, *La Chambre de justice de Guyenne en 1583-4* (Bordeaux, 1874)).

64. *C.S.P. For., July 1583 — July 1584* (1914), p. 252, Stafford to Walsingham, 1/11 December 1583. Referring to the chamber, Stafford said, 'The king has continued the *grands jours* three months longer. Truly justice is done in them marvellously severely. At first it was thought that it was taken in hand to "attrappe" them of the religion, but truly it is common to all men, and more to Catholics than to Protestants. Men of great quality have been executed in it.'

65. E. Coornaert, *Les Corporations en France* (Paris, 1941), pp. 130-3.

66. Drouot, op.cit., pp. 39-44.

67. 'Traicté de tous les estats d'Espaigne', part of a bigger collection of memoirs for the assembly cited by Karcher (op.cit., p. 139), and to be found in B.N. MS. fr. 18481.

68. B.N. MS. fr. 6413, fos. 72ᵛ and ff.; also B.N. MS. Dupuy, 233, fo. 45. The total account was 23,444,998 *livres* ('oultres les levees Cidessus il sen Leve Encores plus de xmons (10,000,000) sur le peuple par plusiers levees particulieres, Comme Octroiz des Villes, Entretenemens de gouverneurs et Capitaines, Remboursements requis d'officiers, Levees de pionniers Chevaulx dartllierie Vivres de munitions Et charroitz dicelle, Estappes Entretenemens des clostures, Et pavez des Villes, Et grands chemins, Et plusieurs aultre(s) Levees particullieres Et extraordinaires, Sans la foulle et oppressions des gens de guerre dont le peuple se sent aultant et plus foulle que desdites Levees').

69. M. Wolfe, op.cit., ch 6, and F.C. Dietz, *English Government Finance, 1558-1640*, p. 111.

70. B.N. MS. fr. 15893 (Revenu et despence, 1576), fo. 390ᵛ, 10,300,000 *livres*, B.N. MS. fr. 6413, fos. 80 and ff. gives the *augmentations de levees* from the reign of Francis I to 1583. There is a slightly different calculation to the same purpose in ibid., fo. 230, but both arrive at a revenue for 1583 of about 24 million *livres*.

71. The debt in 1580, 'Brief Estat des debtes et engaigementz', can be found in B.N. MS. Dupuy 233, fo. 43ᵛ. This arrived at the following figures (i) sold and alienated domain, 6 million *livres*; (ii) *Rentes* upon domain, 1,008,500 *livres*; (iii) the *greffes* and *clercs des greffes* mortgaged, 3.9 million *livres; (iv) Rentes* upon the clergy, 1,024,000 *livres;* (v) *Rentes* at Paris, 10 million *livres*; and (vi) *Rentes* upon other towns, 2 million *livres*. Total capital value of revenues mortgaged, 62,400,000 *livres*; active debts to foreigners and others, 20,490,000 livres; total crown debts, therefore, 82,890,000 *livres*.

72. The cost of the German ritters is to be found in Bibliothèque de l'Institut de France 5605 (*liasses*). The Rouen arrears totalled 89,000 *livres* in 1579 (B.N. MS. fr. 16225). The agitations in Paris in 1578 are mentioned in B.Inst.Coll.Godefroy, 130, fo. 175. In 1579 the Parlement of Paris refused to let the clergy leave or enter Paris until they had offered to pay some of the arrears on the *rentes* mortgaged through the city (de Thou, *Histoire Universelle*, viii.95-97).

73. B.N. MS. It. 1730, fo. 79 (Priuli to the Doge, 14 June 1577).

74. L'Estoile, *Le Journal*, pp. 243, 246, 251.

75. G. Zeller, *La Réunion de Metz à la France, 1552-1648* (2 vols, Paris, 1926), ii. 112.

76. B.N. MS. fr. 25729, fo. 353 (4 Jan. 1580) *Mandement*, Henry III — the *trésorier de l'épargne*, Paris; and L'Estoile, *Le Journal*, pp. 311-12.

77. B.N. MS. fr. 26164 (31 August 1582), quittance to buy Louis d'Adjacet a horse, 600 *écus*; ibid., 26163 (26 August 1580) quittance from Jérome de Gondi for his pension of 106,623 *écus*.
78. Benoît Milon, sieur de Videville, (*C.S.P.For., Aug.1584-Aug. 1585* (1916), p. 69, Stafford to Walsingham, 18 September 1584); L'Estoile, following his disgrace in December 1584 reappeared quite quickly, *Le Journal*, pp. 121-2, 150-1, 351-2 and 363.
79. In 1574 L'Estoile reported that the Court was so poor that courtiers had to pawn their cloaks in order to fund the loan of 5,000 *livres* (ibid., p. 52). In 1576 on the death of one of its servants Brienne sent Bellièvre to lay claim to the 300,000 *livres* of his estate (B.Inst. 5605 (*liasse*)). In August 1582 Henry III reported to Villeroy that 'Je n'avoys pas guere d'argent . . . j'ai pris le payeur d'octobre passe (je ne scai comme il l'avoyt tant guarde) unze mil neuf cent vingt et cinq livres . . .'.
80. The debts of Duke Casimir of the Palatinate were renegotiated in July 1582. The impositions on Paris in the same year included 250,000 *livres* of *rentes*, a forced loan of 1,200 *écus* from councillors of the Parlement (*Registres des délibérations du bureau de Paris*, viii (1896) 276-8).
81. The Crown had a plan for the reformation of provincial governors. Cf. a minute in the hand of Villeroy, the secretary of state, entitled 'Articles concernans les mareschaulx de France, gouvern(eur)s, Lieuten(ant)s g(ener)aulx, Baillifs et seneschaulx de x feb. 1584' in B.N. MS. fr. 15567 fo. 80.
82. L'Estoile, p. 115 (May 1576).
83. R. Mousnier, *La Vénalité des Offices* (Paris, 1971), pp. 455-62.
84. B.N. MS. fr. 3385, fo. 12 (Henry III to Villeroy, 14 August 1584). (I am grateful to M. François, *doyen* of the *Ecole des Chartes*, for permission to consult the transcripts of the correspondence of Henry III made by P. Champion to aid in the deciphering of these letters (B.Inst. MSS. 5077 (*liasse*)).

Glossary

Arrêt	A formal judgement of the *Parlement*.
Assemblée de la salle verte	A short-lived consultative body which was set up in Paris in 1525 during the captivity of Francis I. It was made up of representatives of the sovereign courts and other important Parisian bodies, and was named after its meeting place.
Assemblée de ville	A gathering of the municipal corporation and of representatives of the major interests in Paris.
Avocat	A barrister.
Bonne ville	A description commonly applied to a town exempt from the *taille*, the main royal direct tax.
Bureau de la ville	The municipal corporation of Paris.
Chambre du conseil	A chamber within the Palais de Justice in Paris, where judges of the *Parlement* met in private to discuss cases that had been reserved for further consideration.
Cinquantenier	A local suburban officer of the Paris municipality. Inferior to a *quartenier* and superior to a *dizainier*.
Commissaires enquêteurs	The detectives of the Paris Châtelet.
Conseil étroit	An inner group of the royal council.
Contrôleur des deniers communs	An official created by Francis I in March 1515 to supervise municipal finances.
Deniers communs	Municipal revenues.
Echevin	An alderman in a municipal government.

Fausses-portes	Gateways in Paris dating back to the time of Philip-Augustus, no longer used as such.
Grand conseil	Originally a judicial committee of the royal council. It became an independent sovereign court in 1497.
Grands officiers	The highest officers of state.
Hocqueton	A tunic of cloth or leather worn by troops from the fourteenth to the sixteenth centuries.
Juges-délégués	A special tribunal, consisting of two members of the *Parlement* and two theologians, set up in Paris in 1525 on the pope's authority to judge cases of heresy. It was abolished in 1527.
Lieutenant-civil	A magistrate serving in the *bailliage* courts.
Lit-de-justice	The personal attendance of the king in *Parlement*, usually to enforce registration of an edict.
Morisque	A type of Moorish dance.
Notables	Bourgeois of importance in the magistracy and municipal government. The term is used more loosely in *assemblée des notables*.
Prévôt des marchands	In effect, the mayor of Paris.
Prévôt de Paris	The title given to the king's chief representative in Paris. His jurisdiction (the prévôté) was the same as that of a *bailliage* or *sénéchaussée* elsewhere in France.
Quartenier	An official heading local administration in each of the sixteen districts or quarters of Paris.
Sergents du Châtelet	Executive officers attached to the Châtelet, the tribunal of the *prévôt* of Paris.
Trésoriers de France	Four officials who before 1523 administered the king's ordinary revenues (i.e. those which he drew from his demesne).
Ville franche	Broadly speaking, a town exempt from the *taille*, the main royal direct tax.
Ville prévôtale	A town without a communal charter and directly under the king's authority.

Index

Agenais, *Estates* of, 167

Agramonts, 12

Aguilar, family of, 11

Albi, bishop of, Hughes IV Aubert, 36

Albi, consuls of, 36

Albornoz, Cardinal Gil (d.1367), 15

Aldermen, Court of, see London

Aleyn, Dr, 80

Allmand, Dr C., 14-15

Amboise, Charles d', governor of
Champagne, 136

Amboise, Jean d', duke-bishop of Langres
(1481-97), 139

Amer, Pierre, 120

Amiens, 122-3, 170

Andalusia, 16

Anjou, duke of, see Francis, duke of Anjou

Anjou, Upper, 169

Anne, duchess of Brittany, queen of France
(d.1514), 62-3

Aquinas, St. Thomas, 20

Aquitaine, 92

Aquitaine, dukes of, 12

Archer, John, 98

Aristotle, 10, 20-3, 25

Aristotle, *Art of Rhetoric* by, 22

Aristotle, *Economics* by, 23

Aristotle, *Ethics* by, 23

Aristotle, *Politics* by, 23

Arly, Jean d', 45

Armagnac, Jean d', bishop of Castres
(1460-93), 45

Armourers, guild of, 14

Armourers, warden of, 95

Arras, Treaty of (1435), 131-2, 134

Arras, Treaty of (1482), 139

Arrival of King Edward IV, 89

Arthur, count of Richemont, duke of Brittany,
Constable of France see Richemont, Arthur,
count of,

Assembly of Notables, 171-4

Aubert, Jean, 131

Augustine, St., 20

Aunsell, William, royal sergeant, 90

Autun, 129, 134, 138-9

Autun, bishop of, 134

Autun, diocese of, 132

Autunois, 129

Auvergne, 164

Auvergne, *Estates* of, 167

Auxerrois, 129

Auxois, 129,138, 140

Auxonne, 15, 129, 136-40

Avallon, 129

Avignon, 37

Bacon correspondence, 80

Bailén, count of, Rodrigo Ponce de
León, 11

Bar, Charlotte de, 43

Bar, Denis de, 43-4

Barcelona, 11

Barilh, Guillaume, 41

Barron, Mrs Caroline, 12, 14

Bas-Limousin, 112

Basin, Thomas, 35, 146-8

Basle, Council of, 54

Basque Provinces, 16

Baude, Henri, 112

Baudricourt, Jean, 139

Baynard Castle, 94-5

Beaufitz, William, 94

Beaufort, Henry, bishop of Lincoln
(1398-1404) and Winchester (1404-47),
Cardinal, 91

Beaumanoir, Jean de, lord of le Bois de la
Motte et du Treméreuc, 58, 63

Beaumanoir, Philippe de, 116

Beaumont, Louis de, bishop of Paris (1473-
92), 44-6

Beaumonts, 12

Beaune, 14-15, 129, 133-5, 137-8, 140-1

Beaune, *grande jours* de 132

Beaune, house of Hospitallers, 134

Beaune, *Parlement* of, 139

Beaunois, 129, 138

Beauvais, 33-6, 39, 46, 170

Beauvais, bishops of see Juvenal des Ursins, Jean, and Vincent of,
Bécoisel, 41
Bedford, John, duke of (d.1435), 15
Béjar, duke of, Alvaro de Zúñiga y Guzmán, (d.1533), 11
Bellièvre, *surintendant des finances*, 168
Berbisey, Etienne, mayor of Dijon, 136
Berges, Wilhelm, 23
Bernard, Gui, duke-bishop of Langres (1453-81), 135-6
Berry, 46
Berry, dukes of, 132
Beza, Theodore, 164
Black Death, 24, 56
Blancheappleton, manor of, 100
Blanchfort, Jean de, 43
Blanchet, Maitre Gérard, 37-9, 42, 46
Blois, 26-7
Blois, *Estates General* of (1576), 165-9, 171
Blois, Ordinance of (1579), 169
Blore Heath, battle of (1459), 95
Bolingbroke, Henry (see also Henry IV, king of England), 72, 88
Bordeaux, 35-6, 39, 46, 123, 148
Bordeaux, archbishop of, 25
Bordeaux, *Parlement* of, 175
Boucherat, Nicholas, abbot of Cîteaux, 166
Bourbon, dukes of, 132
Bourgeois de Paris see *Paris, Bourgeois de*
Bourges, 37-8
Bourges, archbishop of, 25, 43
Bourges, Pragmatic Sanction of, 44, 150-1
Bowyers, warden of the, 95
Bretagne, Gilles de, 52
Brewers, guild of, 14
Brézé, Pierre de, 149
Briçonnet, Bertrand, 43
Bristol, 13
Brittany, *Estates* of, 170
Brown, Sir Thomas, 77, 97
Buffart, 38
Burgundy, 14, 60, 120, 122, 129-30, 132-6, 138-41, 167-8, 172
Burgundy, *Estates* of, 166
Burgundy, governor of, 137
Burgundy, *Parlement* of, 141
Caen, 151
Caen, university of, 153-4
Cahors, 123
Calais, 94-6, 99, 146
Calais, garrison of, 101
Calais, mayor and aldermen of, 92
Calais, merchants of, 94

Calais Staple, 91, 93, 101
Calle, Richard, 83
Cam, Professor H.M., 19, 26
Cambridgeshire, 75
Cantelowe, William, alderman, 95
Canterbury, archbishop of, see Chichele, Henry
Capra, P., 57
Caqueran, 37-9
Carné, Adèle de, 61
Casimir, John, duke of the Palatinate (d.1592), 163
Castile, Admiral of, Fadrique Enríquez de Ribera 11
Castile, Constable of, Bernardino Fernández de Velasco, duke of Frías (d.1512) 11
Castres, 45
Catalonia, 16
Catworth, Thomas, mayor of London, 94
Cauchon, Pierre, bishop of Beauvais (1420-32) of Lisieux (1432-42), 33
Caux, *bailli* of, see Havart, Jean
Chabannes, Antoine de, 52
Chabot-Rays, family, 55
Chalon, 14, 129, 134, 136-8, 140
Chalon, diocese of, 132
Chalonnais, 129
Chambre des Comptes (Britanny), 59, 61
Chambre des Comptes (Burgundy), 138, 141
Chambre des Comptes (France), 113, 116, 119-20
Chambre des Comptes (Normandy), 153-4
Champagne, 122, 134, 164
Champagne, *Estates* of, 170
Champagne, governor of, 136
Champdivers, Odinette de, 131
Champeaux, Guillaume, bishop of Laon (1419-41), and of Uzés (1441-2), 42
Champeaux, Isabeau, 42
Champion, Pierre, 33
Charles V, emperor, king of Spain (d.1558), 11
Charles V, king of France (d.1380), 21, 34, 42, 53, 65, 112
Charles VI, king of France (d.1422), 42, 131, 135, 153
Charles VII, king of France (d.1460), 15, 34-5, 37-8, 52, 55, 62, 111-12, 118-9, 123, 131, 146-8, 150-1, 153-5
Charles VIII, king of France (d.1498) 61, 111, 122, 129, 140-1
Charles de France, brother of Louis XI, duke Berry, Normandy and Guyenne (d.1472), 162
Charles the Bold, duke of Burgundy (d.1477), 14, 122, 131-2, 134-7
Charolais, 129, 138

Charrier, 39
Charte aux Normands, 148, 152-3, 167
Chartier, Alain, 43-4
Chastel family, 59, 64
Chastel, Tanguy du, viscount of la Bellière, 55
Chastellier d'Yréac, Jean du, 58
Châtagnier, Maître Jean, 38
Châteugay, 37, 39
Château Thierry, 171
Châtillon-sur-Seine, 129, 134, 138
Châtillon, Coutume de, 132
Châtillonais, 138
Cheval, Guillaume, 140
Chevalier, Professor B., 11, 13-14, 42-3
Chevanne, J.R. de, 137
Chichele, Henry, bishop of St. David's (1408-14), archbishop of Canterbury (1414-43), 13, 91
Chichele, John, 92
Cîteaux, abbot of, see Boucherat, Nicholas
Clermont, 35
Cleves, Jean de, 137
Clifford, Lord, 95
Clisson family, 64
Clisson, Olivier IV, lord of, 53, 59
Clovis, 167
Cobham, Sir Henry, English ambassador, 171
Cobos, Francisco de los (d.1547), 11
Coëtivy, Alain, lord of, 59
Coëtivy brothers, 55
Coëtivy, Guillaume de, 59
Coëtivy, Prigent de, 59, 64
Coëtquis, Philippe de, archbishop of Tours (1427-41), 54
Colinet, 41
Compiègne, 41-2
Compiègne, Edict of (1429), 151-2
'Comuneros' Revolt of the, 15
Condé, prince of, Henri (d.1588), 165
Condomois, *Estates* of, 167
Córdoba, 11
Cordwainers, guild of, 14
Coruña, 36
Cotentin, 116
Cour des Aides (Norman), 15
Coventry, 99
Coventry Parliament (1459), 95

Dagobert (d.639), 27
Damme, John, 79
Dartford, 94
Dauphiné, 37, 122, 164, 168, 170
D'Entrèves, Professor A.P., 25
Derval, lord of, 63
Dieppe, 170
Dijon, 14, 122, 129, 131, 133-41, 168

Dijonnais, 129
Dôle, 136-8
Doriole, Pierre, 43, 45-6
Douhet, Jean, 150
Drapers, company (guild) of, 14, 88
Drury, Sir Robert, 81
Dubec, Jean, 150
Dudesert, Guillaume, 156
Dudley, Edmund, 27
Dudley, Edmund, *Tree of Commonwealth* by 27
Dunois, count of, Jean (d.1465), 147
Dupont-Ferrier, G., 13

Echenon, Monin d', 131
Echiquier, Norman, 15, 148, 153-5
Edict of Pacification (1577), 164, 167, 175
Edward, earl of March, 95-8
duke of York, 88, 91, 98
king of England (Edward IV, d.1483), 12, 74, 97, 99-100, 103-4
Edward, Prince, son of Henry VI (d.1471), 98
Egremont, Lord, 95
Elizabeth I, queen of England (d.1603), 168
Enríquez de Guzmán, Alonso, 11
Erpingham, Sir Thomas, 82
Essars, J. des, 157
Essars, Pierre des, 42
Estoile, Parisian diarist, 171, 173-5
Eu, count of, Charles (d.1472), 35
Exeter, duke of, Henry Holand (d.1475), 98

Faiaust, Henri, 60
Fastolf, Sir John, 80
Fauconberg, Thomas, 89
Fawtier, Professor R., 10
Filescamps, Jacques de, 45
Finistère, 55, 57
Fishmongers, company (guild) of, 14, 88
Flanders, 13, 120
Fletchers, warden of 95
Fortescue, Sir John, 20-1, 25-8
Fortescue, Sir John, *Governance of England* by, 21, 26
Fortescue, Sir John, *De Natura Legis Naturae* by, 26
Fougères, 52
Francis I, king of France (d.1547), 60, 183
Francis, duke of Anjou (d.1584), 163, 168-71, 175-6
Francis I, duke of Brittany (d.1450), 62
Francis II, duke of Brittany (d.1488), 51, 53-4, 62-3, 65
Fresnay, lordship of, 63
Fryde, Professor E.B., 92

Galicia, kingdom of, 11-12, 16

Gascony, 27, 101, 113, 120, 122, 169-70, 175
Gascony, *Estates* of, 167
Gaucourt, Charles de, 44
Gawdy correspondence, 80
Genet, Professor Jean-Philippe, 10
Geneva, 162, 164
'Geney, Mr', 80
Geoffrey, count of Brittany, *Assize of*, 55-6
Gerberoy, 34-5
Germanías, Revolt of the, 15
Ghent, 123
Gibon, Jean, 61
Gibon, Maître Jean, sire du Grisso, 61
Gié, lord of see Pierre, lord of Gié,
Giles of Rome 20-2
Giles of Rome, *De Regimine Principum* by, 24
Gilles, lord of Rays, Marshal of France, 53, 64
Giraldus Cambrensis, 23
Gironde, 116
Gisors, 41, 152
Gisors, *bailliage* of, 153
Goldsmiths, company of, 88
Grancey, 131
Greengrass, Dr M., 15
Gregory, William, 89
Grenade, 36
Grocers, company (guild) of, 88
Grosseteste, Robert, bishop of Lincoln (1235-1253), 23
Guenée, Professor Bernard, 34
Guérande, 1st Treaty of (1365), 53
Guérande, 2nd Treaty of (1381), 53
Guesclin, Bertrand du, 59, 64
Guise, duke of, Henri (d.1588), 172, 175
Guises, 168
Gunners, warden of the, 95
Guyenne, 57, 167

Haberdashers, guild of, 14
Haberdashers, warden of the, 95
Hakedy, Richard, grocer, 90
Hampden, Sir Edmund, 97
Hanse merchants, 99
Harfleur, 147, 149, 151
Harowe, John, mercer, 98
Harriss, Dr G.L., 101
Hastings, 96
Havart, Jean, *bailli* of Caux, 150
Hazardière, Pierre de la, 150
Heigham, Thomas, 80
Henry IV, king of England (d.1413), see also under Bolingbroke, Henry,
Henry V, king of England (d.1422), 88, 101, 135, 154
Henry VI, king of England (d.1471), 13-14, 22, 74, 78, 82, 88-90, 92-8, 100

Henry VII, king of England (d.1509), 58, 75-6, 79, 81, 84
Henry VIII, king of England (d.1547), 79
Henry III, king of France (d.1589), 162-75
Henry of Navarre later Henry IV, king of France (d.1610), 164. 171
Héron, Macé, 42
Hesselin, Denis de, 44
Heydon family, 75
Heydon, John, 77
Hobart, Sir James, 81
Holland, *Estates* of, 168
Holland, Ralph, tailor, mayor of London, 89
Honfleur, 147
Howard, John, duke of Norfolk (d.1485), 84
Huguenots, 162-4, 168-7
Hugotion, Cardinal François, 35-6, 46
Hull, 13
Hungerford, Lord, 96-7
Huntingdonshire, 75

Inteville, d', 175
Ireland, 76, 95
Ironmongers, company of, 88

Jahon, Guillaume, 60
Jarlot, Colin, 37
Jancourt, Jean de, lord of Villarnoul, 140
Jean, lord of Montauban, 64
Jean, lord of Rieux, Marshal of France, 64
Jeffs, Dr, 75
Jenney, John, see also under 'Geney', 80-1
Jerez, 10-11
Jermyn, John, 80
Joan of Arc (d.1431), 35
John II, king of Castile (d.1454), 10
John II, king of France (d.1364), 19, 36, 129, 135
John IV, duke of Brittany (d.1399), 53-4, 57-8, 65
John V, duke of Brittany (d.1442), 61, 63
John of Salisbury, 23
Joiners, warden of, 95
Jones, Dr M., 11-12
Jouard, Jean, 137
Jouguet, Jean, 60
Jouvenel des Ursins, Guillaume, 33, 43, 46, 147-8
Juvenal des Ursins, Jean, bishop of Beauvais (1433-44), of Laon (1444-9), archbishop of Rheims (1449-73), 26-7, 33-6, 46
Juvenal des Ursins, Jean, *Discours touchant les Questions* by, 27
Juvenal des Ursins, Jean, *Epistre* by, 27
Juvenal des Ursins, Jean, *Loquar in tribulacione* by, 33-5

Kendal, earl of, Jean de Foix (d. c.1485), 97
Kent, sheriff of, see Brown, Sir Thomas

La Forêt, lord of, 45
Lagny,
Lamet, Antoine de, *bailli*, 139
La Montagne, 129, 132
Lancaster, duchy of, 73
Langres, 131
Langres, diocese of, 14, 134
Langres, duke-bishops of, see Amboise, Jean d', Bernard, Gui
Langton, Stephen, archbishop of Canterbury (1206-28), 25
Languedoc, 120, 122, 167
Languedoc, *Estates* of, 37, 117
Languedoc, governor of, 172
Languedoc, governor of, secretary of the, 163
Languedoil, 118, 120, 122-3
Languedoil, *Estates* of, 37
Laon, 33
La Rochelle, 40-1, 163
La Trémoille, George de, 137
Laval, André de, lord of Lohéac, 64
Leathersellers, guild of, 14
Leblond, Victor, 33
Le Bouvier, Gilles, 34
Lee, Richard, mayor, 98-9
Leguai, Professor A., 14
Le Jouvencel, 60
Le Molac, lord of, 58
León, 10, 12
Le Paveur, Jean, 131
L'Estat et le gouvernement (1347), 24
Lewis IV, of Bavaria, emperor, (d.1347), 24
Lewis, Dr P.S., 10,57
Liber de informatione Principum, 24
Limeul, lord of, 36
Lippomano, Venetian ambassador, 164
Lobel, Mrs, 13
Lodève, 43
Lollardy, 79
Lomnour, William, 80
London, 88-100, 103
    Clerkenwell, St. John's Fields, 98
    Common Council, 91, 94-9
    Court of Aldermen, 89, 94-6
    Cripplegate, 96
    Dowgate Ward, the 'Erber', 95
    Fleet Street, 95
    Guildhall, 88, 91, 97
    Old Dean Street, house of the earl of Warwick in, 95
    Steward's Inn, 100
The Tower of, 96-8
    The Tower of, constable of, 98

Lorraine, 168
Louis I, the Pious (d.840), 27
Louis, dauphin, son of Charles VII, 52
Louis XI, king of France (d.1483), 14, 42-4, 46, 51, 54, 62, 65, 111, 119, 122, 131-2, 134-6, 138-40, 154
Louis XII, king of France (d.1515), 116, 129, 140, 154, 157
Louis, duke of Guyenne, 131
Lovel, Lord, 97
Lovell, Sir Thomas, 81
Lucas, Thomas, 81
Lucé, Guillaume, bishop of Maillezais, 47
Ludford, Route of (1459), 95
Lynn, 13
Lyonnais, 170
Lyons, 36-9, 42, 120, 122, 167, 171
Lyons, court of the archbishop of, 135
Lyons, sénéchal of, 37
Mâcon, *bailli* of 37
Mâcon, Rolin de, 37-40, 42, 46
Mâconnais, 129
Maddicott, Dr, 82
Machiavelli, Nicolò, 28
Machiavelli, *The Prince* by, 28
Madox, author of the *Firma Burgi*, 13
Maguelone, 43
Malestroit, lord of, 58, 63
Malicorne, Mâitre Geoffroy, 41
Malsafava, 36
Marcel, Claude, 174
Margaret of Anjou, queen of England (d.1482), 89, 92, 94, 98
Marsilius of Padua, 20-1, 25
Marsilius of Padua, *Defensor Pacis* by, 22
Mary of Burgundy (d.1482), 136-8
Matignon, Jacques de, 169, 175
Mauléon, Jean, *tresorier de l'épargne*, 60
Maumont, Gérard de, 44
Maximilian I, emperor (d.1519), 122, 138
McFarlane, K.B., 54, 82
Medici, Catherine de' (d.1589), 171
Mené, Notre Dame du, 61
Mercers, 95
Mercers, company of, 88
Mercers, warden of the, 95
Metz, 173
Meyer, Professor J., 12, 51, 56, 66
Middleton, John, 92
Midi, the 170-1
Milan, Castel Sforzescho, 15
Millau, 164
Milon, Benôit de, lord of Videville, 174
Miroir(s) au(x) Prince(s), 10, 20, 23-4, 28
Molac, lord of le, 58
Montauban, lord of, 58

Montbard, 129, 134
Montcénis, 139
Montfort family, 53-4
Montfort, John IV de, duke of Brittany see
  John IV, duke of Brittany
Montfort, lord of, 58
Montilla, castle of, 11
Montmorency-Damville, Henri de, 163, 172
Montmorency-Laval, family of, 56
Montpellier, 122-3
Morin, Guillaume, 149-50
Mortimer's Cross, battle of (Feb.1461), 98
Morvan, the, 138
Moulins, 171
Mowbray, John, duke of Norfolk (d.1461), 83-4
Moxó, Salvador, de, 12
Multon, Thomas, 90
'Mutemaque', the (June 1477), 137-9

Nancy, battle of (1477), 136
Nantes, 66
Narbonne, archdiaconate of, 43
Navarre, kingdom of, 12
Netherlands, 164, 174
Nevill, earls of Warwick, see also under
  Warwick, 95
Niebla, 3rd count of, Juan Alfonso de Guzmán
  (d.1468), 10
Nîmes, 163
Norfolk, 75-6, 78-9, 81, 83
Norfolk commission, 80
Norfolk, dukes of see Howard, Mowbray
Norfolk, eschaetor of, 77
Norfolk and Suffolk, 78, 80, 83
Normandy, 15, 101, 113, 116, 120, 146-7, 150-5, 167, 169
Normandy, Estates of, 167-8, 170
Northampton, battle of (1460), 97
Northumberland, earl of, Henry Percy
  (d.1461), 95, 98
Norwich, 14
Norwich, Austin Friary, 82
Norwich, bishop of, Thomas Brown (1436-45), 78
Nottingham, 14, 95
Nowell, Charles, 83
Nuits, 138

Orange, Prince of, Jean II (d.1502), 137
Oresme, Nicholas, 21-2
Orléans, Charles d', count of Angoulême
  (d.1496), 45-6
Orléans, duke(s) of, 131-2
Orléans, Estates General of, 171
Orléans, siege of, 33
Outee-Saône, 129, 136

Outre-Seine-et-Yonne, 13, 120
Oxford, 13
Oxford, earl of, John de Vere (d.1513), 76, 84

Papaillon, Jean 41
Papaillon, Jean, son of, 41
Papassol, Hélie de, 41, 46
Paris, 21, 34, 36, 40-1, 55, 58, 152, 164, 171, 174, 183-4
  bishop of, see Beaumont, Louis de
  Châtelet, 183
  Conciergerie, 133
  Hotel de St. Pol, 131
  Hotel de Ville 165
  Parlement of, 14, 21, 40, 132-4, 141, 151, 154, 172, 174
  prévôt des marchands of, 44, 172, 174, 183
  Sainte-Chapelle, 134
  University of, 23
Paris, Bourgeois de 148
Parthenay, lordship of, 40
Paston family, 75
Paston, John, 77, 79-82
Paston, Margaret, 80
Paston Letters, 12, 76-7, 80, 82-3
Peace of the King (1577), 162-3
Pearl, Mrs Valerie, 12
Penthièvre family, 53-4, 57
Pérault, Guillaume, 24
Périgueux, 36-41
Péronne, Treaty of, 134
Perroy, Professor E., 54
Peter II, duke of Brittany, (d.1457), 62-3, 65
Peter of Blois, 23
Petit-Dutaillis, C., 10
Philip II Augustus, king of France (d.1223), 154, 184
Philip IV, king of France (d.1314), 23
Philip II, king of Spain (d.1598), 171, 176
Philip the Bold, duke of Burgundy (d.1404), 132, 134
Philip the Good, duke of Burgundy (d.1467), 61, 131, 135-6
Picardy, 13, 120, 122, 164, 169, 175
Picardy, Estates of, 170-1, 175
Picardy, governor of, 165
Picardy, League of, 164-5
Picquigny, Ferri de, 42
Pierre, lord of Gié, 64
Pierre, son of Jean, lord of Rieux, 64
Platt, Colin, 14
Playter, Thomas, 80
Plessis Bonenffant, 52
Plessis-les-Tours, 140

Ploër, Rivalen de,   58
Ploërmel, count of,   60
Plummer, C.,   24
Plymouth,   36
Poissy,   41
Poissy, Colloquy of,   171
Poitiers, count of,   36
Poitiers, *Parlement* of   37-8
Poitou,   164
Poland,   154
Ponce de León, Rodrigo, 2nd marquis of
   Cadiz,   11
Pons, Michel de,   134
Pont-de-l'Arche,   147
Pont-Sainte-Maxence,   41
Pontbriants, family of,   65
Pontoise,   41
Portsmouth,   14
Portugal,   16
Poulet, Sir Amyas,   162, 168
Poutrell, John,   94
Priego, Marquis of, Pedro Fernández de
   Córdova (d.1517),   11
Priuli, Venetian ambassador,   173
Provence,   120, 164, 169-70
Pseudo-Aristotle, *Secreta Secretorum* by,   23
Ptolemy of Lucca, *De Regimine Principum* by,   24
Putnam, Dr Bertha,   79

Queu, Maître Raymond,   40-1, 46
Quintin, lord of,   63
Quyne, Thomas,   90

Rays, Gilles, lord of, **Marshal of France, 53, 64**
Rebellion, Northern (1569),   15
Rennes,   52
Rennes, diocese of   67
Rey, Professor,   45
Rheims,   33, 118, 122-3
Rheims, archbishop of, see Juvenal, Jean, des
   Ursins
Rheims, *grenetier* of,   45
Rhône,   116
Richard II, king of England (d.1399), 12, 72,
   75, 77, 81, 90
Richard, duke of York, see York, Richard,
   duke of,
Richelieu,   173
Richemont, Arthur, count of, Constable of
   France, duke of Brittany (d.1458), 37-9, 46,
   62, 64
Rieulx, family,   54
Riom,   37-9
Roanne, maison de   37
Rochefort, Rivalen de,   58
Rogers, Dr.   82

Rohan, family,   54, 56, 63
Rohan, viscount of,   65
Rolin, François, captain of Autun,   139
Rolin, Cardinal,   139
Rome,   45, 151, 169
Rosnyvinen family,   64
Rosnyvinen, Guillaume de,   51-2, 59
Ross, Dr C.,   100
Rostrenen, lord of,   58
Rouen,   14-15, 21, 146-54, 167, 173
Rouen, Cardinal of,   43
Rouen, *Chambre des Comptes* see *Chambre des
   Comptes* (Normandy)
Rouen, *Echiquier* see under *Echiquier* (Norman)
Rouen, *Mont-Sainte-Catherine*,   147
Rouen, *Parlement* of,   15, 154, 167, 169
Rouvres, Philippe de, duke of Burgundy
   (d.1361),   129

Sahagún, abbot of,   10
St. Albans, 1st battle of (May, 1455),   94-5
St. Albans, 2nd battle of (Feb. 1461), 89, 97-8
St.-Aubin-du-Cormier,   52
St. Bartholomew, Massacre of,   163
St.-Jean-d'Angély,   40-2, 44
St.-Jean-de-Losne,   136
St. Michael, Order of,   135
Saint-Papoul,   43-4
St. Paul's Cathedral, London,   95-6
St. Quentin,   122
Saintonge,   10
Salisbury, earl of, Richard Nevill (d.1460),
   95-7, 100
Sandwich,   90, 96
Santiago, Order of,   11
Saône, Val de,   138
Saumur,   38
Savoy,   37
Savoy, duke of, Amedeo VIII (d.1434),   42
Scales, Lord,   96-7
Scholz, Richard,   25
Seignourat, Aymeri,   42
Semur,   129, 134, 138
Senlis,   35
Senlis, *bailliage de*,   60
Sens, *bailli* of,   133
Sens, jours de,   134
Seurre,   138
Sévigné, Guillaume,   63
Sforza, the,   15
Short English Chronicle,   89
Shrewsbury, earl of, John Talbot (d.1453), 92
Skinners, company of,   88
Smith, Dr Hassell,   12
Sombernon, lord of,   134
Somerset, duke of, Henry Beaufort (d.1464), 95

Southampton,   13, 36, 90
Spain,   170, 173
Speculum Regis Edwardi III,   28
Staplers,   91, 93, 100
Storey, Professor R.L.,   93
Stubbs, W.,   10
Styce, William,   90
Suffolk,   75-6, 78-9, 82
Suffolk commission,   80
Suffolk, duke of, see Pole, William de la

Tailors, warden of the,   95
Talant,   134
Tanguy du Chastel see Chastel, Tanguy du,
   viscount of La Bellière
Teulier, Jean,   41
Thou, Jacques-Auguste de,   166, 171
Thouars,   38
Tindon, Louis,   45
Toulouse,   36, 122-3, 168
Touraine,   123, 135
Tourangeaux, the,   42
Tournai,   122-3
Tournus,   138
Tours,   117, 134, 151
Tours, *Estates General* of (1468),   155
Tours, Truce of (1444),   33
Tout, T.F.,   10
Towton, battle of (1461),   99
Tractatus de regimine Principum ad Regem
   Henricum Sextum,   22
Trémoille, George de la, see La Trémoille
Troyes,   122, 165
Troyes, Treaty of (1420),   131
Tudert, Maître Jean, dean of Paris,   47
Tudor, Jasper, earl of Pembroke (d.1495), 98
Tulle,   43-5

Ullman, Professor W.,   25
Upholders, warden of the,   95

Val-Notre-Dame,   41
Vale, Dr M.,   147

Valpergue, Théode, de,   38-9, 46
Varye, Guillaume de,   43
Vaudrey, Claude de, governor of Auxonne, 137
Verdun-sur-le-Doubs,   138
Vernon,   152
Vidal, R,   36
Villars, Guillaume de,   41
Villebresme,   46
Villeneuve-le-Roy, prévôt of,   133
Villeroy,   175
Vincennes,   45
Vincent of Beauvais,   34
Vintners,   91
Vintners, company (guild) of,   88, 114
Virgoe, Dr Roger,   12
Vivarais,   164
Vyon, Catherine,   131
Vyon, Chrétiennot,   139
Vyon, Robert,   139

Wakefield, battle of (Dec.1460),   97-8
Wales,   98
Wars of the Roses,   93
Warwick, earl of, Richard Nevill (d.1471), 89,
   95-8, 100
Westminster,   36, 95
Wey, William,   36
Wilks, Professor Michael,   25-6
Wiltshire, earl of, James Butler (d.1461), 96
Wingfield, John, sheriff of Norfolk and
   Suffolk,   76
Wodehouse, Sir Thomas,   79
Worcester, William,   80,83
Wyclif, John,   27
Yolande, of Aragon, Dowager-Countess of
   Anjou, queen of Sicily (d.1442),   37
York,   13, 99
York, duke of, Richard, (d.1460), 76, 83, 93-5,
   98
York, Statute of,   25
Yver, Jean,   43